First World War
and Army of Occupation
War Diary
France, Belgium and Germany

3 DIVISION
Divisional Troops
Royal Army Medical Corps
142 Field Ambulance
12 August 1915 - 31 October 1919

WO95/1408/1

The Naval & Military Press Ltd
www.nmarchive.com
Published in association with The National Archives

Published by

The Naval & Military Press Ltd

Unit 10 Ridgewood Industrial Park,

Uckfield, East Sussex,

TN22 5QE England

Tel: +44 (0) 1825 749494

www.naval-military-press.com

www.nmarchive.com

Contents

Document type	Place/Title	Date From	Date To
Heading	WO95/1408/1		
Heading	142 Field Ambulance 1915 Aug To 1919 Oct. 5 (A) Sanitary Section. 1916 Jan To 1917 Mar. 11 Mobile Veterinary Section. 1914 Aug To 1919 Oct.		
Heading	3rd Division Medical No. 142 Field Ambulance Aug Dec 1915		
Heading	121/6550 3rd Division War Diary of No 142 Field Ambulance From 12 August 1915 To 31 Aug 1915 Vol I		
War Diary	Rouex	12/08/1915	14/08/1915
War Diary	St Omer	15/08/1915	21/08/1915
War Diary	Zuytpeene	22/08/1915	22/08/1915
War Diary	Steenvorde	22/08/1915	23/08/1915
War Diary	Hooqraefe	24/08/1915	24/08/1915
War Diary	Hoograefe near Renenghelst	26/08/1915	26/08/1915
War Diary	Reninghelst	27/08/1915	31/08/1915
Heading	121/6971 3rd Division War Diary of 142 Field Ambulance (3rd Div) From 1 Sept 1915 to 30 Sept 1915 Vol II		
War Diary	Reninghelst	01/09/1915	01/09/1915
War Diary	Near Poperinghe	02/09/1915	04/09/1915
War Diary	Poperinghe	06/09/1915	30/09/1915
Heading	121/7435 3rd Division War Diary of No. 142 Field Ambulance From 1/10/15 To 31/10/15 To The Officer i/c A. G's Office at the Base. Vol III		
War Diary	near Poperinghe	01/10/1915	23/10/1915
War Diary	Godeswaervelde Q 11. G. 6.8. Sheet 27 1/40,000	24/10/1915	24/10/1915
War Diary	Godeswaervelde	25/10/1915	30/10/1915
Heading	121/7637 3rd Division War Diary of No. 142 Field Ambulance From 1st Nov 1915 To 30th Nov 1915 Vol XVI		
War Diary	Winnezeele (Nord)	04/11/1915	20/11/1915
War Diary	Reninghelst	23/11/1915	29/11/1915
Heading	121/7930 3rd Division War Diary of 142 Field Ambulance. From 1 Dec 1915 To 31 Dec 1915 Vol V		
War Diary	Reninghelst	01/12/1915	31/12/1915
Heading	3rd Division Medical No. 142 Field Ambulance Jan-Dec 1916.		
Heading	3rd Div F/119/2 142 Field Ambulance Jan Vol VI		
War Diary	Reninghelst	05/01/1916	31/01/1916
Map	Dispositions Of 142 Field Ambulance 31-1-16.		
Heading	142 Fld Amb Feb 1916 March 1916		
Heading	War Diary of No 142 Field Ambulance. from 1 Feb 1916 to 29 Feb 1916 Vol XIII		
War Diary	Reninghelst	07/02/1916	08/02/1916
War Diary	Zermezeele	09/02/1916	09/02/1916
War Diary	Houlle	10/02/1916	24/02/1916
Heading	Vol VIII War Diary of No 142 Field Ambulance from 1 March 1916 to 31 March 1916		
War Diary	Houlle	01/03/1916	07/03/1916

War Diary	Boeschepe	08/03/1916	31/03/1916
Heading	3rd Div Vol IX War Diary of 142 Field Ambulance. From 1 April 1916 To 30 April 1916		
War Diary	Godewaersvelde	03/04/1916	25/04/1916
War Diary	Westoutre	25/04/1916	30/04/1916
Heading	Vol 10 3rd Div War Diary of No 142 Field Ambulance From 1 May 1916 to 31 May 1916		
Map	Sheet 28		
War Diary	Westoutre	06/05/1916	25/05/1916
War Diary	Godewaersvelde	27/05/1916	31/05/1916
Heading	Vol XI War Diary of No 142 Field Ambulance From 1 June 1916 To 30 June 1916		
War Diary	Godewaersvelde	02/06/1916	19/06/1916
War Diary	Muncq-Nierlet	20/06/1916	30/06/1916
Heading	Vol 12 3rd Division War Diary of No. 142 Field Ambulance From 1 July 1916 To 31 July 1916		
War Diary	Muncq Neurlet	01/07/1916	01/07/1916
War Diary	Bernaville	02/07/1916	02/07/1916
War Diary	Havernas	03/07/1916	03/07/1916
War Diary	Poulainville	04/07/1916	05/07/1916
War Diary	Lahoussoye	06/07/1916	06/07/1916
War Diary	Morlancourt	07/07/1916	07/07/1916
War Diary	Sapper Corner 2509 NE Of Bray	08/07/1916	14/07/1916
War Diary	Sapper Corner Sheet 62 D L 15 b 10.10	14/07/1916	19/07/1916
War Diary	Sapper Corner N Bray	20/07/1916	21/07/1916
War Diary	Billonwood	21/07/1916	24/07/1916
War Diary	Sapper Corner	24/07/1916	26/07/1916
War Diary	XIII Corps Man D. S. (J. 24)	26/07/1916	26/07/1916
War Diary	XIII Corps Main Dressing Station J. 24 Sheet Albert Combined	26/07/1916	26/07/1916
Operation(al) Order(s)	Operation Order No. 17 By Lieut. Colonel W Wiley R.A.M.C. Commanding 142 Field Ambulance.	01/07/1916	01/07/1916
Operation(al) Order(s)	Operation Order No. 18 By Lieut Colonel W Wiley R.A.M.C. Commanding 142 Field Ambulance	07/07/1916	07/07/1916
Operation(al) Order(s)	Operation Order No. 19 By Lieut. Colonel W Wiley R.A.M.C. Commanding 142 Field Ambulances	05/07/1916	05/07/1916
Operation(al) Order(s)	Operation Order No. 20 By Lieut. Colonel W Wiley R.A.M.C. Commanding 142 Field Ambulance	06/07/1916	06/07/1916
Operation(al) Order(s)	Operation Order No. 21 By Lieut. Colonel W. Wiley. R.A.M.C. Commanding 142 Field Ambulance	07/07/1916	07/07/1916
Heading	Vol 13 War Diary of 142 Field Ambulance From 1 Aug 1916 To 31 Aug 1916		
War Diary	Dive Copse (J. 24 Sheet Albert Camp)	01/08/1916	12/08/1916
War Diary	Billon.	14/08/1916	17/08/1916
War Diary	Dive Copse	20/08/1916	22/08/1916
War Diary	Sheet II Lens 1/100000	23/04/1916	31/04/1916
Operation(al) Order(s)	Operation Order No. 23 By Lieut. Col. W. Wiley. R.A.M.C. Commanding 142 Fd. Ambce Gorges.	24/08/1916	24/08/1916
Operation(al) Order(s)	Operation Order No. 22 By Lieut. Colonel Wiley. R.A.M.C.	19/08/1916	19/08/1916
Heading	3rd Div War Diary of No. 142 Field Ambulance From 1 Sept 1916 To 30 Sept 1916		
War Diary	Noeux Les Mines	02/09/1916	21/09/1916
War Diary	Allouagne	22/09/1916	25/09/1916
Operation(al) Order(s)	Operation Order No. 1 By Copy No Capt. A. H. Habgood R.A.M.C.	20/09/1916	20/09/1916

Heading	140/1188 Vol 15 3rd Div War Diary of No 142 Field Ambulance From 011016 To 311016		
War Diary	Cuhem	02/10/1916	04/10/1916
War Diary	Sautrecourt	05/10/1916	06/10/1916
War Diary	Puchevillers	07/10/1916	07/10/1916
War Diary	Bertrancourt	08/10/1916	17/10/1916
War Diary	Bus-Les Artois	18/10/1916	31/10/1916
Heading	140/1849 Vol 16 3rd Div. War Diary Of No 142 Field Ambulance From 1/11/16 To 30/11/16		
War Diary	Bus-Les-Artois	03/11/1916	30/11/1916
Heading	War Diary of No 142 Field Ambulance From 1 Dec 1916 To 31 Dec 1916		
War Diary	Bus Les Artois	02/12/1916	30/12/1916
Heading	3rd Division Medical No. 142 Field Ambulance 1917.		
Heading	140/1947 Vol 18 3rd War Diary of No 142 Field Ambulance To 31/1/17		
War Diary	Bus-Les-Artois	01/01/1917	08/01/1917
War Diary	Beauquesne	09/01/1917	12/01/1917
War Diary	Canaples	14/01/1917	28/01/1917
War Diary	Occoches	29/01/1917	29/01/1917
War Diary	Herlin-Le-Sec	31/01/1917	31/01/1917
Heading	Vol 19 140/1994 3rd Div War Diary of No 142 Field Ambulance From 1 Feb 1917 To 28 Feb 1917		
War Diary	Dieval	01/02/1917	08/02/1917
War Diary	Houvin-Houvigneul	09/02/1917	28/02/1917
Heading	140/2042 Medical Vol 20 War Diary of 142 Field Ambulance R.A.M.C. From March 1/17 To March 31/17		
War Diary	Houvin Houvigneul	02/03/1917	09/03/1917
War Diary	Sars-Les-Bois	11/03/1917	31/03/1917
Heading	140/2086 Medical Vol 21 War Diary of No 142 Field Ambulance From 1/4/17 To 30/4/17		
War Diary	Hauteville	01/04/1917	03/04/1917
War Diary	Wanquetin	04/04/1917	08/04/1917
War Diary	Arras	09/04/1917	30/04/1917
Heading	140/2161 Medical Vol 22 War Diary of No 142 Field Ambulance From 1.5.17 To 31.5.17		
War Diary	Arras	01/05/1917	17/05/1917
War Diary	Liencourt	18/05/1917	31/05/1917
Heading	140/2230 Medical Vol 23 War Diary of No 142 Field Ambulance From 1/6/17 To 30/6/17		
War Diary	Blangy	01/06/1917	18/06/1917
War Diary	Gouy-En-Artois	20/06/1917	30/06/1917
Heading	140/2298 Medical Vol 24 War Diary of No 142 Field Ambulance From 1 July 1917 To 31st July 1917		
War Diary	Ashiet Le Grand	01/07/1917	03/07/1917
War Diary	Lebucquiere	03/07/1917	25/07/1917
Heading	140/2364 Vol 25 War Diary of No 142 Field Ambulance From 1 August 1917 To 31 August 1917		
War Diary	Lebucquiere	01/08/1917	31/08/1917
Heading	140/2438 Sept 1917 No. 142 f. a.		
Heading	No. 142 Field Ambulance From 1.9.17 To 30.9.17		
War Diary	Lebucquiere	01/09/1917	06/09/1917
War Diary	Lechelle	06/09/1917	18/09/1917
War Diary	Luna Farm	19/09/1917	19/09/1917
War Diary	Poperinghe	19/09/1917	22/09/1917

War Diary	Red Farm.	23/09/1917	30/09/1917
Heading	140/2499 Vol 27 War Diary of No. 142 Field Ambulance From 1.10.17 To 31.10.17		
War Diary	Red Farm	01/10/1917	01/10/1917
War Diary	Oudezeele	02/10/1917	04/10/1917
War Diary	Lechelle	05/10/1917	09/10/1917
War Diary	Favreuil	11/10/1917	31/10/1917
Heading	140/2578 Vol 28 War Diary of No 142 Field Ambulance From 1/11/17 To 30/11/17		
War Diary	Favreuil	01/11/1917	30/11/1917
Heading	140/2681 Dec. 1917 No. 142 f. a.		
War Diary	Favreuil	01/12/1917	15/12/1917
War Diary	Bienvillers	15/12/1917	26/12/1917
Heading	3rd Division Medical No. 142 Field Ambulance 1918		
Heading	140/2696 Vol 30 War Diary of No 142 Field Ambulance From 1.1.18 To 31.1.18		
War Diary	Bienvillers	01/01/1918	23/01/1918
War Diary	Ficheux	27/01/1918	31/01/1918
Heading	Medical Vol 31 140/2849 War Diary of No 142 Field Ambulance From 1 Feb 1918 To 28 Feb 1918		
War Diary	Fischeux S. 26.7.4	01/02/1918	28/02/1918
War Diary	Fischeux	28/02/1918	28/02/1918
Heading	140/2849. March 1918 142 Field Ambulance		
War Diary	Fischeux S 26.7.4	01/03/1918	11/03/1918
War Diary	Fischeux	12/03/1918	23/03/1918
War Diary	Fischeux S 26.7.4	24/03/1918	26/03/1918
War Diary	Fischeux (Boisleau Au Mont)	27/03/1918	29/03/1918
War Diary	Bac De Sud	29/03/1918	30/03/1918
War Diary	Ivergny	31/03/1918	31/03/1918
Heading	Vol 33 140/2900 War Diary of No 142 Field Ambulance From 1 April 1918 To 30 April 1918		
War Diary	Ivergny	01/04/1918	01/04/1918
War Diary	Le Vielfort	02/04/1918	06/04/1918
War Diary	Braquemont	07/04/1918	12/04/1918
War Diary	Chateau L'Abbaye	13/04/1918	30/04/1918
Heading	Vol 34 140/2983 War Diary of No 142 Field Ambulance From 1 May 1918 To 31 May 1918		
War Diary	Chateau L'Abbaye	01/05/1918	02/05/1918
War Diary	Lapugnoy	03/05/1918	31/05/1918
Heading	Vol 35 140/3049 War Diary of No 142 Field Ambulance From 1/6/18 To 30/6/18		
War Diary	Lapugnoy	01/06/1918	30/06/1918
Heading	Vol 36 140/3131 War Diary of No 142 Field Ambulance From 1/7/18 To 31/7/18		
War Diary	Lapugnoy	01/07/1918	14/07/1918
War Diary	Lebuvriere	16/07/1918	31/07/1918
Heading	Vol 37 140/3200 War Diary of No 142 Field Ambulance From 1/8/18 To 31/8/18		
War Diary	Lebuvriere	01/08/1918	07/08/1918
War Diary	Auchel	08/08/1918	12/08/1918
War Diary	Brevillers	13/08/1918	19/08/1918
War Diary	Bienvillers	20/08/1918	20/08/1918
War Diary	Ayette	21/08/1918	22/08/1918
War Diary	F4 a 54 (Bucuoy Comb 1/40.000)	23/08/1918	24/08/1918
War Diary	F4a54	25/08/1918	28/08/1918
War Diary	T25C5.8	29/08/1918	31/08/1918

Operation(al) Order(s)	3rd Division R.A.M.C. Operation Order No. 110 Appendix I	20/08/1916	20/08/1916
Operation(al) Order(s)	9th Inf. Bde. Operation Order No. 15 Appendix II	29/08/1918	29/08/1918
Operation(al) Order(s)	9th Infantry Brigade Operation Order No. 17 Appendix III		
Heading	Vol 38 140/3259 War Diary of 142 Field Ambulance. From 1/9/18 To 30/9/18		
War Diary	T 25 C 5.8 (Maison Rouge)	01/09/1918	05/09/1918
War Diary	La Cauchie (V 17d 78)	06/09/1918	10/09/1918
War Diary	Douchy	11/09/1918	11/09/1918
War Diary	Favreuil (H 10 a. 2.5)	12/09/1918	18/09/1918
War Diary	Beugny (I 1.6 C 3.5)	19/09/1918	20/09/1918
War Diary	Beugny I15 b 9.1	21/09/1918	26/09/1918
War Diary	Yorkshire Bank (K 32b 45)	27/09/1918	29/09/1918
War Diary	Beugny (I15 b 9.1.)	30/09/1918	30/09/1918
Operation(al) Order(s)	3rd Division R.A.M.C. Operation Order No. 114.	05/09/1918	05/09/1918
Operation(al) Order(s)	3rd Division R.A.M.C. Operation Order No. 113.	02/09/1918	02/09/1918
Operation(al) Order(s)	9th Infantry Brigade Operation Order No. 21.	02/09/1918	02/09/1918
Operation(al) Order(s)	3rd Division R.A.M.C. Operation Order No. 112.	01/09/1918	01/09/1918
Operation(al) Order(s)	9th Infantry Brigade Operation Order No. 20.	01/09/1918	01/09/1918
Operation(al) Order(s)	9th Inf. Bde. Operation Order No. 19.	01/09/1918	01/09/1918
Heading	140/3324 Oct 1918 142nd Fld. Ambce		
Heading	Vol 39 War Diary of No 142 Field Ambulance From 1.10.18 To 31.10.18		
War Diary	Canal Du Nord. (J 36 b 3.3)	01/10/1918	01/10/1918
War Diary	K 29d 8.9	01/10/1918	02/10/1918
War Diary	K 29 d. 8.9. (57C).	03/10/1918	07/10/1918
War Diary	Masnieres (G 26 C. 5.5)	07/10/1918	09/10/1918
War Diary	K 29C. 8.9	09/10/1918	12/10/1918
War Diary	Noyelles (L 11 b 2. o)	13/10/1918	20/10/1918
War Diary	Bevillers C 22 d 3.2.	20/10/1918	22/10/1918
War Diary	Quievy D 19 b 7.7.	22/10/1918	23/10/1918
War Diary	Solesmes (D 6 d.4.0)	23/10/1918	27/10/1918
War Diary	Le Trousse Minon. W 17 d 1.8 (Sheet 51.4)	28/10/1918	29/10/1918
War Diary	Solesmes (E 1 C 3.2) (Sheet 57 B)	29/10/1918	29/10/1918
War Diary	Solesmes (E 1 C 3.2)	29/10/1918	30/10/1918
War Diary	Cattenieres (H 12 C 9.9.)	30/10/1918	30/10/1918
Miscellaneous	A.D.M.S. 3rd Division App I		
Miscellaneous	Staff Captain 9th Inf Bde App II		
Operation(al) Order(s)	Orders No 5 by Lieut-Col. G.O. Chambers R.A.M.C. Appendix III	12/10/1918	12/10/1918
Miscellaneous	Warning Order by Lieut-col., G. O. Chambers. R.A.M.C. Commanding No. 142 Field Ambulance. App IV		
Operation(al) Order(s)	Orders No 6 by Lieut-Colonel. G. O. Chambers. R.A.M.C. Commanding No. 142 Field Ambulance. App V	20/10/1918	20/10/1918
Operation(al) Order(s)	Order No 6 by Lieut-Col. G. O. Chambers. R.A.M.C. Commanding No. 142 No. Field Ambulance.	22/10/1918	22/10/1918
Operation(al) Order(s)	Addendum To Orders No 6 By Lieut-Col. G. O. Chambers., R.A.M.C. Commanding No 142 Field Ambulance. App VI	22/10/1918	22/10/1918
Operation(al) Order(s)	Orders (No 7) by Lieut-Colonel G. O. Chambers., R.A.M.C. Comdg No. 142 Field Ambulance.	25/10/1918	25/10/1918

Operation(al) Order(s)	Orders (No 8) by Lieut-Col., G. O. Chambers., R.A.M.C. Comdg No. 142 Field Ambulance. Appendix VIII	29/10/1918	29/10/1918
Operation(al) Order(s)	Orders No. 9 By Lieut-Col. G. O. Chambers. R.A.M.C. Commanding Field Ambulance. XI	30/10/1918	30/10/1918
Heading	Vol 40 140/3401War Diary of No 142 Field Ambulance From 1 Nov 1918 To 30 Nov 1918		
War Diary	Cattenieres (H 12 C. 9.9)	01/11/1918	03/11/1918
War Diary	Quievy (D 19 b 6.6)	03/11/1918	08/11/1918
War Diary	Romeries (W 21b 5.0)	08/11/1918	09/11/1918
War Diary	Frasnoy (M 10 b.6.6) Sheet 51	10/11/1918	16/11/1918
War Diary	La Longueville (136 a 6.3)	16/11/1918	17/11/1918
War Diary	La Longueville	18/11/1918	18/11/1918
War Diary	Hospice Sous-Le-Bois	19/11/1918	20/11/1918
War Diary	Colleret (Namur) 3 A.9.1	20/11/1918	20/11/1918
War Diary	Colleret (3 A 9.1)	21/11/1918	23/11/1918
War Diary	Biercee (3 D. 2.8)	24/11/1918	24/11/1918
War Diary	Marbaix (3 E 45.90)	25/11/1918	25/11/1918
War Diary	Villers Poterie	26/11/1918	27/11/1918
War Diary	St Gerard	28/11/1918	28/11/1918
War Diary	Purnode	29/11/1918	29/11/1918
War Diary	Skeuvre	30/11/1918	30/11/1918
Operation(al) Order(s)	Order (No. 10.) by Lieut-Colonel. G. O. Chambers. R.A.M.C. Comdg No. 142 Field Ambulance. Appendix 1	03/11/1918	03/11/1918
Operation(al) Order(s)	Orders (No. 11) by Lieut-Col. G. O. Chambers. R.A.M.C. Comdg No. 142 Field Ambulance. Appendix II	07/11/1918	07/11/1918
Operation(al) Order(s)	Order (No. 12.) by Lieut-Col. G. O. Chambers. R.A.M.C. Comdg No. 142 Field Ambulance. Appendix III	09/11/1918	09/11/1918
Miscellaneous	Orders by Lieut-Colonel. G. O. Chambers., R.A.M.C. Comdg No. 142 Field Ambulance. Appendix VI		
Miscellaneous	A.D.M.S. 3rd Division. Appendix V		
Operation(al) Order(s)	Orders (No. 13.) by Lieut-Col., G. O. Chambers. R.A.M.C. Comdg No. 142 Field Ambulance. Appendix VI	15/11/1918	15/11/1918
Operation(al) Order(s)	Orders (No. 14.) by Lieut-Col., G. O. Chambers. R.A.M.C. Comdg No. 142 Field Ambulance. Appendix VII	17/11/1918	17/11/1918
Miscellaneous	March Discipline Appendix VIII		
Operation(al) Order(s)	Orders (No 15) by Lieut-Colonel G. O. Chambers RAMC Comdg No 142 Field Ambulance. Appendix IX	19/11/1918	19/11/1918
Operation(al) Order(s)	Orders (No. 16) by Lieut-Colonel. G. O. Chambers. R.A.M.C. Comdg No. 142 Field Ambulance. Appendix XI	23/11/1918	23/11/1918
Operation(al) Order(s)	Orders (No. 17.) by Lieut-Colonel. G. O. Chambers. R.A.M.C. Commanding No. 142 Field Ambulance. Appendix XII	24/11/1918	24/11/1918
Operation(al) Order(s)	Orders (No 18) by Lieut-Colonel G. O. Chambers. RAMC Commanding No 142 Field Ambulance Appendix XIII	25/11/1918	25/11/1918
Operation(al) Order(s)	Orders (No. 19) by Major A. F. L. Shields. RAMC Commanding No 142 Field Ambulance App XIV	27/11/1918	27/11/1918
Operation(al) Order(s)	Orders (No.20) by Major A. F. L. Shields. RAMC Commanding No 142 Field Ambulance Appendix XV	28/11/1918	28/11/1918

Operation(al) Order(s)	Orders (No 21) by Major A F L Shields RAMC Commanding No 142 Field Ambulance	29/11/1918	29/11/1918
Heading	Vol 41 140/3481 No 142 Field Ambulance. War Diary For Month Of December 1918.		
War Diary	Skeuvre	01/12/1918	03/12/1918
War Diary	Ry Chateau	04/02/1918	05/02/1918
War Diary	Moinville	05/12/1918	05/12/1918
War Diary	Fisenne	06/12/1918	06/12/1918
War Diary	La Fosse	07/12/1918	07/12/1918
War Diary	Odeigne	08/12/1918	08/12/1918
War Diary	Verleumont	09/12/1918	10/12/1918
War Diary	Deyfeldt	11/12/1918	11/12/1918
War Diary	Crofflinghen	12/12/1918	12/12/1918
War Diary	Schonberg	13/12/1918	13/12/1918
War Diary	Berk	14/12/1918	14/12/1918
War Diary	Lankenheim	15/12/1918	15/12/1918
War Diary	Eichercheid	16/12/1918	16/12/1918
War Diary	Stotzheim	17/12/1918	17/12/1918
War Diary	Euskairchen	18/12/1918	18/12/1918
War Diary	Zulpich	19/12/1918	19/12/1918
War Diary	Binsfeld	20/12/1918	26/12/1918
War Diary	Kelz	27/12/1918	31/12/1918
Operation(al) Order(s)	Order (No 22) by Major A F L Shields RAMC Commanding No 142 Field Ambulance App No. I	03/12/1918	03/12/1918
Operation(al) Order(s)	Order (No 23) by Major A F L Shields RAMC Commanding No 142 Field Ambulance App No. 2	04/12/1918	04/12/1918
Operation(al) Order(s)	Order (No 24) by Major A.F.L. Shields RAMC Commanding No 142 Field Ambulance App No. 3	05/12/1918	05/12/1918
Operation(al) Order(s)	Orders No. 25 by major A. F. L. Shields RAMC Commanding No 142 Field Ambulance App No. 5	06/12/1918	06/12/1918
Operation(al) Order(s)	Orders No. 26 by major A. F. L. Shields RAMC Commanding No 142 Field Ambulance App No. 6	07/12/1918	07/12/1918
Operation(al) Order(s)	Orders (No 27) by Major A F L Shields RAMC Commanding No 142 Field Ambulance App No.7	08/12/1918	08/12/1918
Operation(al) Order(s)	Orders No. 28 by major A. F. L. Shields RAMC Commanding No 142 Field Ambulance App No. 8.	10/12/1918	10/12/1918
Operation(al) Order(s)	Orders No. 29 by major A. F. L. Shields RAMC Commanding No 142 Field Ambulance App No. 9	11/12/1918	11/12/1918
Operation(al) Order(s)	Orders No. 30 by major A. F. L Shields RAMC Commanding No 142 Field Ambulance App No.10	12/12/1918	12/12/1918
Operation(al) Order(s)	Orders (No 31) by major A F L. Shields RAMC Commanding No 142 Field Ambulance App No.11	13/12/1918	13/12/1918
Operation(al) Order(s)	Orders No. 32 by major A. F. L. Shields RAMC Commanding No 142 Field Ambulance App No.12	14/12/1918	14/12/1918
Operation(al) Order(s)	Orders No 33 by major A. F. L. Shields RAMC Commanding No 142 Field Ambulance App. No. 13	15/12/1918	15/12/1918
Operation(al) Order(s)	Orders No 34 by major A F L Shields RAMC Commanding No 142 Field Ambulance App No. 14	16/12/1918	16/12/1918
Operation(al) Order(s)	Orders No. 35 by major A F L Shields RAMC Commanding No 142 Field Ambulance App. No. 15	17/12/1918	17/12/1918
Operation(al) Order(s)	Orders No 36 by major A. F. L. Shields RAMC Commanding No 142 Field Ambulance App No. 16	18/12/1918	18/12/1918
Operation(al) Order(s)	Orders No 37 by major A. F. L. Shields RAMC Commanding No 142 Field Ambulance App No. 17	19/12/1918	19/12/1918
Heading	140/3524 Vol 42 War Diary of O.C. 142 Field Ambulance for the month of January 1919		

War Diary	Kelz (Germany) 1 L 1/100.00	01/01/1919	04/01/1919
War Diary	Kelz	05/01/1919	31/01/1919
Miscellaneous	Medical Arrangements. Appendix 1		
Heading	140/3524 Vol 43 War Diary of O.C. 142nd Field Ambulance. For The Month Of February 1919		
War Diary	Kelz	01/02/1919	23/02/1919
War Diary	Kerpen	24/02/1918	24/02/1918
War Diary	Ehrenfeld	25/02/1918	28/02/1918
Heading	War Diary of O.C. 142 Field Ambulance For The Month Of March 1919 Vol 44 140/3551		
War Diary	Ehrenfeld	01/03/1919	31/03/1919
Heading	Vol 45 140/3552 War Diary of O.C. 14th Field Ambulance For The Month Of April 1919		
War Diary	Ehrenfeld	01/04/1919	30/04/1919
Heading	War Diary of O.C. 142 Field Ambulance For The Month Of May 1919.		
Heading	Ehrenfeld	01/05/1919	30/05/1919
Miscellaneous	Conference At 64 C. C. S., by D. M. S., Army Of The Rhine.		
Heading	June 1919 142 Field Ambulance		
Heading	Cover For Documents. Nature Of Enclosures. 19 Returns (a) Armies-1st Army		
War Diary	Ehrenfeld Cologne.	01/06/1919	05/06/1919
War Diary	Ehrenfeld	06/06/1919	19/06/1919
War Diary	Ehren Feld To Durschield (J-1 Day).	19/06/1919	19/06/1919
War Diary	Durschied to Kurten	20/06/1919	20/06/1919
War Diary	Kurten	20/06/1919	30/06/1919
War Diary	Ehrenfeld	30/06/1919	30/06/1919
Heading	War Diary of O.C. 142nd Field Ambulance for the month of July 1919.		
War Diary	Ehrenfeld (Cologne)	01/07/1919	07/07/1919
War Diary	Ehrenfeld	08/07/1919	31/07/1919
War Diary	Ehrenfeld	01/08/1919	31/08/1919
Heading	Sept: 1919 142nd Field Ambulance		
War Diary	Ehrenfeld (Germany)	01/09/1919	05/09/1919
War Diary	Ehrenfeld	06/09/1919	30/09/1919
Heading	War Diary 142nd Field Ambulance October 1st 1919-October 31st 1919		
Heading	142nd Field Ambulance Original Copy Of War Diary For The Month Of October 1919		
War Diary	Ehrenfeld	01/10/1919	29/10/1919
War Diary	Cologne	30/10/1919	31/10/1919

142 FIELD AMBULANCE
1915 AUG TO 1919 OCT.

5(A) SANITARY SECTION.
1916 JAN TO 1917 MAR.

---

11 MOBILE VETERINARY SECTION.
1914 AUG TO 1919 OCT.

1408

142 FIELD AMBULANCE

1915 AUG TO 1919 OCT.

5(A) SANITARY SECTION.

1916 JAN TO 1917 MAR.

11 MOBILE VETERINARY SECTION.

1914 AUG TO 1919 OCT.

1408

3RD DIVISION
MEDICAL

NO.142 FIELD AMBULANCE
AUG - DEC 1915

3rd Division

CONFIDENTIAL

Joined 3rd Div. 26/8/15.

121/0550

War Diary

of

August 15.

No 142 Field Ambulance

From ~~10~~ 12 August 1915 To 31 Aug 1915

Vol I

Instructions regarding War Diaries and Intelligence Summaries are contained in F. S. Regs., Part II. and the Staff Manual respectively. Title pages will be prepared in manuscript.

WAR DIARY

~~or~~

~~INTELLIGENCE SUMMARY.~~

(Erase heading not required.)

Army Form C. 2118.

1

Place	Date	Hour	Summary of Events and Information	Remarks and references to Appendices
	1915			
Rouen	Aug 12th		No 142 Field Ambulance left Tweezeldown Camp at 4 am on August 10th. Entrained at Farnboro' & left that Station at 7.30 am. Arrived at Southampton 9.15 am & embarked on the S.S Manchester Importer. Three officers and 70 other ranks embarked on the S.S. Duchess of Hamilton. On arrival at Rouen The transport was parked at the Rouen Transport Camp. One officer, one Sergt & 6 men remained there. The remainder of the unit was accomodated at No 5 Infantry Base Depot Auxiliary Camp. Great inconvenience was caused by this splitting up of the unit owing to the distances to be travelled and to the difficulty of co-ordenating the work	
			On arrival I reported to the Base Commandant & the D.D.M.S. Rouen. Sent to Ordnance and Stationery Office to complete deficiencies. Exchanged unsuitable horses at the Remount Depot	
	Aug 13th		Inspected by D.D.M.S. Rouen Base	
	Aug 14th		Entrained at Rouen. Horses, wagons, 5 officers & 43 other ranks in one train the remainder in another	
St Omer	Aug 15th		Billetted at St Martin-au Laert, near Rouen. Tried to draw deficiencies at Ordnance and indented on Stationery Office at Boulogne for Army Forms & Books	

W Hambley
Major RAMC

2353 Wt. W2544/1454 700,000 5/15 D. D. & L. A.D.S.S./Forms/C. 2118.

Instructions regarding War Diaries and Intelligence Summaries are contained in F. S. Regs., Part II. and the Staff Manual respectively. Title pages will be prepared in manuscript.

WAR DIARY
or
~~INTELLIGENCE SUMMARY.~~
(Erase heading not required.)

Army Form C. 2118.

2

Place	Date	Hour	Summary of Events and Information	Remarks and references to Appendices
St Omer	August 16th		Reported to H.Q. H.Q. Troops & to D.D. G of Medical Services. Received instructions from Supply Officer to consume the rations in the train wagon. All rations rendered to H.Q., H.Q. Troops.	
	17th		Visited D.D. G St Omer to enquire about motor transport & personnel	
			Two cases of suspected strangles amongst the horses. Segregated them & sent for the Veterinary Officer	
		7pm.	Received a message from H.Q., H.Q. Troops re arrival of motor workshop unit – unit never arrived	
St Omer	21st		Received Orders from H.Q. Troops to move to ~~STEENVOORDE~~ ZUYTPEENE & await orders	
ZUYTPEENE ~~STEENVORDE~~	22nd		Marched from St Omer. Received Orders to proceed to STEENVOORDE.	
STEENVORDE	23rd		Marched from ~~STEENVOORDE~~ ZUPTEENE	
	24th		arrived from STEENVOORDE	
Hoograefe				
near Reninghelst	26		arrived from HOOGRAEFE	

[Signature] Major RAMC

2353 Wt. W2544/1454 700,000 5/15 D. D. & L. A.D.S.S./Forms/C. 2118.

Instructions regarding War Diaries and Intelligence Summaries are contained in F. S. Regs., Part II. and the Staff Manual respectively. Title pages will be prepared in manuscript.

WAR DIARY
or
INTELLIGENCE SUMMARY.
(*Erase heading not required.*)

Army Form C. 2118.

3

Place	Date	Hour	Summary of Events and Information	Remarks and references to Appendices
RENINGHELST	Aug 27th		"B" tent subdivision proceeded to farm near DICKEBUSCH and opened out a rest station of 50 beds for cases of slight illness. They have also a collecting post at OUDERDOM	
"	Aug 28th		Lieut Snodgrass, 2 Sergts & 6 men proceeded to BRANDHOEK, to no 8 3rd Amb, for instruction. Two Sergts & 6 men proceeded to HOOGRAEFE for the same purpose. I visited the Advanced Depot of Medical Stores & also No 7 Field Ambulance visited DICKEBUSCH	
"	Aug 29th		Sunday – Took church parade.	
"	Aug 30		LIEUT Scott, 2 N.C.Os and 6 men proceeded to BRANDHOEK in relief of LIEUT. Snodgrass and party	
"	Aug 31st		2 N.C.O.s and six men proceeded to HOOGRAEFE for instruction. The water carts supplied to us are already shewing signs of wear and appear to be flimsily constructed.	

William Wiley
Major RAMC
Commanding no 142 F A

2353 Wt. W2544/1454 700,000 5/15 D. D. & L. A.D.S.S./Forms/C. 2118.

3rd Division

CONFIDENTIAL

Summarised

121/6971

Sept '15

War Diary

of

142 Field Ambulance (3rd Divn)

from 1 Sept 1915 to 30 Sept 1915

Vol II

Army Form C. 2118.

Instructions regarding War Diaries and Intelligence Summaries are contained in F. S. Regs., Part II. and the Staff Manual respectively. Title pages will be prepared in manuscript.

WAR DIARY

~~or~~

~~INTELLIGENCE SUMMARY.~~

(Erase heading not required.)

Place	Date	Hour	Summary of Events and Information	Remarks and references to Appendices
RENINGHELST	1915 Sept 1st		Lieut Whitman, 2 N.C.Os & 6 men proceeded to BRANDHOEK to no 8 F.A for instruction	
Near Poperinghe	Sept 2nd		Arrived from RENINGHELST. Very little accomodation in our new farm. Most of the men in bivouacs. Weather very bad and mud ankle deep every where. Advanced dressing station at DICKEBUSCH closed, in change of area, and detachment brought in to Head Quarters. At 10.35 pm. received a message from A.D.M.S to send one officer, 24 bearers & 2 Cars to BRANDHOEK to report to O.C detachment of no 8 Fld amb there. This party returned at 4.a.m	
"	Sept 3rd		In accordance with orders received from A.D.M.S. yesterday, Capt Wallace, Lieut Snodgrass, 3 N.C.Os, 20 men & two motor ambulances & water cart proceeded this morning to KRUISSTRAAT to take over the dug-outs there from the 46th Division (H.24.a.8.9 Sheet 28 1/40,000). This is to be maintained as an advanced collecting post and a sufficient supply of medical and surgical equipment for the troops in the vicinity will be maintained. All cases to be transferred to no.8 Field Ambulance at HOOGRAEFE. Got accomodation in barns of the farm for nearly all the men	
"	Sept 4th		Visited the Collecting post at KRUISSTRAAT. Dug outs very leaky. Capt Wallace is covering them with tarred paper; he is also making brick roads. There was some difficulty in getting the 1/N.M Fld amb 46th Divn to hand over, as they had no orders to move. At Head Quarters, I pitched marquees & unpacked equipment and stored it in them. Am starting to clean farm middens and cow-sheds and to make roads – Visited AD.M.S.	

William Imley(?) Major RAMC Commanding 1/2 Fld amb ...

£353 Wt. W2544/1454 700,000 5/15 D. D. & L. A.D.S.S./Forms/C. 2118.

Instructions regarding War Diaries and Intelligence Summaries are contained in F. S. Regs., Part II. and the Staff Manual respectively. Title pages will be prepared in manuscript.

WAR DIARY
~~or~~
~~INTELLIGENCE SUMMARY.~~
(Erase heading not required.)

Army Form C. 2118.

Place	Date	Hour	Summary of Events and Information	Remarks and references to Appendices
POPERINGHE	Sept 6th		Visited Collecting post at KRUISSTRAAT. The village was shelled last night. Ten wounded admitted, one died of wounds. Visited A D M S. Lieut Scott goes to day to No 8 Fld. Amb. for temporary duty. Capt MacDonald to BRANDHOEK for instruction. Reconnaisance to post of Communication trench E of ZILLEBEKE lake will be undertaken by Officers in turn in order that they may be thoroughly conversant with the Country in the neighbourhood.	
"	Sept 7th		Drew eleven wagon loads of building material from Ypres. Went up to Communication trench at ZILLEBEKE lake, with Lieut Musson, Capt Wallace and Sergt Hardy to reconnoitre the ground. LIEUT MUSSON and Sergt Lambert go to BRANDHOEK to-night for instruction	
"	Sept 8th		Lieut Dowling & Sergt Davenport go to BRANDHOEK for instruction	
"	Sept 9th		Capt Macdonald & Sergt Ballard go to BRANDHOEK for instruction. Visited KRUISSTRAAT	
"	Sept 10th		Visited KRUISSTRAAT Collecting post	
"	Sept 11th		Remainder of Tent-sub. div of "B" Section proceed to KRUISSTRAAT. All bearers at KRUISSTRAAT return to HD. Qrs. Went to MAPLECOPSE with the A.D.M.S.	
"	Sept 13th		Visited KRUISTRAAT DUG-OUTS	
"	Sept 14.		Divisional horse show – won 1st prize for best pair of mules and third for Heavy draught.	
	Sept 15		Visited KRUISSTRAAT DUG OUTS.	
	Sept 16		LIEUT DOWLING proceeded to No 8 Field Ambulance for temporary duty	
	Sept 17		Visited KRUISSTRAAT	
	Sept 19		A' Sec. Tent sub-division opened at HD. Qrs.	

J Mann Miller.

8353 Wt. W2544/1454 700,000 5/15 D. D. & L. A.D.S.S./Forms/C. 2118.

Instructions regarding War Diaries and Intelligence Summaries are contained in F. S. Regs., Part II. and the Staff Manual respectively. Title pages will be prepared in manuscript.

WAR DIARY
or
~~INTELLIGENCE SUMMARY.~~
(Erase heading not required.)

Army Form C. 2118.

Place	Date	Hour	Summary of Events and Information	Remarks and references to Appendices
	1915			
POPERINGE.	Sept 20		LIEUT SCOTT proceeds to medical charge of 23rd Brigade R.F.A., temporarily.	
	" 21st		Saw D.A.D.M.S. In future no 142 Field Ambulance is to make a daily collection of wounded from the wagon Rendez-vous at I.16 d. 8.1 (Sheet 28. 1/40,000); at 7 p.m. Invalid KRUISSTRAAT.	
	23rd		LIEUT DOWLING relieved LIEUT SCOTT in temporary medical charge of 23rd Brigade R.F.A	
			One man slightly wounded at KRUISSTRAAT.	
	24th		Received Operation Orders from the ADMS	Ref Sheet 28 Belgium 1/40,000
	25th		We attacked at 4 a.m. The Ambulance was arranged as follows:-	
			1 Bearer Sub. Division at MAPLE COPSE	
			1 " at ZILLEBEKE	
			1 Tent Sub. Division (for Sick) open at G.15 c. 5.8	
			1 " at H.24 a. 8.9 Kruisstraat	
			The remainder in reserve at G.15 c. 5.8	
			Evacuation:- Collecting posts were formed at MAPLE COPSE + ZILLEBEKE. Advanced Dressing Station at H.24.a.8.9. Casualty Clearing Station at L.23.a (Sheet 27. 1/40,000)	
			Line of evacuation for Walking Cases. MAPLE COPSE — ZILLEBEKE — I.21.b.3.3 — I.21.b.2.10 — Bridge 14 — H.24.a.8.9.	
			Motor Amb. Convoy evacuated from A.D.S. to C.C.S	
			The Brigaded Horsed Ambulances of the Division were in readiness at A.D.S.	

8353 Wt. W2544/1454 700,000 5/15 D. D. & L. A.D.S.S./Forms/C. 2118.

Army Form C. 2118

Instructions regarding War Diaries and Intelligence Summaries are contained in F. S. Regs., Part II. and the Staff Manual respectively. Title pages will be prepared in manuscript.

WAR DIARY
~~or~~
~~INTELLIGENCE SUMMARY.~~
(*Erase heading not required.*)

Place	Date	Hour	Summary of Events and Information	Remarks and references to Appendices
POPERINGHE	1915 Sept 25 (cont)		One bearer Sub-division with 6 Motor Amb Cars were detached for duty with No 8 Fld Amb. at 4 p.m.	Ref Sheet 28 Belgium 1/40000
	26		14 Officers & 822 Other ranks were evacuated between 4 am on 25/9/15 & noon on 26/9/15. 10 German wounded were transferred to No 7 Fld Amb. and one (seriously wounded) was evacuated	
			The Horsed Ambulance Wagons proved extremely useful and covered ground which would have been quite impossible for Motor Ambulance Cars.	
			Wheeled Stretchers proved useful while the ground was dry. But heavy rain set in & they were then found to be of little use off the roads	
			The following men were reported to me as having shown gallantry under Shell fire & rifle fire.	
			No 58203 Pte BATTERSBY, E. — No 58125 Pte PHILLIPS F	
			No ~~58204~~ 58317 Pte RISEAM — No 58893 Pte KNOTT. P. J	
			No 58264 Sergt HILL, F — No 58310 Pte BRAY J. R	
			No 58313 Pte WHITE. S.W — No 58076 CAFFERTY. T.	
			No 58912 ROBERTS. W.D — No 57988 REES. H	
			No 58204 HAMMOND. J — No 58379 DALLIMORE. V. G	
			There are many others who did their work with coolness & pluck under heavy fire	

8353 Wt. W2544/1454 700,000 5/15 D. D. & L. A.D.S.S./Forms/C. 2118.

Instructions regarding War Diaries and Intelligence Summaries are contained in F. S. Regs., Part II. and the Staff Manual respectively. Title pages will be prepared in manuscript.

WAR DIARY

or

~~INTELLIGENCE SUMMARY.~~

(*Erase heading not required.*)

Army Form C. 2[illegible]

Place	Date	Hour	Summary of Events and Information	Remarks and references to Appendices
POPERINGHE	1915 Sept 26th		No 60602 Pte ADKINS, T.H reported wounded & missing. He probably passed through some Fld Amb in another Division.	
	30th		One Officer & 36 bearers were sent at 11.0 pm to MAPLE COPSE in response to a message from the O.C. Advanced Dressing Station there	
			William Wiley Major R.A.M.C.	

W

Oct - 1915

3rd Division

Confidential

121
7435

War Diary

of

No 142 Field Ambulance

From 1/10/15 To 31/10/15

To the Officer
i/c A. G's Office at the BASE.

3rd Div

Vol III

Army Form C. 2118.

Instructions regarding War Diaries and Intelligence Summaries are contained in F. S. Regs., Part II. and the Staff Manual respectively. Title pages will be prepared in manuscript.

WAR DIARY
or
~~INTELLIGENCE~~ SUMMARY.
(Erase heading not required.)

Place	Date	Hour	Summary of Events and Information	Remarks and references to Appendices
	1915			
near POPERINGHE	Oct	1st	"C" Tent-Subdivision relieved "B" Tent sub-division at KRUISSTRAAT	
			LIEUT SNODGRASS proceeded in temporary medical Charge of 2/S. Lancs. Regt.	
			LIEUT MUSSON proceeded in temporary medical charge of 6th Siege Battery, R.G.A.	
		3rd	CAPT WALLACE proceeded in relief of LIEUT Snodgrass.	
		4th	CAPT WALLACE returned to HQ. Qrs. LIEUT SNODGRASS returned to 2/S. LANCS Regt.	
		6th	DDR inspected the horses. LIEUT MUSSON & LIEUT DOWLING returned to HQ. Qrs.	
		13th	D.M.S 2nd Army accompanied by D.D.M.S. 5th Corps visited the Camp.	
		23rd	The division going into rest. The Ambulance marched to GODESWAERVELDE; during our stay near POPERINGHE, a stable was put up for the horses. Q.M. Stores erected also 7 small huts for Officers & a Sergeants' Mess & dining room for personnel. A scheme for a hutted hospital was begun & one hut for 24 patients nearly finished. Handed over to 53 Field Ambulance	
GODESWAERVELDE Q11. b. 6. 8 Sheet 27 1/40,000		24th	Billeted in a factory for making surface drainpipes — most unpromising. In order to make room had to shift thousands of drain pipes and wooden racks on which they are placed to dry. Personnel in barns. Horses in the factory. "A" tent sub-division opened.	

T2134. Wt. W708—776. 500000. 4/15. Sir J. C. & S.

Army Form C. 2118

Instructions regarding War Diaries and Intelligence Summaries are contained in F. S. Regs., Part II. and the Staff Manual respectively. Title pages will be prepared in manuscript.

WAR DIARY

~~or~~

~~INTELLIGENCE SUMMARY.~~

(Erase heading not required.)

Place	Date	Hour	Summary of Events and Information	Remarks and references to Appendices
GODESWAERVELDE	25th		CAPT. WALLACE proceeded on leave to England	
	27th		LIEUT DOWLING returned to Hd. Qrs.	
	28th		LIEUT SNODGRASS proceeded in temporary medical charge of 4/5 LANCS.	
	30		LIEUT SCOTT proceeded in temporary medical charge Liverpool Scottish	
			William Riley Major RAMC O.C. 1/2 W.L.F.A.	

T2134. Wt. W708—776. 500000. 4/15. Sir J. C. & S.

3rd Division

Confidential

3rd Dn

121/7637

WAR DIARY

Nov 1915

of

No 142 Field Ambulance

From 1st Nov 1915 To 30th Nov 1915

Vol XVI

To
The Officer
i/c A.G's Office at the BASE.

Army Form C. 2118

Instructions regarding War Diaries and Intelligence Summaries are contained in F. S. Regs., Part II. and the Staff Manual respectively. Title pages will be prepared in manuscript.

WAR DIARY
~~or~~
~~INTELLIGENCE SUMMARY.~~
(*Erase heading not required.*)

Place	Date	Hour	Summary of Events and Information	Remarks and references to Appendices
	1915 Nov			
WINNEZEELE (NORD)	4th		arrived from GODWAERSVELDE. Opened out "A" tent-subdivision in a small "brasserie" Personnel billetted in barns. H.D. horses under cover, but mules outside.	
	7th		LIEUT SNODGRASS returned from 4th S. Lancs	
	8th		LIEUT SCOTT returned from 10/ Liverpool Scottish.	
	11th		LIEUT SNODGRASS proceeded to 1/ Lincoln Regt.	
	16		LIEUT SNODGRASS returned from 1/ Lincoln Regt	
	20th		Marched with 76th Infantry Brigade via STEENVOORDE – EECKE – GODEWAERSVELDE – BOESCHEPE to RENINGHELST. On arrival took over dispositions of No 73 Field ambulance	
			HdQrs at RENINGHELST	
			A.D.S. at BEDFORD HOUSE (I 26.A)	
			A.D.S at DICKEBUSCH	
			D.S at OUDERDOM	
			with parties of bearers at VOORMEZEELE and the "BRASSERIE" (I s. 6.	

T2134. Wt. W708—776. 500000. 4/15. Sir J. C. & S.

Instructions regarding War Diaries and Intelligence Summaries are contained in F. S. Regs., Part II. and the Staff Manual respectively. Title pages will be prepared in manuscript.

WAR DIARY
or
~~INTELLIGENCE SUMMARY.~~
(Erase heading not required.)

Army Form C. 2118

Place	Date	Hour	Summary of Events and Information	Remarks and references to Appendices
	1915 November			
RENINGHELST	23rd		No 58236 Pte Perry E.W. No 58207 Pte Johnson W & No 57987 Pte Greave T. were wounded near trench 28 while collecting wounded & conveying them to the A.D.S. at Bedford House	
	25th		Visited DICKEBUSCH, OUDERDOM, BEDFORD HOUSE and Regimental Aid posts.	
	28th		Proceeded on leave to U.K. Capt A.S. Wallace in Command. Maj. M. Macmillan Major RAMC	
	28th		The D.A.D.M.S. 5th Corps visited the dressing station at OUDERDOM today	
	29th		1 N.C.O. and 12 men of B. Section proceeded to A.D.S. BEDFORD HOUSE to relieve a similar party which returned to H.Qrs	
			Alex. G. S. Wallace Capt RAMC	

T2134. Wt. W708—776. 500000. 4/15. Sir J. C. & S.

3rd Dⁿ

Confidential

F/119/1

J Dec 1915

3rd

121/7930

WAR DIARY

of

142 FIELD AMBULANCE

from 1 Dec 1915 to 31 Dec 1915

Vol V

To/ The Officer

i/c A.G's Office at the BASE.

Army Form C. 2118.

Instructions regarding War Diaries and Intelligence Summaries are contained in F. S. Regs., Part II. and the Staff Manual respectively. Title pages will be prepared in manuscript.

WAR DIARY
or
~~INTELLIGENCE SUMMARY.~~
(Erase heading not required.)

Place	Date	Hour	Summary of Events and Information	Remarks and references to Appendices
	Dec 1915			
RENINGHELST	7th		12 men proceeded to A.D.S. BEDFORD HOUSE to relieve a similar party which returned to Hd Qrs. Alex G C Wallace Capt RAMC	
	7th		Returned from leave. William Riley, Major RAMC	
	9th		LIEUT WHITMAN proceeded on leave	
	11th		The Condition of the roads is very bad & breakages to Motor Ambulance Cars are, in consequence, numerous. The road to DICKEBUSCH is especially bad and is in places almost impassable. CAPT WALLACE proceeded yesterday to D.S. at OUDERDOM.	
	13th		LIEUT A.M. CLARK, No 7 Field Ambulance attached for duty & posted to A.D. Station at BEDFORD HOUSE. LIEUT SNODGRASS returned to Head Quarters	
	15th		Heavy shelling all around BEDFORD HOUSE. Privates JACKSON No 58234, MEEHAN T.F. 60933, and DUNSTONE No 58261 carried in a man of 9th SEAFORTHS under heavy fire.	
	16th		LIEUT SNODGRASS proceeds to OUDERDOM in relief of CAPT. MACDONALD.	
	17th		CAPT. MACDONALD proceeded on leave. No. 57823 Pte Johnstone was in the party which carried in a wounded man under heavy fire on 15th inst.	

Instructions regarding War Diaries and Intelligence Summaries are contained in F. S. Regs., Part II. and the Staff Manual respectively. Title pages will be prepared in manuscript.

WAR DIARY
or
INTELLIGENCE SUMMARY.
(Erase heading not required.)

Army Form C. 2118.

Place	Date	Hour	Summary of Events and Information	Remarks and references to Appendices
	Dec 1915			
RENINGHELST	19th		Very heavy cannonade starting at 4.30 am. Orders for Division to stand-by. An attack was made, preceded by gas, against the 6th Corps. Detachment at DICKEBUSCH had to wear their gas helmets. 1 Officer & 44 O.R. wounded evacuated during the day, the majority from shell fire. [illegible] Major RAMC	
	21st		LIEUT. BOWEN proceeded on leave.	
	23rd		LIEUT. N. MACDONALD proceeded on leave	
	26th		CAPT. MACDONALD returned from leave	
	31st		During the past month the Ambulance has evacuated sick & wounded from the whole line held by the Division. The main dressing Station at OUDERDOM has been enlarged & improved & a hut built for the accomodation of personnel. At HdQrs huts have been built, roads made, bath room completed & various other improvements. Owing to the state of the roads and the distance to the Divisional Rest Station I have found it necessary to have 4 horses in each Ambulance wagon. [illegible] Major RAMC	

T2134. Wt. W708—776. 500000. 4/15. Sir J. C. & S.

3RD DIVISION
MEDICAL

NO. 142 FIELD AMBULANCE

JAN - DEC 1916.

3

3rd Div

142 Fd Ambulance

Jan

Vol VI

F/119/2.

S/Jan 1916

142 F.A

Instructions regarding War Diaries and Intelligence Summaries are contained in F. S. Regs., Part II. and the Staff Manual respectively. Title pages will be prepared in manuscript.

WAR DIARY
or
INTELLIGENCE SUMMARY.
(Erase heading not required.)

Army Form C. 2118.

Place	Date	Hour	Summary of Events and Information	Remarks and references to Appendices
	1916			
RENINGHELST	Jan	5th	Have built a shed for a Quarter-Masters Stores. Hitherto equipment not in use has been kept in a marquee & considerable trouble has to be taken to prevent the equipment from being damaged by damp. Medical Comforts and medical Stores for the Division will also be kept in the same hut.	
		7th	A draft of 10 men arrived from the base	
			[illegible signature] Major RAMC	
		8th	LIEUT SNODGRASS proceeded on leave	
			LIEUT WHITMAN proceeded to OUDERDOM	
		14th	LIEUT DOWLING proceeded on leave	
		20th	LIEUT SNODGRASS returned from leave	
		~~27~~	LIEUT MUSSON returned to HD Qrs	
		~~21st~~	2LIEUT MacDONALD proceeded to Bedford House	
		21	CAPT MACDONALD returned to HD Qrs. LIEUT WHITMAN proceeded to BEDFORD HOUSE, LIEUT SNODGRASS to OUDERDOM.	
		23	LIEUT MUSSON proceeded to DICKEBUSCH	
			LIEUT DOWLING returned from leave	
			[illegible signature] Major RAMC	

T2134. Wt. W708—776. 500000. 4/15. Sir J. C. & S.

Instructions regarding War Diaries and Intelligence Summaries are contained in F. S. Regs., Part II. and the Staff Manual respectively. Title pages will be prepared in manuscript.

WAR DIARY
or
INTELLIGENCE SUMMARY.
(Erase heading not required.)

Army Form C. 2118.

Place	Date	Hour	Summary of Events and Information	Remarks and references to Appendices
RENINCHELST	1916 Jan	24	While the motor ambulances were proceeding to the Advanced Dressing Station at BEDFORD HOUSE & taking the weekly relief of Stretcher bearers heavy shell fire was begun over the POPERINGHE – YPRES road. One of the cars in the convoy was hit & the following men were wounded:-	
			No 58843 Pte ATKINSON A., No 58378 Pte BALL. H.V., No 58251 Pte OAKEY L.T and M2 053708 Pte DOUGHTY W. – A.S.C (M.T.) attached.	
			Pte Doughty died of wounds in No 10 Casualty Clearing Station	
		31	During the month the Ambulance continued to clear the whole line occupied by the Division	
			The head Quarters are at RENINCHELST. No sick or wounded are received here. The main dressing Station (A. section tent subdivision) is at OUDERDOM. The ADVANCED DRESSING STATIONS are at BEDFORD HOUSE and "the creamery" at DICKEBUSCH. BEDFORD HOUSE clears the trenches North of the Canal and DICKEBUSCH the trenches South of the Canal.	
			There are posts at VOORMEZEELE and the BRASSERIE, which consist of small detachments to conduct walking cases to the A.D. Stations and	

Instructions regarding War Diaries and Intelligence Summaries are contained in F. S. Regs., Part II. and the Staff Manual respectively. Title pages will be prepared in manuscript.

WAR DIARY
or
INTELLIGENCE SUMMARY.
(Erase heading not required.)

Army Form C. 2118.

Place	Date	Hour	Summary of Events and Information	Remarks and references to Appendices
			and to help to load the cars at the Regimental Aid posts	
			A map showing the dispositions of the Ambulance & the sites of the Regimental Aid posts is attached	
			Wm Moore [illegible] Lieut - Colonel RAMC Commanding 142 Fld Ambulance	

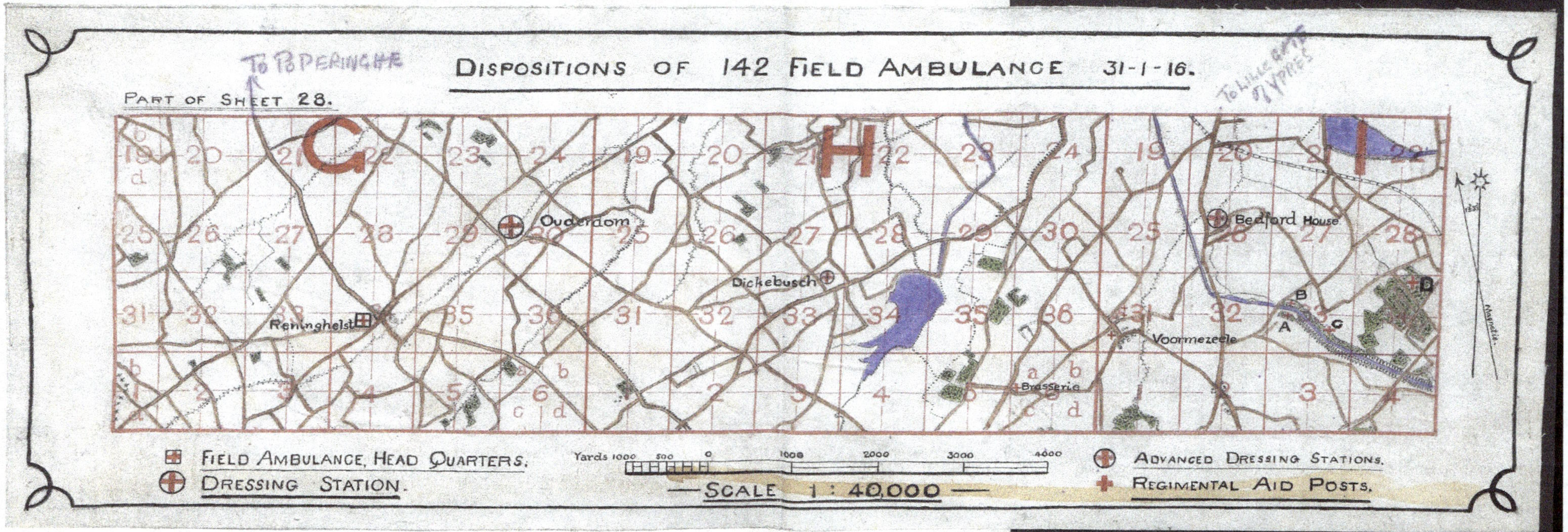

Dispositions of 142 Field Ambulance 31-1-16.
Part of Sheet 28.
To Poperinghe
To Lille Gate of Ypres
Ouderdom
Reninghelst
Dickebusch
Voormezeele
Bedford House
Brasserie
Magnetic
Field Ambulance, Head Quarters.
Dressing Station.
Advanced Dressing Stations.
Regimental Aid Posts.
Yards 1000 500 0 1000 2000 3000 4000
Scale 1 : 40,000

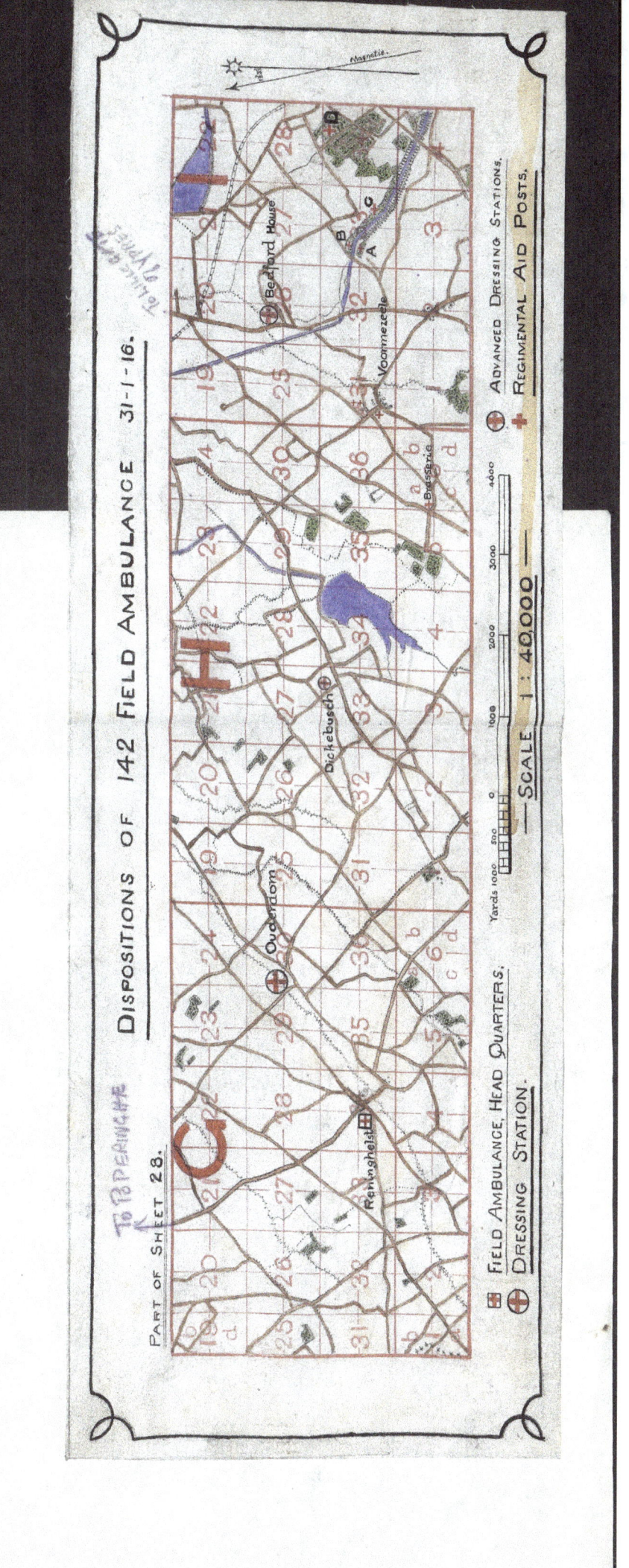

S/

142nd Fld Amb

Feb 1916

March 1916

Confidential

WAR DIARY

of

No 142 FIELD AMBULANCE.

from 1 Feb 1916 to 29 Feb 1916

Vol XIII

To The Officer

i/c Adjutant-General's Office at the BASE

Instructions regarding War Diaries and Intelligence Summaries are contained in F. S. Regs., Part II. and the Staff Manual respectively. Title pages will be prepared in manuscript.

WAR DIARY
or
~~INTELLIGENCE SUMMARY.~~
(Erase heading not required.)

Army Form C. 2118.

Place	Date	Hour	Summary of Events and Information	Remarks and references to Appendices
1916 RENINGHELST				
Feb	7th		Handed over Advanced Dressing Station at BEDFORD HOUSE on 6/2/16. Handed over A.D.S. at Dickebusch on the same date. At 4 pm. on the 7th the handing over to No 52 Field Ambulance was completed	
	8th		Marched out at 8.30 am via WESTOUTRE, BOESCHEPE, STEENVOORDE OUDEZEELE to ZERMEZEELE. Billetted here for the night. The men marched well considering the fact that they have had no practice in marching for past 3 months. Distance of march 21 miles.	
ZERMEZEELE	9th		Marched from ZERMEZEELE to Rest billets at HOULLE.	
HOULLE	10th		Arrived at 4 pm. yesterday.	
	11th		"B" Section opened for the accomodation of sick at the "Malterie", HOULLE There is accomodation for about 20. The weather being very wet, no out-door parades could be held. Lectures given to the men on first aid. In the evening Capt D.C. MACDONALD gave a lecture to Officers & N.C.O's on "Gas Defence.	
	12th.		Inspection of Gas Helmets. Lectures & Gas helmet drill.	

Instructions regarding War Diaries and Intelligence Summaries are contained in F. S. Regs., Part II. and the Staff Manual respectively. Title pages will be prepared in manuscript.

WAR DIARY
or
~~INTELLIGENCE SUMMARY.~~
(Erase heading not required.)

Army Form C. 2118.

Place	Date	Hour	Summary of Events and Information	Remarks and references to Appendices
HOULLE	14/2/16		CAPT. WALLACE proceeded in temporary medical charge of 10 ROYAL WELSH FUS.	
	15/2/16		LIEUT. COL. WILEY. proceeded on leave to U.K. CAPT. MACDONALD in command.	
			LIEUT. MUSSON proceeded in temporary medical charge of 2nd SUFFOLK REGT.	
	18/2/16		Issue of two "P.H." Tube Helmets per officer and man completed.	
			Inspection of Gas helmets and instruction in use of same.	
			[signature] Capt. RAMC	
	23/2/16		Returned from leave [signature] Lt Col RAMC	
	29/2/16		The Ambulance has been at rest at HOULLE, in the back area, since the 5th inst. While here kits & equipment have been thoroughly inspected & brought up to date and the men have been trained daily in field work. A small dressing station with accomodation for about 20 was opened. This was found to be ample, as the 76th Brigade moved up to the YPRES Salient leaving very few troops in our vicinity	
			During the month the health of the personnel has been excellent. Eight men arrived as reinforcements from Rouen Base during the month	
			[signature] Lieut. Colonel O.C. 142 Field Ambulance	

T2134. Wt. W708—776. 500000. 4/15. Sir J. C. & S.

142 F Amb
Vol VIII

Confidential

WAR DIARY

of

No 142 FIELD AMBULANCE

From 1 March 1916 To 31 March 1916

To Officer i/c A.G's Office at the BASE

Instructions regarding War Diaries and Intelligence Summaries are contained in F. S. Regs., Part II. and the Staff Manual respectively. Title pages will be prepared in manuscript.

WAR DIARY
~~or~~
~~INTELLIGENCE~~ SUMMARY.

(Erase heading not required.)

Army Form C. 2118.

Place	Date	Hour	Summary of Events and Information	Remarks and references to Appendices
HOULLE	1/3/16		T/Lieut J.T. O'BOYLE reported his arrival and is taken on the strength.	
			T/Lieut J.P.T. MUSSON is posted to the medical charge of the 2nd Suffolks and is struck off the strength with effect from the 29/2/16	
			Two Officers and 67 Other ranks with 8 Motor Drivers and 4 Cars proceeded to the YPRES Salient with the 8th Brigade entraining at ST. OMER at 11.50 a.m. (Capt D.C. MACDONALD in command)	
			1914 Infantry pattern equipment received from the Ordnance.	
			[signature] Lieut Col RAMC	
"	2/3/16		Temp. Lieut McGRATH arrived and was taken on the strength & to be supernumary	
"	4/3/16		Temp Lieut R.R Scott proceeded to take over medical charge 1st R Scots Fusiliers & is struck off the strength accordingly	
"	6/3/16		CAPT SNODGRASS, Lieut McGRATH & tent subdivision of "C" Section proceeded to NORDAUSQUES & took over the D.R.S. there from No 8. Field Ambulance.	
"	7/3/16		An advance party consisting of CAPT WALLACE, LIEUT WHITMAN & 10 other ranks proceeded to BOESCHEPE to take over the D.R.S. there from 53rd F.A, 17th Division	

T2134. Wt. W708—776. 500000. 4/15. Sir J. C. & S.

Instructions regarding War Diaries and Intelligence Summaries are contained in F. S. Regs., Part II. and the Staff Manual respectively. Title pages will be prepared in manuscript.

WAR DIARY
or
INTELLIGENCE SUMMARY.
(Erase heading not required.)

Army Form C. 2118.

Place	Date	Hour	Summary of Events and Information	Remarks and references to Appendices
BOECHEPE	8/3/16		HdQrs arrived at Boechepe.	
			The Ambulance marched from HOULLE (less one tent subdivision which remained at NORDAUSQUES & two bearer subdivisions, with 17th Div, Advance party & HdQrs. The ambulance billetted for the night 8/9th at WEMAERS-CAPPEL.	
	9/3/16		The Ambulance arrived at BOECHEPE	
	10/3/16		Sergt O'Brien & 30 bearers arrived from being attached to 17th Division	
	11/3/16		Capt Snodgrass, Lieut McGrath & "C" section tent sub-division arrived from NORDAUSQUES. CAPT PERRIN temporarily attached from 8 Kings Own (R.L.) Regt.	
			3 Horsed Ambulance wagons transferred temporarily to No 7 F.A.	
			1 motor cyclist transferred temporarily to No 8 F.A.	
			2 motor ambulances transferred temporarily to No 7. F.A.	
			Baths started.	
	12/3/16		CAPT DOWLING & men returned to HdQrs	
	15/3/16		Sergt. FAWBERT & 6 men returned from No 7 Field Ambulance	
	16/3/16		CAPT SNODGRASS proceeded in temporary medical charge of	
	17/3/16		Took over D.R. Stations at METEREN & GODESWAERSVELDE.	
			CAPT G.S. GLYNN arrived from 1 Northumberland Fusiliers [signature]	

T2134. Wt. W708—776. 500000. 4/15. Sir J. C. & S.

Instructions regarding War Diaries and Intelligence Summaries are contained in F. S. Regs., Part II. and the Staff Manual respectively. Title pages will be prepared in manuscript.

WAR DIARY
or
INTELLIGENCE SUMMARY.
(Erase heading not required.)

Army Form C. 2118.

Place	Date	Hour	Summary of Events and Information	Remarks and references to Appendices
BOESCHEPE	March	1916		
	18		Visited D.R. Stations at GODEWAERSVELDE and METEREN.	
			Capt SNODGRASS permanently attached to 1/Northumberland Fus.	
			Lieut J.T. O'BOYLE permanently attached to 8th K.O. (R.L.) Regt.	
	23rd		A practice has grown up of shewing a number of patients, such as cases of Scabies, dental & eye cases as remaining on the books of Field Ambulances while they are undergoing treatment in Casualty Clearing Stations & General Hospitals. The only result, in my opinion, is to make the evacuation figures quite fictitious. Reliance can no longer be placed on the A & D book as a source of information as to the movements of a patient; Considerably more Clerical work has to be done and the only advantage appears to be that the number of evacuations (as shewn) in the division is lower than it ought to be.	
			[signature]	
	24th		Capt A.S. GLYNN. posted to 3rd Divn. Amm. Col.	
	26th		LIEUT WHITMAN & 50 stretcher bearers proceeded to RENINGHELST.	

T2134. Wt. W708—776. 500000. 4/15. Sir J. C. & S.

Instructions regarding War Diaries and Intelligence Summaries are contained in F. S. Regs., Part II. and the Staff Manual respectively. Title pages will be prepared in manuscript.

WAR DIARY
or
INTELLIGENCE SUMMARY.
(Erase heading not required.)

Army Form C. 2118.

Place	Date	Hour	Summary of Events and Information	Remarks and references to Appendices
	March			
BOESCHEPE	29th		LIEUT. WHITMAN and party returned from RENINGHELST. During their absence they were employed in the engagement near St ELOI, which resulted in the occupation of "the mound" & the taking of 600 yards of the enemy's trenches. LIEUT WHITMAN reports that the detachment cleared the crater of wounded, under orders received from the G.O.C. 9th Infantry Brigade. All the party behaved extremely well under heavy fire. The names of No 58330 Corporal H GRIMMITT, No 58912 Corporal W.D. ROBERTS and No 57998 Pte D. SCOTT are especially mentioned. Corporal GRIMMITT was severely wounded and evacuated to the Base.	
"	31st		The Ambulance has been at BOESCHEPE since 8/3/16. At present it is running the Divisional Rest Station, the Special Hospital for self-inflicted wounds, the Baths at BOESCHEPE, and Dressing Stations at GODESWAERSVELDE & METEREN.	

[illegible]
Lieut Col RAMC

T2134. Wt. W708—776. 500000. 4/15. Sir J. C. & S.

3rd / Dw

Confidential

S/ April 1916.

WAR. DIARY.

of

142 FIELD AMBULANCE.

From 1 April 1916 to 30 April 1916

To The Officer

i/c A.G's. Office at the BASE

Vol IX

Instructions regarding War Diaries and Intelligence Summaries are contained in F. S. Regs., Part II. and the Staff Manual respectively. Title pages will be prepared in manuscript.

WAR DIARY
or
INTELLIGENCE SUMMARY.
(Erase heading not required.)

Army Form [illegible]2118.

Place	Date	Hour	Summary of Events and Information	Remarks and references to Appendices
GODEWAERSVELDE	3rd April		Handed over D.R.S at BOESCHEPE, also Special Hospital for Self-Inflicted wounds and Divisional Baths at the same place to No 4 Canadian Field Ambulance	
			Handed over Dressing Station at METEREN to No 8 Field Ambulance	
			Concentrated at GODEWAERSVELDE. Opened "B" Tent Sub-division	
			CAPT MACDONALD proceeded on leave	
	6th April		LIEUT MACDONALD proceeded on leave	
	9th "		CAPT PERRIN proceeded in M/c 7th K.S.L.I. (temporarily)	
	11th April		CAPT. G.A. BERKELEY COLE and LIEUT R. TIBBLES reported and were taken on the strength	
	15th Ap		LIEUT A. McGRATH proceeded to England on expiration of Contract	
	23rd		LIEUT WHITMAN & advance party proceeded to A D.S KEMMEL	
	24th		CAPT MACDONALD & advance party to WESTOUTRE. Lt E.7 REEVE arrived for duty	
	25		Marched to WESTOUTRE. Capt G.A COLE proceeded to XIV Corps for duty and is struck off the strength	
WESTOUTRE	29th		LIEUT. TIBBLES proceeded to temporary medical charge of 40th Brigade RFA	

Instructions regarding War Diaries and Intelligence Summaries are contained in F. S. Regs., Part II. and the Staff Manual respectively. Title pages will be prepared in manuscript.

WAR DIARY
or
INTELLIGENCE SUMMARY.
(Erase heading not required.)

Army Form C. 2118.

Place	Date	Hour	Summary of Events and Information	Remarks and references to Appendices
	1916			
WESTOUTRE	April 30		The Division moved into the new area; H.Q. 142 Field Amb. took over from 2nd Northumbn. 2 a m 25th. The advanced dressing station is at KEMMEL. Serious wounded are evacuated direct to C.C.S. Sick & slightly wounded are sent to Main Dressing Station at WESTOUTRE, where there is accommodation for 100 patients.	
			On the night of the 29/30 the alarm for a gas attack sounded; The unit stood by. Reinforced A.D.S. Only two cases of Gas poisoning passed through my Ambulance, the wind having apparently carried gas to the right, where the trenches were cleared by No 7 Field Amb.	
			On the night of 30 Ap/1st May the alarm again sounded, but was apparently a false one.	

[illegible signature]
Lt Col RAMC
O.C. 142 Fld Amb.

T2134. Wt. W708—776. 500000. 4/15. Sir J. C. & S.

5/ May 1916

CONFIDENTIAL 3rd. Div

3

Vol 10

WAR DIARY

of

No 142 FIELD AMBULANCE

From 1 May 1916 To 31 May 1916

To/

The Officer

i/c A.G's Office BASE

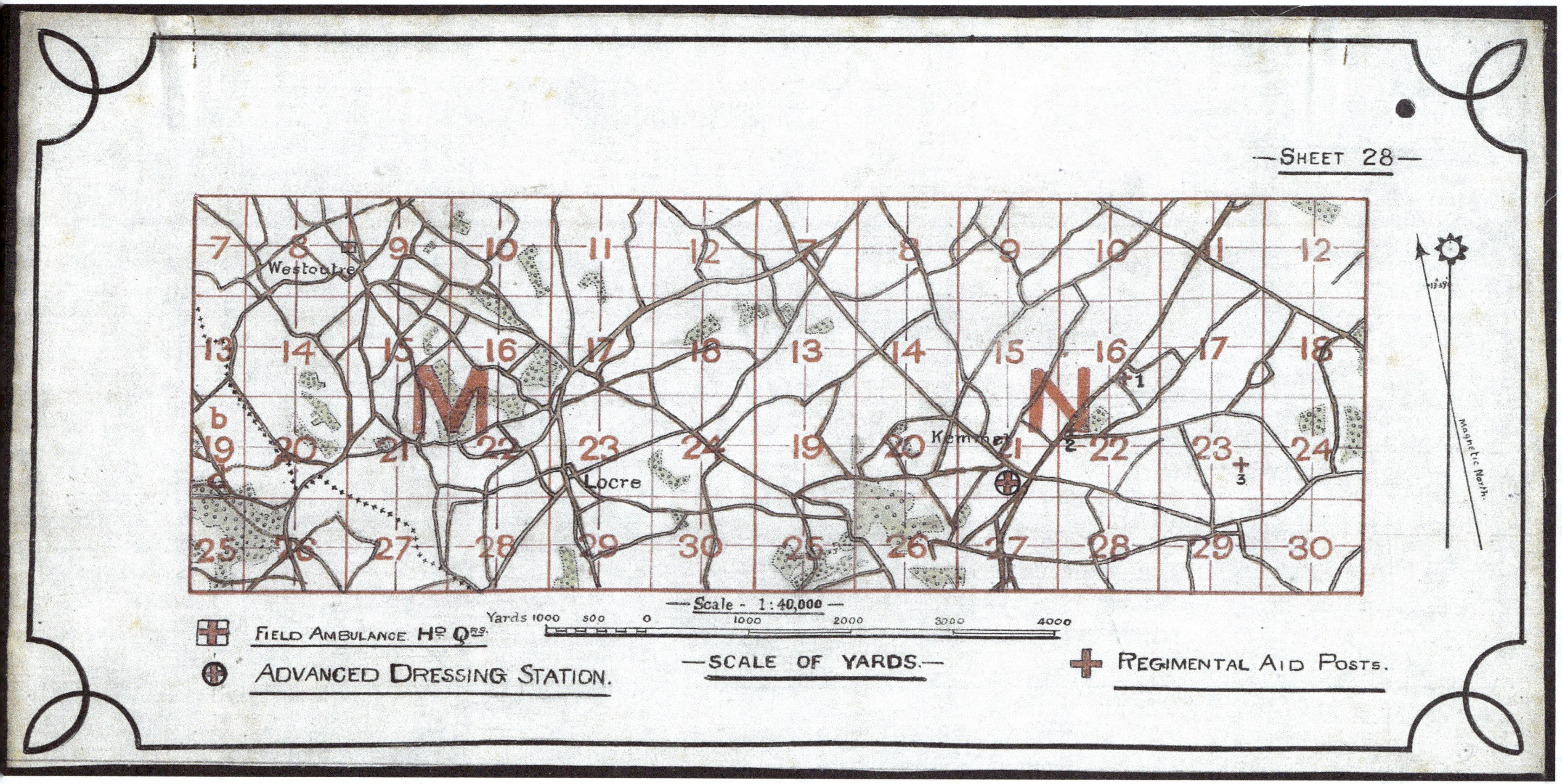

—Sheet 28—
Westoutre
Locre
Kemmel
M
N
Magnetic North.
—Scale - 1:40,000—
Yards 1000 500 0 1000 2000 3000 4000
Field Ambulance. H^d Q^rs.
Advanced Dressing Station.
—Scale of Yards.—
Regimental Aid Posts.

Instructions regarding War Diaries and Intelligence Summaries are contained in F. S. Regs., Part II. and the Staff Manual respectively. Title pages will be prepared in manuscript.

WAR DIARY
or
~~INTELLIGENCE SUMMARY.~~
(Erase heading not required.)

Army Form C. 2118.

Place	Date	Hour	Summary of Events and Information	Remarks and references to Appendices
	1916			
WESTOUTRE	May	6	CAPT W.J. DOWLING proceeded on leave	
"	"	11	LIEUT TIBBLES returned from temporary duty with 40th Brigade R.F.A.	
"	"	12	LIEUT REEVE proceeded for temporary duty to 30th Brigade R.F.A.	
		13	CAPT PERRIN proceeded on leave	
		14	LIEUT REEVE returned	
		15	CAPT A.G.S WALLACE proceeded on leave	
		15	CAPT W.J. DOWLING returned from leave	W MacArthur, Lieut Col R.A.M.C.
		17.	Lieut Col. W. WILEY proceeded on leave. CAPT D.C. MACDONALD in command.	
			LIEUT E.F. REEVE proceeded for temporary duty with ~~3rd Divisional Train~~ 8th K.O.R.L.	
			LIEUT N. MACDONALD for duty with 3rd Divisional Train.	
		21	CAPT PERRIN returned from leave.	
		23.	CAPT PERRIN M.N. proceeded for duty with 3rd D.A.C. & struck off strength	
		24.	CAPT WALLACE A.G.S. returned from leave.	
		25.	CAPT SNODGRASS. W.M. reported for duty. & taken on strength	
			LIEUT MACDONALD and advance party proceeded to GODEWAERSVELDE	
			An urgent message was received at 6 p.m. from 149th Brigade for twenty	

Instructions regarding War Diaries and Intelligence Summaries are contained in F. S. Regs., Part II. and the Staff Manual respectively. Title pages will be prepared in manuscript.

WAR DIARY
or
~~INTELLIGENCE SUMMARY.~~
(Erase heading not required.)

Army Form C. 2118.

Place	Date	Hour	Summary of Events and Information	Remarks and references to Appendices
			stretchers with bearers to collect 50 casualties. It was passed to CAPT. DOWLING at A.D.S. KEMMEL and reinforcements were sent up. CAPT. DOWLING reported all clear at 11 pm.	
GODEWAERSVELDE		27th	The ambulance marched from WESTOUTRE to GODEWAERSVELDE on relief by the 50th Div.	
			Lt Col WILEY returned from leave.	
		31st	Until the 27th of this month, the Ambulance was engaged collecting from the KEMMEL trenches, with its HQ Quarters at WESTOUTRE. Seriously wounded were evacuated direct to C.C.S & were not brought to HQ Qrs. The A.D.S at KEMMEL was improved & rendered much safer by sand-bagging – A gas proof dug-out was constructed. Numerous improvements were made at the HQ Qr Camp. Map attached.	
			William Wiley Lt Col RAMC OC 142 Fd Amb.	

T2134. Wt. W708—776. 500000. 4/15. Sir J. C. & S.

June 1916
5/

3

142. F. Amb

Vol XI

SECRET

WAR DIARY

of

No 142 FIELD AMBULANCE.

From 1 June 1916 To 30 June 1916

To/ D.A.G.
3rd Echelon.

Army Form C. 2118.

Instructions regarding War Diaries and Intelligence Summaries are contained in F. S. Regs., Part II. and the Staff Manual respectively. Title pages will be prepared in manuscript.

WAR DIARY
or
~~INTELLIGENCE SUMMARY.~~
(Erase heading not required.)

Place	Date	Hour	Summary of Events and Information	Remarks and references to Appendices
	1916			
GODEWAERSVELDE	June 2.		LIEUT E.F. REEVE took over medical charge of 7th Kings Shropshire L.I. & is struck off the strength accordingly.	
			[illegible] Lt Col.	
	4th		CAPT H.L. MANN taken on strength.	
	15th		CAPT W.J. DOWLING proceeded to temporary medical charge of 12th W. Yorks. and returned the same day, CAPT SUGARS leave having been cancelled	
			LT J.R. TIBBLES rejoined from temp medical charge of 10/R.W. Fus.	
	16		CAPT WALLACE, CAPT DOWLING & "B" tent subdivision proceeded to the Chateau at EPERLECQUES, in the training area to prepare to receive the sick of 9th Infty Brigade on their arrival	
	17		CAPT H.L. MANN took over temporary medical charge of 12/West Yorks	
	18		LT J.R. TIBBLES proceeded on leave	
			The Field Ambulance marched via CAESTRE and WAEMARS CAPPELLE to OCHTEZEELE where it billetted for the night	
	19		Marched from OCHTEZEELE to HAYERSHERGE FARM (M.2.c Sheet 27 (1/40000) & billetted there for the night	

T2134. Wt. W708—776. 500000. 4/15. Sir J. C. & S.

Instructions regarding War Diaries and Intelligence Summaries are contained in F. S. Regs., Part II. and the Staff Manual respectively. Title pages will be prepared in manuscript.

WAR DIARY
or
INTELLIGENCE SUMMARY.
(Erase heading not required.)

Army Form C. 2118.

Place	Date	Hour	Summary of Events and Information	Remarks and references to Appendices
MUNCQ-NIERLET 1916				
	June	20	Arrived at Billet in Training Area (E.26.C)	Ref
		21	D.D.G. A.V.S, D.V.S and D.D.V.S (Second Army) inspected the horses.	Sheet 27A N.E (B Series)
		24	LIEUT TIBBLES returned from leave	
			CAPT MANN returned from temporary duty with 12/W. Yorks.	
		30	Since June 20th the Ambulance has been in the training area, looking after the sick of the 9th Infantry Brigade and 56th Field Coy. R.E. The Ambulance is billetted in the farm "à la Motte Aubin" (E.26.C) There is indoor accomodation for about 25 sick. Personnel in barns. Officers in the adjoining Château Herbaut. The personnel has been trained daily in March Discipline; wagon loads reduced to scale & equipment brought up to date. Wagons painted.	

M Shaw [illegible]
Lieut Col RAMC
Commanding 142 F.A.

July 1916

Confidential

3rd Division

3

Vol 12

WAR DIARY

of

No 142 Field Ambulance

From 1 July 1916 To 31 July 1916

To A. G.

BASE

Army Form C. 2118.

Instructions regarding War Diaries and Intelligence Summaries are contained in F. S. Regs., Part II. and the Staff Manual respectively. Title pages will be prepared in manuscript.

WAR DIARY
or
~~INTELLIGENCE SUMMARY.~~
(Erase heading not required.)

Place	Date	Hour	Summary of Events and Information	Remarks and references to Appendices
	1916 July			5a HAZEBROOK 1/100000
MUNCQ NEURLET	1st			2. B.
BERNAVILLE	2nd		Marched at 10 minutes after midnight & entrained at AUDRICQ. CAPT MANN 1 corporal & 6 men proceeded on detachment to 35 C.C.S. DOULLENS.	11. LENS 1/100000
"	"		arrived at DOULLENS 1.15 pm & marched to BERNAVILLE	5. C.
HAVERNAS	3rd		marched to HAVERNAS.	11. LENS 1/100000 6 B
POULAINVILLE	4th		marched to POULAINVILLE	17. AMIENS 1/100000
"	5th		arrived POULAINVILLE 1. am. marched out at 10.30 pm	1. D.
LAHOUSSOYE	6th		arrived at LAHOUSSOYE 3. am. marched out at 10.30 pm	17. AMIENS 1/100000 1. F.
MORLANCOURT.	7th		arrived at MORLANCOURT	17. AMIENS 1/100000 1. H.
SAPPER CORNER 250 yds N.E. of BRAY	8th		Took over the dispositions of 55 Field Ambulance, 18th Division	62D 1/40000
			Bearer Division marched with the 9th Infantry Brigade.	L.15.b.10.10
"	14th		The XIII Corps attacked at Dawn (3rd, 9th & 18th divisions). The disposition of No 142	
			Field Ambulance was as follows; Tent Division (less personnel for HQ Qrs & A.D.S	Sheet ALBERT
			at BRONFAY FARM) forming an Advanced Dressing Station at CARNOY (A 13.b)	Combined 1/40 000
			Bearer Division clearing from Regimental Aid Posts of 9th Infantry Brigade in	"
			CATERPILLAR Wood (S.20.d & 26.b). An advanced Dressing Station at BRONFAY	
			FARM (F.29.d.7.8). HQ Quarters at SAPPER CORNER (L.15.b.10.10)	"

Instructions regarding War Diaries and Intelligence Summaries are contained in F. S. Regs., Part II. and the Staff Manual respectively. Title pages will be prepared in manuscript.

WAR DIARY
or
~~INTELLIGENCE SUMMARY.~~
(Erase heading not required.)

Army Form C. 2118.

Place	Date	Hour	Summary of Events and Information	Remarks and references to Appendices
SAPPER CORNER Sheet 62D L 15 b 10.10	1916 July		The Motor Ambulances of the XIIIth Corps were at my disposal & arrangements for Clearing cases from all A.D. Stations of the Corps were in my hands. The cars were parked at DIVE COPSE (J 24) & sent for to SAPPER CORNER as required whence they were distributed to ADVANCED DRESSING STATIONS. About 1 pm (14th) The nine horsed Ambulance wagons, which had been carrying walking cases from SAPPER CORNER to DIVE COPSE were ordered up to A.D.S CARNOY & worked on the CARNOY - MONTAUBAN ROAD, relieving the stretcher bearers who were becoming exhausted; extra horses & drivers were also sent up so that the wagons could work continuously. The wounded from the 8th Infantry brigade were cleared by the bearers of No 8 Field Ambulance to my A.D Stations. Bearers of No 7 Field Ambulance were in reserve with 76th Infantry Brigade. Great assistance was rendered by the Cavalry to the stretcher bearers (19th Hussars ?) the 3rd Divisional Band and R.G.A (59th Siege Bty) ∧ The latter very kindly offered their services to O.C A.D.S. CARNOY. CAPT MANN & 9 other ranks rejoined from 35 C.C.S & immediately proceeded to CARNOY to reinforce the bearers	
	19		CAPT WALLACE proceeded to 8/KORL & is struck off the strength	

T2134. Wt. W708—776. 500000. 4/15. Sir J. C. & S.

Instructions regarding War Diaries and Intelligence Summaries are contained in F. S. Regs., Part II. and the Staff Manual respectively. Title pages will be prepared in manuscript.

WAR DIARY
or
~~INTELLIGENCE SUMMARY.~~
(Erase heading not required.)

Army Form C. 2118.

Place	Date	Hour	Summary of Events and Information	Remarks and references to Appendices
SAPPER CORNER N^r BRAY	20th		There has been continual fighting since my last entry. The evacuation of the wounded has been going on with clockwork regularity.	
			The following casualties have occurred in 142 Field Ambulance: –	
			on the 14th inst killed in action No 35749 Staff Sergt CANTON, J	Buried at CARNOY
			" No 58310 Pte BRAY, J.R	
			" No 58272 Pte HAYWARD, C	
			wounded No 56408 Sergt BURTT, R.E	
			" (slightly, to duty) No 60967 Pte LENNETT. C	
			On the 17th inst, wounded slightly, to duty No T4/038304 Dr STEVENSON, F.R (A.S.C)	
			" 18th inst, wounded (gassed) No 9097 a/L Cpl MANTLE, A.B.	
			On the 17th inst two heavy draught horses were wounded. As my spare pair of H.D horses has been taken away, there will be obvious difficulty if my Ambulance has to march before remounts arrive.	
			In the evening H^d Quarters moved to BILLON WOOD (Sheet Albert comb. F.24.b.8.2)	
	21st		Handed over A.D.S CARNOY & A.D.S BRONFAY FARM to O.C. 107 Fld Amb.	
			Opened a new A.D.S at "CARNOY RAILHEAD" (i.e. where the trolley line crosses the road at A 13.d.4.8) – evacuating down the trolley line from BERNAFAY WOOD	

Instructions regarding War Diaries and Intelligence Summaries are contained in F. S. Regs., Part II. and the Staff Manual respectively. Title pages will be prepared in manuscript.

WAR DIARY
or
INTELLIGENCE SUMMARY.
(Erase heading not required.)

Army Form C. 2118.

Place	Date	Hour	Summary of Events and Information	Remarks and references to Appendices
	1916			
BILLON WOOD	July 20th		Bearers in North BERNAFAY WOOD, clearing from LONGUEVAL	
	"		CAPT MANN despatched on temporary duty with 23rd Brigade R.F.A.	
	22nd		CAPT FARRANT joined & sent to A.D.S. CARNOY	
	24th		Bearers relieved by bearers of No 5 Field Ambulance	
SAPPER CORNER	"		Owing to the position at BILLON WOOD becoming untenable owing to heavy shell fire, removed HdQrs & Car rendez-vous back to SAPPER CORNER	
	26		Handed over to No 5 Field Ambulance	
			Tent Division marched to XIII Corps Main Dressing Station	
			Bearer Division to VILLE-SUR-ANCRE	
XIII Corps Main D.S (J.24)			Further casualties as follows; On 22/7/16 No 57823 Pte JOHNSTONE (wounded) On 23/7/16 No 58095 Pte CHESSAR J (Killed in action), On 24/7/16 No 58190 Pte TEW, J.F (Killed in action) On 23/7/16 No 58127 Pte COYNE, H, No 48628 Pte Pritchard A.A, No 58311 Pte WILLIAMS. J No 58366 Pte LESVEUR FJ, No 58898, Pte BIRHET J.H, No 74892 Pte OSBORN, W.N, (all wounded). On 24/7/16 No 58246 SERGT FAWBERT J, No 58379 Pte DALLIMORE. V.G No 58273 Pte SMALL, S, No 58241 Pte SCHOFIELD, No 58114 Pte FURSDEN, J, No 58376 Pte BLAIR R (all Killed in action), No 58042 Pte KNIGHT, C	

T2134. Wt. W708—776. 500000. 4/15. Sir J. C. & S.

Army Form C. 2118.

WAR DIARY
or
~~INTELLIGENCE SUMMARY.~~
(Erase heading not required.)

Instructions regarding War Diaries and Intelligence Summaries are contained in F. S. Regs., Part II. and the Staff Manual respectively. Title pages will be prepared in manuscript.

Place	Date	Hour	Summary of Events and Information	Remarks and references to Appendices
XIII Corps Main Dressing Station J.24 Sheet ALBERT combined			No 60929 Pte KIRK. W, No 58358 Pte OAKLEY, E.J., No 57988 Pte REES, H., No 58153 Pte ROBERTS, W., No 58292 Pte JONES, I.S, No 70566 Pte ANDREWS, A, No 57863 a/L. Sgt DEAS, J.M (all wounded)	
			The following were wounded & remained at duty:- Lt & Qr Mr E.C. BOWEN, No 58338 Pte DOUGAL, J, No 58219 Pte NASH, A No 58281 Pte CLOSE, R.M No 58148 Pte REYNOLDS	
			The following are especially noted for gallantry in action CAPT W.M. SNODGRASS, CAPT W.J. DOWLING & Lieut J.R TIBBLES No 18734 Sgt WILSON. S. No 4692 Cpl DALE No 6414 Pte TILL W.L. No 78836 Cpl CHANDLER A.C No 57606 Pte GILL.S. No 31114 Sgt WESTON S.F No 57863 Cpl (a/L Sgt) DEAS J.M No 58909 Pte SAMSON A. No 58308 Pte WORSWICK H. No 58148 Pte REYNOLDS. F T3 10560 Dr SHIPP. J.G.V – A.S.C. attached 1427A. No T4 038304 Dr STEVENSON E.R A.S.C. attached 1427A and No 57928 Pte ADAMS W.S.	
			[signature]	

SECRET

Copy No 3

Operation Order No. 17 by
LIEUT. COLONEL W. WILEY R.A.M.C.
Commanding 142 Field Ambulance.

1/7/16

Ref- Sheet 11 LENS. 1/100000.

MOVE 1. The Ambulance will march tomorrow at 10 minutes past midnight and entrain at AUDRUICQ station for CANDAS via CALAIS and ABBEVILLE.
Train leaves AUDRUICQ at 2.39 am.
Entrainment must be completed ½ hr. before the departure of the train.

RATIONS 2. Troops will entrain with
(a) Unexpended portion of the days ration.
(b) Iron rations
(c) One days rations in Supply waggon.
Water carts will be entrained full.

FORAGE 3. One days Forage in the trucks with the horses and one days supply in the Supply waggon.

ROPES. 4 Breast ropes for horse trucks will be provided by the Ambulance. Ropes for lashing vehicles on the flat trucks will be provided by the railway.

LOADING PARTY 5 CAPT. N. MACDONALD, Sgt FAWBERT, + "B" Section Bearers.

BILLETING 6. The Billeting Officer will be CAPT. DOWLING

MOTOR 7. Motor Cars will proceed by road under CAPT WAITMAN via DOULLENS to BERNAVILLE.
Detailed Orders will be issued later.
Motor Cyclists will proceed by train.

Issued at 2pm.

(signed) William Wiley.
Lieut. Col. R.A.M.C.
Comdg. 142 Field Ambce.

Copy. 1. A.D.M.S.
2 Filed
3 War Diary

SECRET

Copy No 1

Operation Order No. 18 by
LIEUT-COLONEL W. WILEY RAMC.
Commanding 142 Field Ambulance 4/7/16.

Ref. 1/100000 Sheets 11/17.

MOVE 1. The ambulance will march tonight at 7.50 pm and join the column of "B" group. Starting point of column 250 yds N. of V in VIGNACOURT

BILLETS 2. CAPT DOWLING with the interpreter and a mounted orderly will proceed at once for to the MAIRIE at POULAINVILLE. for billeting duties

MOTOR TRANSPORT 3. Motor Cars will proceed direct to POULAINVILLE and await orders. They must be clear of FLESSELLES by 8 pm

(signed) William Wiley.
Lieut. Col. RAMC
O/C 142 Field Ambulance.

Issued at 7 pm.
Copy 1 War Diary
2 ADMS.
3 Files.

SECRET

Copy No 1.

Operation Order No. 19 by
LIEUT-COLONEL W WILEY R.A.M.C.
Commanding 142 Field Ambulance

5/7/16.

Ref. Map. 1/100000. Sheet 17.

MOVE 1. March out this evening at 10.30 pm
Starting point of column. crossroads 200 yds south of CARDONNETTE. Ambulance passes starting point at 11.15 pm.
Route ALLONVILLE - QUERRIEU - PONT NOYELLES - LA HOUSSOYE.

BILLETING 2. LIEUT BOWEN, the Interpreter and an Orderly will proceed in the FORD car and report to the Staff-Captain at the MAIRIE of LA HOUSSOYE at 6pm.

MOTOR TRANSPORT 3. Motor Ambulance Cars to be clear of the starting point by 10 pm.

(signed) William Wiley.
Lieut. Col. R.A.M.C.
Comdg 142 Field Ambce

Issued at 12.10 pm

Copy 1. War Diary
2 A.D.M.S.
3 Files

SECRET

Copy No 2

Operation Order No 30 by
LIEUT. COLONEL W. WILEY R.A.M.C.
Commanding 142 Field Ambulance

6/7/16

Ref. Sheet 17. AMIENS. 1/100000.

1 Ambulance will march at 9.30 pm.
Starting point of column the forked roads 650 yds. east of the final E in ESCARDONNEUSE. Ambulance passing starting point at 10.10 pm. Route BONNAY - main CORBIE-BRAY Road to cross roads due South of the L of MORLANCOURT. First halt at 10.30 pm and afterwards at 11.30 pm, 12.30 pm and so on.

2 LIEUT BOWEN will report to 2nd LIEUT. R.H. SCOTT at the MAIRIE MORLANCOURT at 6 pm.

3 Motor Ambulance Cars start before 9 pm

(signed) William Wiley
Lieut. Col. R.A.M.C.
Comdg. 142 Field Ambulance

Issued at 2 pm

Copy 1 A.D.M.S.
2 War Diary
3 File.

SECRET

Copy No 2

Operation Order No. 21 by
LIEUT.-COLONEL W. WILEY. R.A.M.C.
Commanding 142 Field Ambulance.

Ref. - 1/40000. Sheet 62D. 7/7/16

MOVE 1. The Field Ambulance will take over the disposition of No 55 Field Ambulance to-morrow.

ADVANCE PARTY. 2. CAPT. D. C. MACDONALD, CAPT. W. J. DOWLING and 3 Sergeants will proceed at 8.30 a.m. to CARNOY and reconnoitre.

TENT DIVISION 3. The Tent-division will march at 10 o'clock to CARNOY and take over the A.D. STATION there and the A.D. STATION at BRONFAY FARM.

BEARER DIVISION 4. The Bearer Division will march with the 9th Infantry Brigade on the night of the 8a/9a.

HORSE TRANSPORT 5 Horse Transport will proceed at 2.30 p.m. to K. 20. b. 3. 9.

MOTOR TRANSPORT 6. Motor Transport will report to Senior Transport N.C.O. at DIVE COPSE (J.24).

(signed) William Wiley.
Lieut Colonel R.A.M.C.
O.C. 142 Field Ambulance.

Issued at 10 pm

Copy 1. A.D.M.S.
2 War Diary
3 Filed.

Aug. 1916

SECRET

Vol 13

WAR DIARY of No 142 Field Ambulance

From 1 Aug 1916 To 31 Aug 1916

To/ A. G

A. G's Office
BASE

Instructions regarding War Diaries and Intelligence Summaries are contained in F. S. Regs., Part II. and the Staff Manual respectively. Title pages will be prepared in manuscript.

WAR DIARY
or
INTELLIGENCE SUMMARY.
(Erase heading not required.)

Army Form C. 2118.

Place	Date	Hour	Summary of Events and Information	Remarks and references to Appendices
	1916			
DIVE COPSE	Aug	1st	Tent Division working in XIII Corps Main Dressing Station	Ref sheet
(J.24 Sheet Albert Comb.)			Bearer Division with 9th Infty Brigade at VILLE-SUR-ANCRE	Albert
		12th	Bearer Division marched with 9th Infantry Brigade to "the Sandpits" (E.18 d.0.6)	(Combined)
BILLON.		14th	Bearer Division proceeded to CASEMENT TRENCH (A10.b.5.8) & worked from Regimental Aid posts at (A12.a.2.7) and (S.32.c.0.5)	
			Tent Division left XIII Corps Main Dressing Station and took over the Advanced Dressing Stations at BILLON FARM (F.30.a central) & WEST PERONNE (A.20.b.8.8) from 1st 2 West Lancs Fld Amb. and 1/3 West Lancs Fld Amb	
		17th	3rd Division came under XIV Corps from midnight 16/17 Aug.	
			Capt R. FARRANT proceeded to temporary medical charge of 7/K.S.L.I.	
			At 7 pm the Bearer Division was relieved by No 7 Field Ambulance & proceeded to BRONFAY FARM	
DIVE COPSE		20th	handed over to 105 F.A. BILLON WOOD, WEST PERONNE & TALUS BOISE. Tent Division proceeded to DIVE COPSE & Bearer Division joined 9th Brigade at the Sand Pits, Meaulte	
		21	Bearers moved with 9th Infantry Brigade to VILLE-SUR-ANCRE.	
		22nd	HORSE TRANSPORT marched to MONTONVILLERS.	

T2134. Wt. W708—776. 500000. 4/15. Sir J. C. & S.

Army Form C. 2118.

WAR DIARY
or
INTELLIGENCE SUMMARY.
(Erase heading not required.)

Instructions regarding War Diaries and Intelligence Summaries are contained in F. S. Regs., Part II. and the Staff Manual respectively. Title pages will be prepared in manuscript.

Place	Date	Hour	Summary of Events and Information	Remarks and references to Appendices
	1916			
SHEET 11-LENS 1/100000	Aug	23rd	RAMC Personnel entrained at MERICOURT for FIONVILLERS-CANDAS.	
			Motor transport proceeded by road to BERNAVILLE	
			Unit concentrated at GORGES	
		25th	Marched to MEZEROLLES.	
		26th	Marched to BUNEVILLE	
		27	Marched to ANVIN. All motor Ambulance Cars & Cycles & ASC (MT) personnel transferred to 3rd Divisional Supply Column, for duty with 18th Division	
		28	Two motor ambulances arrived from 1st Corps on loan	
		29	Marched to TANGRY	
		30	Marched to MARLES-LES-MINES	
		31	"C" Section took over Billets at NOEUX-les-MINES	

[illegible] Lt Col RAMC
OC 142 Field Ambulance

T2134. Wt. W708—776. 500000. 4/15. Sir J. C. & S.

Copy No. 2.

SECRET

Operation Order No. 23. by
Lieut. Col. W. WILEY, RAMC
Commanding 142 Fd. Ambce.
GORGES.

Ref. Sheet 11. LENS - 1/100000.

MOVE 1. The Field Ambulance will march at 8.30 am tomorrow, and march with the 9th Brigade GROUP to an area about MEZEROLLES - RESMAISNIL. - BARLY. Starting-point; cross-roads northern exit of FIENVILLERS. Hour of passing starting-point 9.30 am.

BILLETING 2. Orders regarding Billeting will be issued later.

MOTOR AMBULANCES 3. The Cars will proceed independently; - detailed orders later.

Issued at 4.30 pm
24/8/16.

(Sd.) William Wiley
Lieut Col.
........................, R.A.M.C.
COMDG: 142ND FIELD AMBULANCE.

Copies to (1) ADMS.
(2) War Diary

Operation Order No 22 by Copy No 2

Lieut. Colonel W. Wiley R.A.M.C.

Commanding 142 Field Ambulance.

Ref. Sheet ALBERT (combined) BILLON FARM.

19.8.16

MOVE 1. The 35th Division will relieve the 3rd Division in the line on the night of Aug 19/20.

TENT DIVISION. 2 Tent division will hand over the A.D. Stations at WEST PERONNE, BILLON FARM, and TALUS BOIS to in-coming Field Ambulances of 35th Division by 12 am on 20th August and on completion of relief march to K 15 a. 5.0 on the BRAY - CORBIE Road and bivouac.

BEARER DIVISION 3. Bearer divisions with Horsed Ambulances, Wagons, Water Cart and One Limber Wagon and necessary equipment will rejoin the 9th Infantry Brigade at the CITADEL by 11 am. on Aug. 20th.

SURPLUS EQUIPMENT &c. 4 All equipment and stores surplus to Field Ambulance Scale to be handed over to in-coming Field Ambulance.

TRANSPORTS 5 Staff Sgt Major WALFORD will arrange for two empty G.S. Wagons and two empty limbered wagons to be at BILLON FARM by 6 am. on the 20th August.

(sd) William Wiley

Lieut. Colonel R.A.M.C.

O/C. 142 Field Ambulance

Issued at 10 pm.

Copies to

1 A.D.M.S.

2 War Diary

Sept 1916

Secret — 3rd Div

Vol 14.

WAR DIARY

of

No 142 Field Ambulance

From 1 Sept 1916 To 30 Sept 1916

To A. G.

A.G.'s Office
BASE.

Army Form C. 2118.

WAR DIARY
or
INTELLIGENCE SUMMARY.
(*Erase heading not required.*)

Instructions regarding War Diaries and Intelligence Summaries are contained in F. S. Regs., Part II. and the Staff Manual respectively. Title pages will be prepared in manuscript.

Place	Date	Hour	Summary of Events and Information	Remarks and references to Appendices
	1916			Sheet 36B 1/40000
NOEUX-Les MINES	Sept	2	Main party arrived at NOEUX-les-MINES.	
		8	Handed over Command to CAPTAIN D.C. MACDONALD [signature] Wiley Lieut Colonel R.A.M.C.	
		8	LIEUT-COLONEL WILEY was evacuated to No 1 C.C.S. sick.	
		12.	CAPT. H.L. MANN rejoined from Temporary Duty as Officer in Medical Charge of 23rd Brigade of Artillery.	
		13.	LIEUT. J.R. TIBBLES was evacuated sick to WEST RIDING C.C.S.	
		12.	CAPT. G.W. WHITMAN and CAPT. N. MACDONALD proceeded on leave to CANADA for 30 days. Authority W.O. Letter 121/Medical/2693. A.M.D.1 of 24/7/16. D.C. Macdonald Capt RAMC	

T2134. Wt. W708—776. 500000. 4/15. Sir J. C. & S.

Instructions regarding War Diaries and Intelligence Summaries are contained in F. S. Regs., Part II. and the Staff Manual respectively. Title pages will be prepared in manuscript.

WAR DIARY
or
INTELLIGENCE SUMMARY.
(Erase heading not required.)

Army Form C. 2118.

Place	Date	Hour	Summary of Events and Information	Remarks and references to Appendices
NOEUX LES MINES	Sept.	15th	Took command of the Field Ambulance with effect from 9/9/16 Authority DMS First Army No P.L. 966 d/13-9-16	
			During the period the Ambulance was in NOEUX LES MINES a large School was occupied as a hospital with accommodation for about 40 patients. Sick from the 9th Brigade and I Corps Cavalry Regt VAUDRICOURT were accommodated. There was also an Officers ward capable of accommodating five patients.	
			Shoemakers tailors and Hairdressers shops were opened and operations were begun on two huts to accommodate personnel for the winter. The personnel were billeted in the upper storey of the Hospital and in tents pitched in an adjoining garden and in neighbouring houses. One N.C.O and twelve men were employed at working the Divisional Baths, an average of 700 men being bathed daily.	
			A site was selected in the vicinity of NOEUX LES MINES and a scheme was prepared for opening a hospital for Cholera patients under CAPT. MANN should the necessity for it arise.	
			Visits were made by D.G.M.S of British Army in the Field, D.D.M.S I Corps and ADMS 3rd Division.	
			The wagons were repainted.	

T2134. Wt. W708—776. 500000. 4/15. Sir J. C. & S.

Instructions regarding War Diaries and Intelligence Summaries are contained in F. S. Regs., Part II. and the Staff Manual respectively. Title pages will be prepared in manuscript.

WAR DIARY
or
INTELLIGENCE SUMMARY.
(Erase heading not required.)

Army Form C. 2118.

Place	Date	Hour	Summary of Events and Information	Remarks and references to Appendices
NOEUX LES MINES	Sept.	21st	Marched to ALLOUAGNE via MARLES LES MINES and LOZINGHEM, and were billeted in a school	
			Sick were collected from the 8th Brigade.	
ALLOUAGNE	Sept	22	Marched by LOZINGHEM, CAUCHY LA TOUR, FERFAY, RELY, ESTREE BLANCHE to CUHEM (FLECHIN)	
			Hospital opened for 16 patients. Personnel billeted in barns. Collected sick of 8th Brigade	
	"	23	Visited by A.D.M.S. 3rd Division. Collected sick of 9th Brigade	
		24	Accommodation for 12 extra patients provided	
		25	Visited by A.D.M.S. 3rd Division.	

C. H. Watson
Major RAMC

O.C. 142 Field Ambulance

T2134. Wt. W708—776. 500000. 4/15. Sir J. C. & S.

SECRET

Operation Order No I by CAPT. A.H. HABGOOD R.A.M.C. Commanding No 142 Field Ambce

Copy No 2

Ref Sheet	36 B. -1/40000	20-9-16
MOVE 1.	The Field Ambulance will march tomorrow at 10 am independently via FOUR-A-CHAUX - MARLES-LES-MINES - LOZINGHEM to ALLOURGNE area.	
BILLETING 2.	CAPT. DOWLING will meet Staff Captain 8th Brigade at MARLES-LES-MINES at 9 am to arrange for billets	
MOTOR AMBULANCES 3	Motor Ambulance Cars will proceed independently under command of CAPT MANN.	
STORES ETC, 4	No 58313 Pte S.W. WHITE will remain behind in charge of Stores and will hand over to the incoming Unit. He will rejoin his Unit on Completion of this duty.	
RATIONS 5.	Unexpended portion of days Rations will be carried on Cooks Cart	

Issued at 11.10 pm
Copies to.
1. A.D.M.S
2. War Diary

(Signed) A.H. Habgood
Captain

Oct. 1916

SECRET

140/1/88
Vol 15

War Diary of

No 142 Field Ambulance — 3rd Div

From 1 October 1916 To 31 October 1916

To A. G. BASE

Instructions regarding War Diaries and Intelligence Summaries are contained in F. S. Regs., Part II. and the Staff Manual respectively. Title pages will be prepared in manuscript.

WAR DIARY
or
~~INTELLIGENCE SUMMARY.~~
(Erase heading not required.)

Army Form C. 2118.

Place	Date	Hour	Summary of Events and Information	Remarks and references to Appendices
				Sheet 5A HAZEBROUCK 1/100000
CUHEM	Oct.	2nd/16	CAPT. D. C. MACDONALD ~~left~~ proceeded on Special leave.	
	"	3rd	LIEUT. S. SIMONS and LIEUT. E. EVANS joined for duty	
	"	4th	LIEUT. G. S. CLANCY joined for temporary duty	
SAUTRECOURT	"	5th	Marched to SAUTRECOURT the transport proceeding with the brigade transport	Sheet 11 LENS 1/100000
		6	Field Ambulance Transport under CAPT. MANN marched to ZAVETTEMENT	
PUCHEVILLERS		7	R.A.M.C. personnel entrained at St POL and detrained at PUCHEVILLERS. where they were joined by the Transport.	
BERTRANCOURT		8th	Took over from No. 5 F. Ambulance H.Q. BERTRANCOURT, Advanced Dressing Stations, COLINCAMPS and EUSTON, bearer posts in OBSERVATION WOOD and FLAG AVENUE	Sheet 57.D 1/40000
			Took in sick and wounded from 3rd Division 2nd 51st, 39th 63rd and Corps (V) troops. Accommodation for 150 patients and a small officers' ward	
		13th	Visited by D.D.M.S. V Corps.	
		14th	CAPT. D. C. MACDONALD returned from leave	
		17	CAPTS G. W. WHITMAN and N. MACDONALD returned from Special leave to Canada	
			LIEUT. G. S. CLANCY proceeded to 13th King Liverpools for duty	
BUS-LES-ARTOIS		18	Headquarters took over from 1/3 Highland Field Ambulance at BUS LES ARTOIS	

T2134. Wt. W708—776. 500000. 4/15. Sir J. C. & S.

Army Form C. 2118.

Instructions regarding War Diaries and Intelligence Summaries are contained in F. S. Regs., Part II. and the Staff Manual respectively. Title pages will be prepared in manuscript.

WAR DIARY
or
INTELLIGENCE SUMMARY.
(Erase heading not required.)

Place	Date	Hour	Summary of Events and Information	Remarks and references to Appendices
BUS-LES-ARTOIS	Oct.	18/16	One N.C.O. and 5 men were sent as a holding party to huts in BOIS DE WARNIMONT.	Sheet 57.D. 1/40000
		19th	These huts were handed over to No 8. Field Ambulance.	
		21st	The Bearer subdivision at COLINCAMPS relieved by No 8 F.A	
		22nd	The Bearer subdivision at EUSTON relieved by No 8. F.A.	
		24th	Capt. D.C. Macdonald proceeded to A.D.M.S. Office for temporary duty as D.A.D.M.S. vice Capt. C.M. Nicol killed in action.	
		25th	No 61598 Pte RANSOM R.J. wounded at COLINCAMPS	
		29th	LIEUT. E. EVANS proceeded on temporary duty to No. 49 C.C.S. & One N.C.O + 4 men to COURCELLES for duty at the Divisional Baths.	
		30.	G.O.C. 3rd Division inspected the camp. Lieut + Q.M. E.C. BOWEN rejoined the unit	
		31.	D.D.M.S. V Corps inspected the camp.	
			During the last three weeks a hospital has been established at H.Q. for sick + wounded receiving on an average seventy ~~sick~~ daily. Sick came from the 2nd, 3rd, 18th, 31st, 49th, 51st, 63, 1st and 2nd Canadian Divisions and Vth + XIIIth Corps Troops. C. Section tent subdivision has during this time been open as an advanced Dressing Station at COLINCAMPS and all wounded have	

T2134. Wt. W708—776. 500000. 4/15. Sir J. C. & S.

Instructions regarding War Diaries and Intelligence Summaries are contained in F. S. Regs., Part II. and the Staff Manual respectively. Title pages will be prepared in manuscript.

WAR DIARY
or
INTELLIGENCE SUMMARY.
(Erase heading not required.)

Army Form C. 2118.

Place	Date	Hour	Summary of Events and Information	Remarks and references to Appendices
			passed through this station. For the last fortnight those have been sent direct to the Main Dressing Station FORCEVILLE under Corps arrangements – penetrating abdominal wounds to the Corps Operating Station AUTHIE. The bearer post at EUSTON was occupied by each subdivision in turn and dumps were established at OBSERVATION WOOD and FLAG AVENUE for the accumulation of reserve stretchers, blankets, rations, water and medical comforts. All wounded from the line held by the Division and numbers from the adjoining Divisions passed through EUSTON and were evacuated to COLINCAMPS by the FORD cars. The large motor ambulances worked between COLINCAMPS and the Main Dressing Station. Improvements were made in the dugouts both at EUSTON and COLINCAMPS – and in the half finished huts at Head Quarters.	

R. A. [illegible] Lieut Col
, R.A.M.C.
COMDG: 142ND FIELD AMBULANCE.

T2134. Wt. W708–776. 500000. 4/15. Sir J. C. & S.

Nov. 1916

3rd Div.

SECRET

140/1849

Vol 16.

WAR DIARY

OF

No. 42 Field Ambulance

From 1/11/16 To 30/11/16

Army Form C. 2118.

Instructions regarding War Diaries and Intelligence Summaries are contained in F. S. Regs., Part II. and the Staff Manual respectively. Title pages will be prepared in manuscript.

WAR DIARY
or
INTELLIGENCE SUMMARY.
(Erase heading not required.)

Place	Date	Hour	Summary of Events and Information	Remarks and references to Appendices
BUS-LES-ARTOIS	Nov 3rd/16		The bearers of A and C Section ~~—~~ relieved at COLINCAMPS + EUSTON ~~by~~ No 7. Field ambulance bearers	Map Reference
		10th	Bearers relieved by No 8 Field ambulance	Sheet 57.D
		13th	B. Section bearers proceeded to COLINCAMPS and A + C to the Walking wounded Post at COURCELLES	J.26 c.1.8
			This was the beginning of the action during which B. Tent subdivision were employed at the A.D.S	and
			COLINCAMPS. All serious cases from the SERRE sector, wounded and sick, of the 3rd and	K.25 a 1.1
			other divisions passed through this dressing station. From 6 am 13th to 12 noon on the 14th	
			36 officers and 412 O.R.s were dressed and evacuated. On the night of the 13th the bearers	
			went up to EUSTON and assisted in clearing the wounded. CAPT W M SNODGRASS and	
			N. MACDONALD were in charge of the A.D.S. + the bearers were under Captns. DOWLING + WHITMAN.	
			Casualties during this period among our own men. Killed in action Pte A SAMSON (58909)	
			wounded 58912 Corpl ROBERTS W.D., 58270 Pte SMITH A L., 80248 Pte GREEN G.	
			58345 Pte TURNER J.	
		15th	B + C Bearers returned to Head Quarters.	
		17th	A. Section bearers took over at EUSTON, OBSERVATION WOOD + FLAG AVENUE	
		18th	Lieut. S. SIMONS proceeded to England on expiry of contract	
		19th	A. Sect. bearers returned to Head Quarters.	

T2134. Wt. W708—776. 500000. 4/15. Sir J. C. & S.

Army Form C. 2118.

Instructions regarding War Diaries and Intelligence Summaries are contained in F. S. Regs., Part II. and the Staff Manual respectively. Title pages will be prepared in manuscript.

WAR DIARY
or
INTELLIGENCE SUMMARY.
(Erase heading not required.)

Place	Date	Hour	Summary of Events and Information	Remarks and references to Appendices
BUS LES ARTOIS	Nov. 28th/16		Capt. G.W. WHITMAN - evacuated sick.	Map reference
	29th		Tent subdivision at COLINCAMPS relieved by No 7. F.A. Capt. H.L MANN proceeded on leave.	Sheet 57D
	30th		Capt E.C. RAYNER posted for duty - and Lieut. E. EVANS rejoined from temporary duty at 49. C.C.S.	J. 26 c. 1. 8 and
			During the month the A.D.S was continuously occupied and the dugouts were strengthened and various improvements made. The dugouts only were used this month as the buildings were shelled on several occasions. During the action which took place on the 13th & 14th the horsed ambulance wagons were used to supplement the FORD cars & did very valuable work between EUSTON DUMP and the A.D.S. The large motor ambulances worked continuously from the A.D.S to the M.A.S at FORCEVILLE and the special abdominal hospital (Corps Operating Station) at AUTHIE.	K. 25 a. 1. 1
			At headquarters a great many improvements have been made. The paths have been laid & drained - 2 large huts built - Bricked horse lines and a brick incinerator with disinfecting and hot water apparatus attached, have been built. Accommodation for 120 patients was provided by the huts & slight cases of wounded have been taken in.	
			30/11/16 C.H. Hobbs(?) Lieut Col. RAMC O.C. 142 Field Ambulance	

Dec 1916.

SECRET

3rd Div.

140/1900.

Vol 17

WAR DIARY

OF

No 142 Field Ambulance

From 1 Dec 1916 To 31 Dec 1916

To/ A. G.

BASE

Instructions regarding War Diaries and Intelligence Summaries are contained in F. S. Regs., Part II. and the Staff Manual respectively. Title pages will be prepared in manuscript.

WAR DIARY

or

INTELLIGENCE SUMMARY.

(Erase heading not required.)

Army Form C. 2118.

Place	Date	Hour	Summary of Events and Information	Remarks and references to Appendices
			Leaving Capt SNODGRASS in temporary command	
BUS LES ARTOIS	Dec 2nd /16		I proceeded on 10 days leave to the U.K. ↑ Lieut EVANS went to the 2nd Royal Scots for temporary duty.	Sheet 57D.
	6th		Lieut J. PRYCE-DAVIES posted to this unit	J.26.c 1.8
	7th		Bearers returned to H.Q. from EUSTON	1/40000
	10th		Lieut J. PRYCE-DAVIES proceeded on temporary duty as M.O i/c 42nd Bde R.F.A.	
	11th		Capt. W.J. DOWLING proceeded on leave to U.K.	
	12		Capt H.L. MANN rejoined from leave. Lieut	
	13		I returned from leave. Lieut. T.M. BELLEW was posted to this unit for duty & was reposted to 1st N. Fus on the 14th	
	15th		Capt MANN proceeded to the 7th K.S.L.I. on temporary duty.	
	18		Capt MANN rejoined on completion of duty.	
	19		Capt E.P. RAYNER and 14 squads of Bearers relieved No 8 F.A. at the bearer posts in the trenches.	
	20		Capt SNODGRASS proceeded on leave to the U.K.	
	21		Lieut E. EVANS rejoined for duty	
	22		Lieut EVANS proceeded on temporary duty to the 10th R.W. Fus. Five extra squads were sent up to EUSTON	
			to take over bearer posts on the SUCERIE, WHITE CITY, and ROMAN ROAD from the 23rd F.A. 7th Division	
			Capt W.J. DOWLING returned from leave	
	25		Bearers were relieved by No 7. F.A and returned to Headquarters	
	26		Capt W.J. DOWLING went to the 4th Royal Fus for temporary duty.	

Instructions regarding War Diaries and Intelligence Summaries are contained in F. S. Regs., Part II. and the Staff Manual respectively. Title pages will be prepared in manuscript.

WAR DIARY
or
INTELLIGENCE SUMMARY.
(Erase heading not required.)

Army Form C. 2118.

Place	Date	Hour	Summary of Events and Information	Remarks and references to Appendices
BUS LES ARTOIS	Dec 30th 16		Lieut A. H. ERNST was posted to this unit. ~~Yesterday~~ Ten men were attached to the 3rd Div. Train for temporary duty as woodcutters. During this month a considerable amount of work has been done in the vicinity of HOME AVENUE in the construction of a large dug out – a working party of a Sergt and 10 men being continuously employed. Materials have been carried daily from BEAUSSART via COLINCAMPS an exceedingly difficult journey as the tracks have been in a bad condition. At Headquarters the huts already built have been improved and a ~~[illegible]~~ hut has been erected. The old canvas huts have been bunked, thus doubling their accommodation & keeping the men off the ground – All this work including the building of the huts has been done by the men of the unit. A concert troupe has been formed and has given entertainments to the Regiments when they return ~~from~~ rest billets and to the patients in hospital.	Map – Sheet 57D – J.26.c.1.8.

R. A. Bagshawe [?]
Lieut R.A.M.C.
O.C. 142 Field Ambulance

31/12/16

T2134. Wt. W708—776. 500000. 4/15. Sir J. C. & S.

3RD DIVISION
MEDICAL

NO. 142 FIELD AMBULANCE

1917.

Jan 1917

S[illegible]T

149/947

WAR DIARY 3rd Division Vol 18

S

of

No 142 Field Ambulance

From 1/1/17 To 31/1/17.

Instructions regarding War Diaries and Intelligence Summaries are contained in F. S. Regs., Part II. and the Staff Manual respectively. Title pages will be prepared in manuscript.

WAR DIARY
or
INTELLIGENCE SUMMARY.
(Erase heading not required.)

Army Form C. 2118.

Place	Date	Hour	Summary of Events and Information	Remarks and references to Appendices
BUS-LES-ARTOIS	Jan 1st/1917		Capt SNODGRASS returned from leave. Lieut A. H. ERNST proceeded to 23rd Bgde RFA on temporary duty.	Ref Sheet 57 D. 1/40000 J. 26 C.
	2nd		Lieut. J. W. MACKIE posted to this unit for duty.	
	3rd		Two horsed ambulance wagons ~~proceeded~~ to COURCELLES to meet the 7th KSLI. on their way down from the trenches.	
	6th		An advance party of one NCO and 25 men under Lt MACKIE marched to FIEFFES. The same day Capt SNODGRASS and 5 OR went to the same village in a motor ambulance. Lt MACKIE was detailed for temporary duty with the Fifth Army Signal School at LA HAYE FARM DOMART	
	7th		Handed over the area at BUS to the 90th Field Ambulance 32nd Division.	
	8th		Marched to BEAUQUESNE via AUTHIE and MARIEUX and billeted for the night.	
BEAUQUESNE	9th		Marched to FIEFFES. A schedule of training was drawn up and submitted to ADMS.	Sheet 11 LENS
	12th		Marched to CANAPLES. Capt DOWLING rejoined from temporary duty with 4th Roy. Fus	
CANAPLES	14th		One Sergt and 36 OR were sent to 47 CCS for fatigue duties - by orders of DMS Fifth Army.	" "
	16		Capt. N. MacDONALD proceeded on leave to the U.K	
	19		Ten OR employed on woodcutting at CANDAS rejoined the unit	
	28th		Sick were collected from the Brigade Groups and were sent to XIII Corps Rest Station BEAUVAL as there was no accomodation for sick in the rest area. The training was much restricted owing to the number	

T2134. Wt. W708—776. 500000. 4/15. Sir J. C. & S.

Instructions regarding War Diaries and Intelligence Summaries are contained in F. S. Regs., Part II. and the Staff Manual respectively. Title pages will be prepared in manuscript.

WAR DIARY
or
INTELLIGENCE SUMMARY.
(Erase heading not required.)

Army Form C. 2118.

Place	Date	Hour	Summary of Events and Information	Remarks and references to Appendices
			of men detached for various fatigues. Horse standings, latrines, were erected and a large NISSON hospital hut was in process of construction, but was never completed.	Sheet 11 LENS 1/100000
CANAPLES	28th		One Sergt and 33 men rejoined at OCCOCHES to which place the unit marched during the day and billeted for the night. From midnight 28th/29th the division came under the orders of the Third Army and from the night of the 30th 31st under the orders of XVII Corps.	" "
OCCOCHES	29th		Marched to HERLIN-LE-SEC and rested there during the 30th.	" do "
HERLIN-LE-SEC	31st		Marched to DIEVAL collecting the sick of the Brigade Group on the march.	" do "

C. G. Watson
Lieut Col. RAMC
OC 142 Field Ambulance

T2134. Wt. W708—776. 500000. 4/15. Sir J. C. & S.

Feb. 1917

SECRET

3rd Div

140/1994

Medical

Vol 19

WAR DIARY

of

No 142 FIELD AMBULANCE

From 1 Feb 1917 To 28 Feb 1917

Instructions regarding War Diaries and Intelligence Summaries are contained in F. S. Regs., Part II, and the Staff Manual respectively. Title pages will be prepared in manuscript.

WAR DIARY
or
INTELLIGENCE SUMMARY.
(*Erase heading not required.*)

Army Form C. 2118.

MEDICAL

Place	Date	Hour	Summary of Events and Information	Remarks and references to Appendices
				Ref LENS. 11 1/100000
DIEVAL	Feb. 1st 1917		One horsed ambulance wagon was sent to accompany the 12th W. Yorks to LOUEZ and a motor ambulance to HAUTE AVESNES with the 4th Roy. Fusiliers.	F. 1.
	2nd		Car sent with Capt RAYNER to accompany the 1st North. Fus. to ARRAS.	
			Capt N. MACDONALD returned from leave	
	4th		Horsed ambulance sent to accompany 250 men of the 13th Kings Liverpool Regt. to ERIN. and another horsed ambulance with an officer to accompany the 250 men of 13th Kings to WANQUETIN.	
			A small barn was converted into a hospital sufficient in size to take 20 patients. Morning sick parade included troops from the brigade and Corps. and averaged about 100	
	8th		Marched to HOUVIN-HOUVIGNEUL	
HOUVIN-HOUVIGNEUL	9th		Hospital provided for 30 patients. – Lt J. W. MACKIE returned to duty from the Fifth Army Signal School	Ref 51 C H 14 b. 5. 5
	11th		One car to ERIN to follow the 13th Kings to this village. and one to HAUTE. AVESNES to follow the 12th W. Yorks on their march to the village.	
	18th		Capt E. C. RAYNER proceeded on Temporary duty with D. D. M. S. VI Corps.	
	19th		Lieut J. W. MACKIE proceeded on permanent duty with 1st North. Fus.	
			Detachments were ~~posted~~ detailed for temporary duty under O.C. Baths. Ten privates to	

2353 Wt. W2544/1454 700,000 5/15 D. D. & L. A.D.S.S./Forms/C. 2118.

Instructions regarding War Diaries and Intelligence Summaries are contained in F. S. Regs., Part II. and the Staff Manual respectively. Title pages will be prepared in manuscript.

WAR DIARY
or
INTELLIGENCE SUMMARY.
(Erase heading not required.)

Army Form C. 2118.

Place	Date	Hour	Summary of Events and Information	Remarks and references to Appendices
				Ref 51 C.
HOUVIN-HOUVIGNEUL	Feb 19		to FREVENT. One N.C.O and 5 men to BERLENCOURT. One N.CO & 3 men to baths in the village and one private to LE CAUROY	H.14 b 5.5.
	20		Capt. W.S. MARTIN posted to this unit.	
	21		Capt MANN posted to 4th Roy. Fus. for temporary duty	
	22		Capt W.J. DOWLING evacuated sick	
	23		Capt W.S. MARTIN and 26 O.R proceeded to ARRAS attached to 1st New Zealand Tunneling C	
	25		Capt MANN returned from Tempy duty with 4th Roy. Fus	
	27		Capt MANN proceeded on 14 days Special leave to U.K on completion of 2nd years contract.	
			During the last fortnight - sick have been collected from the 9th Infy Brigade and evacuated to No 6 Stationary Hospl FREVENT. New latrines & incinerators have been built, and for about ten days, during which we had no appreciable numbers of men both regimentally employed or on detachment the opportunity was taken to carry out as much of the scheme of training as possible. Drills every morning, Route marches, lectures practical instruction in gas protection, formation of stretcher squads, inoculation by T.A.B. Kit inspection. For the first time in their experience, the men were billeted in bunked	

Army Form C. 2118.

Instructions regarding War Diaries and Intelligence Summaries are contained in F. S. Regs., Part II. and the Staff Manual respectively. Title pages will be prepared in manuscript.

WAR DIARY
or
INTELLIGENCE SUMMARY.

(*Erase heading not required.*)

Place	Date	Hour	Summary of Events and Information	Remarks and references to Appendices
HOUVIN-HOUIGNEUL	Feb 28-1917		barns, and it was found necessary to provide straw for the bunks, as it was impossible for them to sleep owing to the intense cold.	Ref 51.C. H.14.b. 5.5.
			A. A. Hatherd [illegible] Lt Col RAMC. Commanding 142 Field Ambulance	

140/2042

Confidential

Medical

Mar. 1917

Vol 20

WAR DIARY

of

142 Field Ambulance.

R.A.M.C.

From March 1/17 to March 31/17.

(1)

Instructions regarding War Diaries and Intelligence Summaries are contained in F. S. Regs., Part II. and the Staff Manual respectively. Title pages will be prepared in manuscript.

Army Form C, 2118.

WAR DIARY
or
INTELLIGENCE SUMMARY.
(Erase heading not required.)

MEDICAL.

Place	Date	Hour	Summary of Events and Information	Remarks and references to Appendices
HOUVIN-HOUVIGNEUL	March 2/17.		Capt N. MacDONALD and 14 OR. proceeded to MANIN to take charge of VI Corps Rest Station for Officers.	Ref. Sheet 51.C 1/40,000
			Capt MARTIN returned from Cave dressing station at ARRAS.	
	Mar. 3		Capt RAYNER rejoined from temporary duty with DDMS. VI Corps.	
			While at HOUVIN-HOUVIGNEUL sick were collected from 3rd. 12th. 37th and 46th Divisions – Hospital accommodation was provided in the village for from 30 to 40 patients – Evacuations were made to No 6. Stationary Hospital FREVENT and special cases to No 12 Stat. Hospital ST POL. Bath parties were provided for work at FREVENT, BERLENCOURT and LE CAUROY and a working party of 1 officer + 25 OR. were attached to No 1. New Zealand Tunnelling Co in the Cave dressing Station ARRAS.	
	9th		Marched to SARS-LEZ-BOIS	
SARS-LES-BOIS	11th		Capt W.S. MARTIN went on temporary duty in Medical charge of 12th W. Yorks	
			Capt W.M. SNODGRASS admitted to hospital sick	
	14th		Detachment at ARRAS relieved by 28 OR.	
	15.		One horsed-ambulance wagon followed the 2nd Suffolks to MILLY to pick up stragglers.	
			Capt H.L MANN returned from leave.	
	16		Original party from ARRAS rejoined	
	18		Lieut E.A. RUNTING joined for duty.	

2353 Wt. W2544/1454 700,000 5/15 D. D. & L. A.D.S.S./Forms/C. 2118.

Instructions regarding War Diaries and Intelligence Summaries are contained in F. S. Regs., Part II. and the Staff Manual respectively. Title pages will be prepared in manuscript.

WAR DIARY
or
INTELLIGENCE SUMMARY.
(Erase heading not required.)

Army Form C. 2118.

(2)

Place	Date	Hour	Summary of Events and Information	Remarks and references to Appendices
SARS-LES-BOIS	Mar 20th		Capt H.K. MANN admitted to Hospital sick. There was no accomodation for sick in the village small sick were transferred to 36th F.A. (VI Corps Rest Station)	
		22	Marched to HAUTEVILLE	
		24	Capt W.M. SNODGRASS returned to duty. Capt H.A. CUTLER joined for duty. Summer time at 11 p.m.	
		25	Capt W.W. UTTLEY joined for duty.	
		26	One N.C.O. and 3 men were detailed to the Baths at HAUTEVILLE.	
		30	Capt MARTIN rejoined from temporary duty with 12th W. York.	
		31.	During the past month a fair amount of training has been undertaken — lectures & demonstrations on the application of Thomas' splint and Gas defense, & drills & route marches. Inoculation of anti-typhoid serum have been carried out — the Equipment and Kit have been overhauled. Arm badges of blue squares 2" square have been introduced for the bearer division to be worn square by the bearers and diamond shaped by the officers N.C.O. and squad leaders	
			31/3/17 C. W. Hartgill Lieut Col. RAMC Commanding 142nd Field Ambulance	

2353 Wt. W2544/1454 700,000 5/15 D. D. & L. A.D.S.S./Forms/C. 2118.

April 1917

S

SECRET

140/2086

MEDICAL

Vol 21

WAR DIARY

of

No 142 Field Ambulance

From 1/4/17 To 30/4/17

Army Form C. 2118.

Instructions regarding War Diaries and Intelligence Summaries are contained in F. S. Regs., Part II. and the Staff Manual respectively. Title pages will be prepared in manuscript.

WAR DIARY
or
INTELLIGENCE SUMMARY.
(Erase heading not required.)

Place	Date	Hour	Summary of Events and Information	Remarks and references to Appendices
HAUTEVILLE	April	2nd 1917	Capt CUTLER. Lt RUNTING and 1 clerk proceeded to 19 CCS. for temporary duty.	Sheet 51B 51C France 1/40000
		3rd	Sgt Maj TELLING and 5 O.R. RAMC to WARLUS railhead in charge of Walking Wounded entraining post. Men detached at baths were recalled from FREVENT + BERLENCOURT	
WANQUETIN		4th	Marched to WANQUETIN - Capt W.M SNODGRASS and 3. O.R. proceeded to ARRAS as an advance party. Later in the day Capt. RAYNER + Capt UTTLEY with 103 bearers followed.	
		7th	3 large ambulance cars were attached to 15 MAC for temporary duty. Capt MANN returned to duty from Officers Rest Station. No 64958 Pte WOOD - F. Killed in action.	
		8th	Horsed ambulance wagons joined divisional pools at ARRAS + WAGONLIEU - Hospital at WANQUETIN was cleared in anticipation of a move.	
ARRAS.		9th	Marched to No 1. Transport Camp at ARRAS - 1 NCO detailed for sanitation duties of Camp	
		12.	Lieut. F.W. HARROWELL - joined for duty.	
		13.	Bearers returned to Transport Camp and the following were reported wounded. 58348 Pte BUDD. H 88511 Pte DAVIS. W.J. 34418 Pte ROEBUCK J.A 105688 Pte GREENWOOD - W. 28909 Pte BEALE - B. 27599 Pte WATERS. S. Evacuated. The following were wounded and remained at duty - 58281 A/Corpl CLUSE. R M 58370 A/L/Corpl SMITH. A.L 34224 Pte READ - J.W. 58229 Pte LEE - A. 79321 Pte TOWLE. R - 77885 Pte MORGAN. D.J. From the 9th to the 13th the bearers were employed in clearing the ground between ARRAS	

Instructions regarding War Diaries and Intelligence Summaries are contained in F. S. Regs., Part II. and the Staff Manual respectively. Title pages will be prepared in manuscript.

WAR DIARY
or
INTELLIGENCE SUMMARY.
(Erase heading not required.)

Medical

Place	Date	Hour	Summary of Events and Information	Remarks and references to Appendices
ARRAS			and the trenches in front of TILLOY. Bearer posts were established in TILLOY village. The section were employed loading & unloading cars at the Car[?] dressing station RUE DE ST. QUENTIN	Sheet 51B 51 C France 1/40000
	14th		Moved to HOPITAL ST. JEAN - Rue GAMBETTA - (VI Corps Main Dressing Station). The tent subdivisions available were employed under O.C. VI C.M.D.S. (O.C. 87 F.A.) - Bearers were employed in construction work & loading cars	
	26th		Took over command of VI Corps M.D.S. from O.C. 87 F.A.	
	27th		Tent Division of 2/2 London F.A. joined for duty. Capt C.M. KENNEDY joined M.D.S. as abdominal surgical specialist. Capt SCARBOROUGH anaesthetist	
	28		Bearers proceeded to FEUCHY LA CHAPEL A.D.S. and gun pits behind MONCHY LE PREUX under Capts RAYNER and UTTLEY.	
	29		Capt W.J. DOWLING rejoined for duty. Capt MACNAUGHTON attached for temporary duty	
	30		Capt DOWLING took over command of the bearers - Capt RAYNER rejoined & was posted for temporary duty to A.D.M.S. ~~[illegible]~~ 3rd Division.	
			During the first part of the month the unit was prepared to move forward at short notice and open as an advanced dressing station. The bearers were employed to the East of ARRAS and there took for the first time since the advance to the AISNE approached the methods of the text books. During the latter part of the month a great deal of work has been done at the HOPITAL	

Instructions regarding War Diaries and Intelligence Summaries are contained in F. S. Regs., Part II. and the Staff Manual respectively. Title pages will be prepared in manuscript.

WAR DIARY
or
INTELLIGENCE SUMMARY.
(Erase heading not required.)

Army Form C. 2118.

Place	Date	Hour	Summary of Events and Information	Remarks and references to Appendices
ARRAS			ST. JEAN which was in a very filthy and knocked about condition – Repairs have been made where possible. wagon loads of rubbish have been removed. Many yards of calico have been put into the windows – incinerators, latrines, urinals, kitchens have been built. One part of the hospital was converted into a dressing station and another into ~~[illegible]~~ accommodation for the retention of both sick and wounded. The operating theatre was reconstructed and a ward in the proximity converted into a surgical ward – Two surgical specialists were attached to the M.A.S. Capt. K. WALKER and Cpt. KENNEDY, and a great many operations were undertaken – including abdominals. A quantity of stores has been received from the Red Cross. The Dressing Station has been visited frequently by D.M.S. Third Army – D.D.M.S. VI Corps & COL. GRAY Consulting Surgeon to Third Army	
			C. H. Watson Lt Col. RAMC Commanding 142 Field Ambulance	

2353 Wt. W2544/1454 700,000 5/15 D. D. & L. A.D.S.S./Forms/C. 2118.

SECRET

MEDICAL

May 1917

S

140/2161

Vol 22

WAR DIARY

OF

No 142 FIELD AMBULANCE

From 1.5.17 To 31.5.17

Army Form C. 2118.

WAR DIARY
or
INTELLIGENCE SUMMARY.
(Erase heading not required.)

Instructions regarding War Diaries and Intelligence Summaries are contained in F. S. Regs., Part II. and the Staff Manual respectively. Title pages will be prepared in manuscript.

Place	Date	Hour	Summary of Events and Information	Remarks and references to Appendices
ARRAS	May 1st 1917		A ward in the hospital was fitted with 48 beds and prepared to accommodate abdominal cases	Ref. Sheet 51B S.W. FRANCE 1/20,000
	2nd		Three nursing sisters, Sister JAMES, Sister STRACHAN and Sister MAUDE arrived for duty in the abdominal section of the Hospital. Bearers returned to H.Q. Twelve Nursing orderlies of 87 Field Amb. detailed for temporary duty. Sgt Major & party from entraining station at WARLUS returned to H.Q.	
	3rd		Twenty wounded officers & 259 wounded O.R. passed through the main dressing station during the day. ARRAS was shelled during the evening and the hospital hit several times killing 3 O.R. RAMC & wounding 17 (87 Field Amb.). In consequence of this the abdominal & other cases in the ward were removed to the ground floor. The Sisters were sent back to 20 CCS. As many cases as would travel were evacuated to CCs. and the wounded diverted to No 1 VI Corps M.D.S. for a time.	
	3rd		Bearers under Capt DOWLING relieved the bearers of No 7 & 8 FA. at N.3 Central and Gunpits(?) at N.5.d.7.2. Four casualties were reported No 56773 Pte ARNSWORTH. R 77885 Pte MORGAN, D.J.	
	4th		73947 Pte DELAFIELD. J.J. 55952 Pte PRICE. T.	
	5th		Capt McNAUGHTON posted to No 8 Field Amb. Capt McMACDONALD(?) rejoined from Officers Rest Station & the section remained under an officer of No 26 F.A.	
	6th		Capt. E.C. RAYNER detailed for temporary duty with 8th E. York. Bearers returned to H.Q.	
	7th		Sgt Major & 2 ORs to WARLUS entraining station for Walking Wounded. 87 F.A. left the Hospital	

Instructions regarding War Diaries and Intelligence Summaries are contained in F. S. Regs., Part II. and the Staff Manual respectively. Title pages will be prepared in manuscript.

WAR DIARY
or
INTELLIGENCE SUMMARY.
(Erase heading not required.)

Army Form C. 2118.

Place	Date	Hour	Summary of Events and Information	Remarks and references to Appendices
ARRAS			and received the 12 nursing orderlies	Ref - Sheet 11 - LENS 1/100000
	9th		Lieut T. MOHAN joined for duty	
	12th		Bearers relieved No 7 - 8 Field Ambulance. Six nursing orderlies of No 7 were attached for duty.	
	13th		87 Field Ambulance occupied part of the Hospital as a billet	
	14th		B Section bearers returned with Lt MOHAN to H.Q.	
	15th		A + C section bearers returned to H.Q. The bearer division under Capt SNODGRASS marched to SIMENCOURT	
	17		Capts C.M. KENNEDY + SCARBOROUGH and orderly proceeded to VII Corps M.D.S. Handed over the Main Dressing Station to O.C. 2/2 London Field Ambulance.	
LIENCOURT	18		Bearers marched from SIMENCOURT to LIENCOURT and the tent division from ARRAS to LIENCOURT. Nursing orderlies of No 7 returned to their unit.	
	19		Capt MacDONALD proceeded to England on leave - Capt UTTLEY to A.D.M.S. 37th Division - Capt RAINER rejoined for duty. Lt MOHAN visits daily the sick of 25th Canadian Forestry Co. BEAUVINCOURT.	
	20		Lt MOHAN proceeded to 7 K.S.L.I. for temporary duty. CAPT A. GILMOUR evacuated to 9 C.C.S.	
	23		Lt T. MOHAN proceeded to 50th Div. for permanent duty, CAPT H.L. MANN took over medical charge of 7 K.S.L.I.	
	24		LIEUT. COL. A.H. HABGOOD proceeded on leave to U.K. CAPT E.C. RAYNER Took over command.	

2353 Wt W2544/1454 700,000 5/15 D. D. & L. A.D.S.S./Forms/C. 2118.

Instructions regarding War Diaries and Intelligence Summaries are contained in F. S. Regs., Part II. and the Staff Manual respectively. Title pages will be prepared in manuscript.

WAR DIARY
or
INTELLIGENCE SUMMARY.
(Erase heading not required.)

Army Form C. 2118.

Place	Date	Hour	Summary of Events and Information	Remarks and references to Appendices
LIENCOURT	28th		LIEUT + QM E.C. BOWEN proceeded on leave to IRELAND.	Ref Sheet 11- LENS 1/100000
	30th		CAPT. W.W. UTTLEY rejoined from temporary duty with 27th Div.	
	31st		Marched to NOYELLETTE	
			During the period 18th–31st the Field Amb. acted as divisional rest station accommodating up to 100 patients, special arrangements were made for dealing with scabies cases. Sick were collected daily from 9th Inf. Bde. The Bearers were undergoing a course of training for 5 hours a day.	
			E C Rayner Capt. a/OC 142 Field Ambulance	

SECRET

6

MEDICAL

Vol 23

WAR DIARY

140/2230

June. 1917.

of

No 142 Field Ambulance

From 1/6/17 To 30/6/17

Army Form C. 2118.

Instructions regarding War Diaries and Intelligence Summaries are contained in F. S. Regs., Part II. and the Staff Manual respectively. Title pages will be prepared in manuscript.

WAR DIARY
or
INTELLIGENCE SUMMARY.
(Erase heading not required.)

Place	Date	Hour	Summary of Events and Information	Remarks and references to Appendices
BLANGY	June 1st/17		Proceeded here from NOYELLETTE – the personnel by bus, the transport by road under Capt. UTTLEY	Sheet 51.B FRANCE 1/40000
	2nd		Took over dressing station, the advanced dressing station at FEUCHY (Capt SNODGRASS and C section) the relay post H.29.c. and bearer collecting Post H.26.A.3.6. A section + half of B section took over these bearer posts under Capt MARTIN. (Capt DOWLING with the half section of B in reserve at FEUCHY)	
	3rd		Capt N. MacDONALD struck off the strength.	
	4th		I returned from leave.	
	5th		104558 Pte CRISP. J. evacuated wounded 33184 Pte WHITBY J.A died of wounds	
	6th		Capt MARTIN and A Sect. bearers returned to H.Q. Capt UTTLEY and C Sect. bearers proceeded to FEUCHY	
			Pte WHITBY buried at FEUCHY Cemetery H.21.c.7.6 by the Revd G. BEECH. CF. VI Corps H.A.G.	
	7th		Capt W.S. MARTIN proceeded on leave to U.K.	
	9th		Capt H.L. MANN rejoined from temporary duty with 7th K.S.L.I.	
	10th		Lieut + Q.M. BOWEN rejoined from leave	
	11th		A Sect. bearers went to FEUCHY A.D.S and C Sect. bearers relieved B Sect at the aid posts.	
			B. Sect – Capt DOWLING returning to H.Q	
	12th		No. M/2 105616 Pte CUNNINGHAM A Killed in action. N. 5889 Pte DAVIES T.J evacuated wounded.	
	13th		Capt RAYNER and 3 squads of B Sect proceeded to detraining post at RIVAGE – Capt DOWLING + 3	

2353 Wt. W2544/1454 700,000 5/15 D. D. & L. A.D.S.S./Forms/C. 2118.

Army Form C. 2118.

Instructions regarding War Diaries and Intelligence Summaries are contained in F. S. Regs., Part II. and the Staff Manual respectively. Title pages will be prepared in manuscript.

WAR DIARY
or
INTELLIGENCE SUMMARY.
(Erase heading not required.)

Place	Date	Hour	Summary of Events and Information	Remarks and references to Appendices
BLANGY			Squads of B sect. to FEUCHY entraining point. Capt. H.L. MANN to A.D. Dres. Stn. FEUCHY. Four large motor ambulance cars were ~~attached~~ sent to RIVAGE under Capt RAYNER.	
	14th		Two horsed ambulances & one Ford car were sent to the pool under O.C. No 8 F.A. Eight nursing orderlies were attached to No 7. F.A.	
	15th		Capt SNODGRASS returned to H.Q. leaving Capt MANN in command	
	16th		Nursing orderlies, cars & wagons returned to H.Q. Capt RAYNER went on leave to U.K.	
			B section took over bearer posts and C sect under Capt UTTLEY returned to HQ	
	18th		Relieved by 38 F.A. and marched to billets in ARRAS.	
GOUY-EN-ARTOIS	20th		Marched to GOUY-EN-ARTOIS. Capt MARTIN rejoined from leave	
	22		Twenty six reinforcements from the base.	
	23		Capt SNODGRASS went to 1st N. Fus. for temporary duty.	
	25		Capt DOWLING proceeded on leave to U.K.; Capt UTTLEY to PARIS. – I inspected the camps of the 1st N. Fus.	
	26		I inspected the camps: & new drafts of 1st Norfk. Fus. 4th Ry. Fus. 12th W. Yorks, 13th Kings L & 9th T.M.B. & 9th M.G.C.	
	27		Inspection of unit by D.D.M.S. VI Corps	

2353 Wt. W2544/1454 700,000 5/15 D. D. & L. A.D.S.S./Forms/C. 2118.

Instructions regarding War Diaries and Intelligence Summaries are contained in F. S. Regs., Part II. and the Staff Manual respectively. Title pages will be prepared in manuscript.

WAR DIARY
or
INTELLIGENCE SUMMARY.
(Erase heading not required.)

Army Form C. 2118.

Place	Date	Hour	Summary of Events and Information	Remarks and references to Appendices
GOUY-EN-ARTOIS	29th June/17		B Tent subdivision was sent to No 19 CCS for duty in relief of a subdivision of No 8 FA which joined us temporarily. Capt. CUTLER rejoined from 19 CCS.	
	30th		Transport marched via BAILLEULMONT, BERLES AU BOIS to ACHIET LE PETIT. Personnel proceeded by bus.	
			During the month, sick and wounded were collected from the 9th Regt Group with artillery formations. Wounded were brought down from the RAP. to the A.D.S. & subsequently entrained on the Decauville railway. At first they were detrained at BLANGY railhead for attention in the dressing station at BLANGY before being transferred to the M.D.S. ECOLE NORMALE. During the latter part of the month the detraining took place at the RIVAGE & the cases were transferred to the M.D.S. by cars from this station.	
			Capt W. J. DOWLING and Capt N. MacDONALD were mentioned in despatches and No 58308 Pte H. WORSWICK — No. 56267 Pte G.C. TURNER & No. 58163 Corpl. acting Sergt. D. KEENAN received the Military Medal.	
			C. A. [illegible] Lt Col RAMC Commanding 102 Field Ambulance	

2353 Wt. W2544/1454 700,000 5/15 D. D. & L. A.D.S.S./Forms/C. 2118.

SECRET

4

July 1917

141/2298

MEDICAL

Vol 24

WAR DIARY

of

No 142 FIELD AMBULANCE

From 1 July 1917 To 31st July 1917

Instructions regarding War Diaries and Intelligence Summaries are contained in F. S. Regs., Part II. and the Staff Manual respectively. Title pages will be prepared in manuscript.

WAR DIARY
or
INTELLIGENCE SUMMARY.
(Erase heading not required.)

Army Form C. 2118.

Place	Date	Hour	Summary of Events and Information	Remarks and references to Appendices
ACHIET LE GRAND	July 1st/17		Capts RAYNER and UTTLEY returned from leave	Sheet 57c 1/40000
	2nd		Capts MARTIN, CUTLER and UTTLEY with part of A + C section proceeded to LEBUCQUIERE to take over the Bearer Relay Posts at DOIGNIES, BEAUMETZ and HERMIES from ½ S Midland F.A.	
			Capt K.O. WALKER was posted to this unit	
	3rd		Marched to LEBUCQUIERE and took over from ½ S. Midland F.A. at 12 noon	
LEBUCQUIERE			The remainder of A + C section proceeded to DOIGNIES and HERMIES respectively	
			Capt R.A. CUTLER proceeded on leave to UK.	
	4th		Capt CUTLER transferred for duty to No 8 Field Ambulance	
	5th		Capt SNODGRASS rejoined from temporary duty with 12 N.F.s	
	6		Lieut RUNTING and 15 OR rejoined from temporary duty with (9 CCS)	
			Capt UTTLEY returned to HQ on relief by Capt RAYNER	
	7th		Lt RUNTING to temporary duty with 13 Kings	
	8		Capt W.J. BOWLING rejoined from leave.	
			Capt UTTLEY posted to 4th Kings Own for permanent duty in relief of Capt A.G.S WALKER who was posted permanently to this unit. Corps Commander inspected the camp.	
	9th		Capt K.O. WALKER joined from temporary duty with 4 [illegible] F.A	

Instructions regarding War Diaries and Intelligence Summaries are contained in F. S. Regs., Part II. and the Staff Manual respectively. Title pages will be prepared in manuscript.

WAR DIARY
or
INTELLIGENCE SUMMARY.
(Erase heading not required.)

Army Form C. 2118.

Place	Date	Hour	Summary of Events and Information	Remarks and references to Appendices
LEBUCQUIERE		9th	Eleven O.R. and one motor ambulance proceeded to BAZENTIN as hutting party	Sheet 57c 1/40000
			D.A.D.V.S. IV Corps inspected horses & horse lines	
		10th	Capt SNODGRASS proceeded on leave	
		12	Capt K.M. WALKER in temporary medical charge of 3rd D.A.C.	
		15	Capt F.E. CARR HARRIS posted to this unit in exchange with Lt RUNTING	
			Inspection of Camp by G.O.C. 3rd Division	
		16	Capt CARR-HARRIS to 13th Kings – Lt RUNTING to 255 Tunnelling Coy	
		20	Inspection of Camp by D.D.M.S. IV Corps	
		23	Capt RAYNOR to 42 C.C.S. for temporary duty – Capt SNODGRASS returned from leave – Capt DOWLING went	
			to HERMIES in relief of Capt RAYNOR – Capt CARR-HARRIS transferred to No 8 F.A. Nissen Hut party	
		2	rejoined.	
		24	Capt RAYNOR posted to Third Army Trench Mortar School for permanent duty	
		25	Capt MAIN proceeded on leave	
			During this month sick and wounded from the Divisional sector of the	
			South of the CAMBRAI road were collected & evacuated through the posts at DOIGNIES & HERMIES	
			A great deal of work has been done both under and above the ground – at DOIGNIES	

Instructions regarding War Diaries and Intelligence Summaries are contained in F. S. Regs., Part II. and the Staff Manual respectively. Title pages will be prepared in manuscript.

WAR DIARY
or
INTELLIGENCE SUMMARY.
(Erase heading not required.)

Army Form C. 2118.

Place	Date	Hour	Summary of Events and Information	Remarks and references to Appendices
			and [illegible] underground dressing stations have been constructed on an elaborate scale with accommodation for the personnel at a depth of about 20 ft. below the surface. A dug-out dressing station at BEAUMETZ has been completed and a sliding gallery for stretchers has been dug to the surface.	Sheet 51/c 1/40000
			At H.Q. a camp has been constructed, paths laid and railed. A Canteen has been inaugurated and installed in a large wood and canvas hut built specially for it. Thirteen Nissen Huts have been put up. Horselines and standings for cars have been laid. A large demolished building has been re-roofed and tiled and now serves as a Q.M. Stores. The wagons have been repainted and the cars overhauled & ~~one~~ one is now being painted. At the present time a drying room & incinerator combined is being erected. Grazing for the horses has been good and they are all in a very fit condition.	
			[illegible] Lt Col. RAMC Commanding 142 Field Ambulance	

2353 Wt. W2544/1454 700,000 5/15 D. D. & L. A.D.S.S./Forms/C. 2118.

SECRET

Aug 1917 9

140/2304

Vol 25

WAR DIARY

OF

No 142 FIELD AMBULANCE

From 1 August 1917 To 31 August 1917

Instructions regarding War Diaries and Intelligence Summaries are contained in F. S. Regs., Part II. and the Staff Manual respectively. Title pages will be prepared in manuscript.

WAR DIARY
or
INTELLIGENCE SUMMARY.
(Erase heading not required.)

Army Form C. 2118.

Place	Date	Hour	Summary of Events and Information	Remarks and references to Appendices
LEBUCQUIERE	Aug.	1st/17.	D.D.M.S. IV Corps inspected the camp.	FRANCE Sheet 57C 1/40000
		3rd	D.M.S. Third Army inspected the camp.	
		4th	Handed over HERMIES bearer collecting Post to 1st S.A. Field Ambulance. Capt DOWLING and bearers returned to HQ.	
		6th	One N.C.O. + 12 men took over post on LAGNICOURT road at I. 7. c. 10. 10	
		7th	Capt K.M. WALKER posted to 12th W. Yorks for temporary duty.	
		8th	D.A.D.V.S inspected the horses.	
		10th	Visit from D.D.M.S IV Corps. Lt T.M. HOLMES - M.O.R.C. - USA posted for duty.	
		17th	D.D.M.S IV Corps went to DOIGNIES to inspect the B.C.P.	
		20th	Lt HOLMES proceeded to DOIGNIES for instruction.	
		21.	Capt WALKER rejoined from 12th W. Yorks. Capt SNODGRASS evacuated sick	
		24.	Brood mares of the ambulance were inspected for selection by B. Gen OLIPHANT with a view to the breeding of Artillery horses. None selected	
		27.	Lt HOLMES and 9 OR, to 21 CCS for temporary duty on construction work	
		28	12 OR's reinforced the party at 21 CCS for fatigue duties	
		29.	Lt W.G. MASEFIELD posted for duty. Capt SNODGRASS rejoined for duty from C.C.S.	

2353 Wt. W2544/1454 700,000 5/15 D. D. & L. A.D.S.S./Forms/C. 2118.

Instructions regarding War Diaries and Intelligence Summaries are contained in F. S. Regs., Part II. and the Staff Manual respectively. Title pages will be prepared in manuscript.

WAR DIARY
or
INTELLIGENCE SUMMARY.
(Erase heading not required.)

Army Form C. 2118.

Place	Date	Hour	Summary of Events and Information	Remarks and references to Appendices
LEBUCQUIERE	Aug 31		From the 9th of the month the sick and wounded from the 76th and 8th Brigades have been evacuated through our bearer posts. The 9th Brigade which shifted its position to the north of the CAMBRAI road has been served by the 8th F. Amb.	FRANCE Sheet 57C 1/40000
			At DOIGNIES the dug out has been finished and provides accommodation for 40 patients. The construction has been excellently carried out under Capt MARTIN and numerous visits have been paid by both Corps and Divisional Staff Officers to inspect the work. Visitors included the Army Commander, Corps Commander, Divisional Commander, CRE. To Corps CRE [illegible]. Relay posts have been taken over at the Beetroot factory on the CAMBRAI - DOIGNIES road junction and LAGNICOURT Road, and the roads between DOIGNIES and BEAUMETZ and DOIGNIES and the CAMBRAI road have been repaired.	
			At H.Q. a large amount of constructional work has been accomplished. The hutting has been completed - a model kitchen built, incinerator, drying room, horse lines and shelters and the roads repaired. At present a brick waiting room is being built by at the station and a brick officers mess. Concerts have been given by the Bluelights to the troops in the vicinity. Cricket matches have been played [illegible] and the Canteen has taken on an average fcs 500 daily.	

A. L. Hobson
Hon. Lieut.
Commanding 142 Field Ambulance

Sept. 1917

5/

140/2438

No. 142 7.0.

11

Instructions regarding War Diaries and Intelligence Summaries are contained in F. S. Regs., Part II. and the Staff Manual respectively. Title pages will be prepared in manuscript.

WAR DIARY

~~or~~

~~INTELLIGENCE SUMMARY.~~

(Erase heading not required.)

SECRET

Army Form C. 2118.

Vol 26

Place	Date	Hour	Summary of Events and Information	Remarks and references to Appendices
			No 142 FIELD AMBULANCE	
			From 1.9.17 To 30.9.17	

(A7092). Wt. W12839/M1293. 750,000. 1/17. D. D. & L., Ltd. Forms/C.2118/14.

Instructions regarding War Diaries and Intelligence Summaries are contained in F. S. Regs., Part II. and the Staff Manual respectively. Title pages will be prepared in manuscript.

WAR DIARY
or
INTELLIGENCE SUMMARY.
(*Erase heading not required.*)

Army Form C. 2118.

Place	Date	Hour	Summary of Events and Information	Remarks and references to Appendices
LEBUCQUIERE.	1-9-17	9 am	The day opens with consternation and wild excitement – a thief has broken into the Canteen in the night and from under the head of the canteen N.C.O. L/Corpl. WILKINS has stolen the pillow, which happened to be a jacket containing £7 in postal orders. The loose cash box containing about fr 120 is missing also. The thief must have entered hard by the beer barrel and escaped across the fields at the back of the camp	Sheet 57 C 1/40,000 FRANCE
		10 am	O.C. 8th S Yorks paid a call & said that an attempted robbery had been made in his canteen during the night.	
		12 noon	We are going to move. I learnt this yesterday from the A.D.M.S. who came along to get a hair cut & have a game of Badminton – so accompanied by the Q.M. I went to [illegible] this morning to spy out the land. Felt very depressed when I saw our new site, for nothing has been done towards winter quarters – no huts – no horse lines, no cook house, only a few tattered and torn marquees and a few tumbledown sheds – the place looked like a laundry on drying day. It means starting all over again. Thought very deeply of the proverb "Fools build houses for wise men to live in". The town major protested that it was an excellent camp. And more in sorrow than in anger as he was of an inferior nature than myself, being a full colonel, I protested that it wasn't.	
		1.30.	A new R.C. Padre appeared – the Revd. BAINES C.F.	
		4.30.	Rained all the afternoon – so went to the Divisional Cinema.	

2353 Wt. W2544/1454 700,000 5/15 D. D. & L. A.D.S.S./Forms/C. 2118.

Instructions regarding War Diaries and Intelligence Summaries are contained in F. S. Regs., Part II. and the Staff Manual respectively. Title pages will be prepared in manuscript.

WAR DIARY
or
INTELLIGENCE SUMMARY.
(Erase heading not required.)

Army Form C. 2118.

Place	Date	Hour	Summary of Events and Information	Remarks and references to Appendices
LEBUCQUIERE	2/9/17	9. am	SUNDAY. Church Service in the Cinema. Rev. ADAMS. and M. le Lieut. VILDA - French Interpreter called on their way up the line. Lieut MASEFIELD was sent for temporary duty with the 13th Kings. One officer and 20 men from 2/3 LONDON. F.A.	FRANCE Sheet 57C 1/40000
		4.0	56th Div. appeared. Took the officer round the BEAUMETZ - CAMBRAI road posts in the afternoon & they all went	
		9.30 pm	to DOIGNIES in the evening. Seven of our bearers returned to H.Q.	
	3/9/17		Sixteen barrels of beer with L/Corpl WILKINS i/c proceeded from ALBERT to H.Q. by lorry. Very good light beer & much appreciated.	
		3. pm	Lt Col DUCAT attended by his QM and a G.S. officer called & stayed to tea. Took him round the camp and round DOIGNIES & the other posts. He seemed very pleased to find that so much work had been done & that we were carrying on with it up till the last moment. The canteen took frs. 1000 during the day.	
	4/9/17		Capt K. Macfarlane WALKER who is a member of the Church Committee Third Army visited the 36th Div. on propaganda work. Capts WALLACE & SNODGRASS with 20 OR's went to LECHELLE to prepare the way	
	5/9/17	9. am	Had a brain wave & invented a Security Wire for the Caps of Petrol Tins. Made drawings & got Sergt SHARP ASC MT. to make some. Showed them to ADMS who suggested Q might like to see them. Perfected the diagram & account of petrol tins. Party at DOIGNIES and CAMBRAI road relieved by 2/3 Lond F.A. The Rev. T. M. O'CONNOR. C.F. went to HAVRE	
	6/9/17	9. am	Lt & QM. BOWEN with cooks went to LECHELLE. Men paraded at 9.45 and marched at 10 under Capt MARTIN	
		10.30	Transport under Capt MANN - horses very fit & wagons newly painted, marched to LECHELLE	

Instructions regarding War Diaries and Intelligence Summaries are contained in F. S. Regs., Part II. and the Staff Manual respectively. Title pages will be prepared in manuscript.

WAR DIARY
or
INTELLIGENCE SUMMARY.
(*Erase heading not required.*)

Army Form C. 2118.

Place	Date	Hour	Summary of Events and Information	Remarks and references to Appendices
LEBUCQUIERE	6/9/17	11 am	Advance party of 2/3 Home. F.A. now in sight – Our motor transport left – also looking very fine – I have had the cars painted a milk chocolate brown upon which the blue & yellow of the Div. sign and the red & white of the red cross look very artistic.	
		11.15.	Attended by mounted orderly rode across country to LECHELLE.	
LECHELLE		12.15.	All detachments arrived within ½ an hour of each other – Unloaded wagons & apportioned billets. Canteen opened – very hot day – beer very refreshing. Lt. MASEFIELD proceeded to 20 KRR for permanent duty.	
		2.30 pm	Settled in during afternoon, erecting sheds, kitchens & making beds, tables & seats.	
	7/9/17		A.D.M.S. called and took away my petrol tin patent to Div. HQ. Morning spent in renovation, clothing parades, haircutting. Attached temporarily to 8th Brigade for sick & casualties.	
	8/9/17		Gas helmet & Box respirator parade. Nine P.B. men arrived to replace 10 Category A.1 A.S.C. Six of the P.B. men knows nothing of horses. One was discovered removing horse bugs with a broom handle!	
	9/9/17	12 noon	Baseball match at BUS between Canadian & American Railway Engineers – Plenty of excitement. Lecture in afternoon by G.O.C. Division who explained new method of attack and hinted at our move to YPRES.	
	10/9/17		Started Training. Adopted a new scheme, forming the bearers into 2 subdivisions instead of 3, keeping only a few men in A. Sect. in Staff Employ & putting all officers' servants, car & wagon orderlies, bootmakers, tailors & hairdressers into A Sect. Capt. SNODGRASS visited 3rd Div. Train daily. Lectures daily.	
	13/9/17		D.D.M.S. IV Corps visited the camp his business being to look at the new incinerator drying room we had built.	

2353 Wt. W2544/1454 700,000 5/15 D. D. & L. A.D.S.S./Forms/C. 2118.

Instructions regarding War Diaries and Intelligence Summaries are contained in F. S. Regs., Part II. and the Staff Manual respectively. Title pages will be prepared in manuscript.

WAR DIARY
or
INTELLIGENCE SUMMARY.
(Erase heading not required.)

Army Form C. 2118.

Place	Date	Hour	Summary of Events and Information	Remarks and references to Appendices
LECHELLE	14/9/17		Capt MARTIN's magpie has found a mate – They are terrible thieves. Lt HOLMES, MORC USA to the 2nd [illegible] for temporary duty. Grand dinner of the three ambulances last night at 1st R. F.A. 20 officers present, myself in the chair – ADMS STORMS & Area commandant Lt Col CRAIG – A. & S. Highlanders guests.	
	15/9/17	8 am	Capt DOWLING, the QM. & cooks went as advanced party to WATOU. Letter from DDMS II Corps expressing his appreciation of the work done in the IV Corps area. Capt SNODGRASS + 2 OR to the V & XIX Corps Reinforcement Camp.	
	16/9/17		Another American, Lt F.G. HALL MORC USA posted to us, seems an excellent fellow.	
	17/9/17		Lt. G.R PHILLIPS from 36 – Div – vice Capt KM WALKER posted to that Division.	
	18/9/17		The Div Ambulance Convoy under myself Capt LLOYD of No 8, Lt PINCOFFS USA of No 7 went to WATOU via ST POL, St VENANT & HAZEBROUCK. Owing to a confusion of orders we wandered round the area a bit finally reaching BRANDHOEK which we found occupied & went back to WATOU & put up with No 8 for the night.	
LUNA FARM POPERINGHE	19/9/17		The main body of the Ambulance came by train & marched to the AUX Corps Rest Station which we had proceeded there, taking over from 2/3 N. Mid. F.A. Capt SNODGRASS, R.C. proceeded to England having expressed a wish to go to MESOPOTAMIA.	Belgium Sheet 27 1/40000
	20/9/17		Capts WALLACE, MANN & Lt PHILLIPS with 32 ORs attached for duty to V Corps M D S Red Farm – Left with bearer officers to carry on the Rest Station. Stalled building – some outhouses & a drying room.	
	22/9/17		Capt MARTIN & C Sect bearers with 20 Regtl Stretcher bearers from 4th Bde went up the line.	

Instructions regarding War Diaries and Intelligence Summaries are contained in F. S. Regs., Part II. and the Staff Manual respectively. Title pages will be prepared in manuscript.

WAR DIARY
or
INTELLIGENCE SUMMARY.
(Erase heading not required.)

Army Form C. 2118.

Place	Date	Hour	Summary of Events and Information	Remarks and references to Appendices
RED FARM	23/9/17	12 noon	Took over the V Corps M.D.S from 2/1 WESSEX F.A. Found attached here 3 officers of 9th Division + 72 O.Rs, 2 officers of 59th Division + 32 O.R's also 42 temporarily unfit infantrymen. Capt DOWLING and B sub. bearers went up the line. There were a great many Corps orders to be read and understood.	Sheet 28 Belgium 1/40000
	25/9/17		The 2 Ford cars and 2 horsed ambulances were sent to the Division at YPRES for duty between POTIZE and BAVARIA House. Rations were sent up daily to BAVARIA House. Capt WALLACE and 4 officers were posted for duty to undertake the loading of cars. The D.D.M.S. visited here during the day. We were to take all the Corps wounded with the exception of walking cases, fractured femurs, penetrating chest & abdominal wall except the W.W. were to pass through our books. The special cases were to have a label attached to the stretcher handle & were not to be unloaded but passed straight on to the special hospital at DOZINGHAM. All other cases went to MENDINGHEM. Two-hourly returns of numbers were required by the D.D.M.S. and each A.D.M.S. received a daily state.	
	26/9/17		The M.D.S. worked well. A resuscitation ward with hot air chambers made by an oil drum & piping was most interesting. The D.M.S. Fifth Army, D.D.G.M.S. and D.D.M.S. V + II Anzac Corps called during the day. Admissions were as follows from 6 a.m. 26th to 8 am 29th	

26th		27th		28th		29th		Totals	
Officers	58	Offs	12	Offs	22	Offs	7	Offs	99
ORs	730	ORs	234	ORs	270	ORs	111	ORs	1346
P.O.W	49	P.O.W	10	POW	8	POW	2	POW	69

Instructions regarding War Diaries and Intelligence Summaries are contained in F. S. Regs., Part II. and the Staff Manual respectively. Title pages will be prepared in manuscript.

WAR DIARY
or
INTELLIGENCE SUMMARY.
(Erase heading not required.)

Army Form C. 2118.

Place	Date	Hour	Summary of Events and Information	Remarks and references to Appendices
RED FARM	30/9/17	8 am	The total number of cases passed through the M.D.S. now amount to over 2000. The last two or three nights have been rather busy owing to casualties in the district from aeroplane bombs a great number of which have been dropped on BRANDHOEK and the surrounding camps. The work of the bearers under Capts MARTIN and DOWLING has been excellent and our casualties have been light. No. 50473 Pte INGRAM. H.C. killed. 69151 Pte McCAUSLAND, 72546 Pte MARLOW. E, 101373 Pte CROSS. W. evacuated wounded. ~~Sergt~~ 58203 Sergt BATTERSBY. S., 462 Pte CARR G.E, wounded and at duty. One of the FORD cars was destroyed by a shell. 30 bearers were relieved on the night of the 29th and the remainder are to be relieved tonight	Belgium Sheet 28 1/40,000
			R. W. Walford Lt Col RAMC Commanding 142 Field Ambulance	

11 SECRET

Oct. 1917

140/2499 Vol 27

WAR DIARY

OF

No 142 FIELD AMBULANCE

From 1·10·17 To 31·10·17

Instructions regarding War Diaries and Intelligence Summaries are contained in F. S. Regs., Part II. and the Staff Manual respectively. Title pages will be prepared in manuscript.

WAR DIARY
or
INTELLIGENCE SUMMARY.
(Erase heading not required.)

Army Form C. 2118.

Place	Date	Hour	Summary of Events and Information	Remarks and references to Appendices
				Sheet
RED FARM	1/10/17	10 am	Transport under Capt. MANN marched to WAEMARS CAPPEL. Personnel under Capt WALLACE embussed at VLAMERTINGE debussed at WINNEZEELE and marched to OUDEZEELE – whilst I had proceeded with the Motor Transport.	LENS 11 1/100000
OUDEZEELE	2/10/17		Billeted in HARLEY CAMP which turned out to be a bare field.	
	3/10/17		Visited Brigade HQ. and battalions of 9th Brigade. G.O.C. 3rd Div. inspected the brigade in the afternoon and specially mentioned the field ambulance and its work in the operations – owing to mental aberration on the part of someone we were not informed of this & in consequence not on the parade.	
	4/10/17		Personnel embussed to St OMER and entrained for BAPAUME with transport – Capt WALLACE went on leave from St OMER – Motor transport by road to our old camp at LECHELLE.	
LECHELLE	5/10/17		Unit detrained at BAPAUME and marched to LECHELLE. Kit inspection parade revealed 147 deficiencies – a great number from carelessness and 17 were demanded on repayment.	
			Time was spent in cleaning up, clothing parades, reformation of squads.	France Sheet 57.C.
	8/10/17		Lieut BOWEN went on leave to the U.K. Lt PHILLIPS detailed for duty to 3rd Div. RE.	
	9/10/17		Capt DOWLING with 40 O.R's went to H.16.d.9.8 as advance party. I went round the line with the ADMS.	

Instructions regarding War Diaries and Intelligence Summaries are contained in F. S. Regs., Part II. and the Staff Manual respectively. Title pages will be prepared in manuscript.

WAR DIARY
or
INTELLIGENCE SUMMARY.
(Erase heading not required.)

Army Form C. 2118.

Place	Date	Hour	Summary of Events and Information	Remarks and references to Appendices
FAVREUIL	11/10/17		Marched to FAVREUIL H 16 d 9 8 & took over from 2/3 W. Riding F.A. 62 Div. who exchanged sites with us. Found the HQ hutted and used as a M.D.S. Very large camp with huts and canvas capable of taking over 600 patients. No 7 across the road in a camp of similar dimensions. Work practically none except for sick. Started painting the huts, building fireplaces of brick, digging deep pit latrines to replace the buckets and erecting a Drying room ... with hot water and disinfector.	Sheet 57 C FRANCE
	12/10/17		Found a bugler who blew the reveille, midday and lights out. Ordered to dig plots for 2500 cabbages and 3000 onions. Put the police and prisoners on the job. Canadian stoves were fitted in the Nissen huts, duck boards laid. Canteens built. Two huts formed into dining room.	
	13/10/17		Personally inspected the instruments and prickers for Primus Stoves.	
	14/10/17		D.D.M.S. VI Corps inspected us.	
	15/10/17		Capt MARTIN went on leave. Lt HALL - MORC USA struck off strength.	
	16/10/17		Capt WALLACE returned from leave. Several musical instruments arrived.	
	17/10/17		Lt. BOWEN returned from leave. Visited the A.D.S. with Capt MANN and found all correct. The cabbage patch is finished – waiting for cabbages & onions.	
	23/10/17		Lt HURD - MORC USA attached for a week's instruction.	

Instructions regarding War Diaries and Intelligence Summaries are contained in F. S. Regs., Part II. and the Staff Manual respectively. Title pages will be prepared in manuscript.

WAR DIARY
or
INTELLIGENCE SUMMARY.
(Erase heading not required.)

Army Form C. 2118.

Place	Date	Hour	Summary of Events and Information	Remarks and references to Appendices
FAVREUIL	24/10/17		Capt DOWLING relieved by Capt MANN went on leave. Capt WALKER [illegible] in and stopped the [illegible]	
	25/10/17		Building proceeds - First that the stable was built in a very ramshackle manner and requires complete rebuilding - Football team played No 8 and lost by one goal. Cabbage patch [illegible] - waiting for cabbages & onions. AMIENS leave has been open for the men in couples every other day	
	26/10/17		Lt HURD joins Capt MANN at the ADS	
	27/10/17		Ten men detailed for dugout building to No 7.	
	28/10/17		Lt HURD rejoins his unit and is struck off the strength.	
	29/10/17		Military Medals were awarded to 57998 Pte SCOTT W.D., 69252 Pte MILLINGTON W.G. and 2/Cpl 58336 BURBIDGE J. all of RAMC and M/2/272217 Pte OTTLEY P.D. ASC for gallantry in the field.	
	30/10/17		Capt W.S. MARTIN returned from leave.	
	31/10/17		Capt WALLACE rejoined - Lt HARPER RAMC, 1/Lt SULLIVAN [illegible] and 1/Lt BINGER [illegible] MORC USA taken on strength - the two Americans for a week's instruction. Wounded have been collected from the 8th Brigade in the line and sick from the 9th Brigade. A great many improvements have been made around the camp. An orchestra of [illegible], violin, bass, violins, flute, piccolo, side drum & clarinet has been practising daily.	

[illegible] Lieut Col RAMC
Commanding 142 Field Ambulance

Nov. 1917

7

SECRET

140/2578

Vol 28

WAR DIARY

OF

No 142 FIELD AMBULANCE

From 1/11/17 To 30/11/17

Instructions regarding War Diaries and Intelligence Summaries are contained in F. S. Regs., Part II. and the Staff Manual respectively. Title pages will be prepared in manuscript.

WAR DIARY
or
INTELLIGENCE SUMMARY.
(Erase heading not required.)

Army Form C. 2118.

Place	Date	Hour	Summary of Events and Information	Remarks and references to Appendices
FAVREUIL	Nov 1st 1917.		Lieut. R. S. HARPER posted for duty. 1/Lt. J. F. SULLIVAN and 1/Lt. C. S. L. BINGER – MORC. USA attached for one week's instruction – Lt. SULLIVAN went to the ADS at VAULX with Capt MANN for three days – Lt. BINGER to follow after three days at H.Q. Both very interested and keen on looking into everything – Capt WALLACE. MC. rejoined from 3rd Div. Depot Batts	FRANCE Sheet 57 C 1/40,000
	4th		At 4 pm a parade was held at No 7 F.A. and the G.O.C 3rd Division presented medal ribbons won by the unit since last year.	
			MILITARY CROSS – Capt W. S. MARTIN	
			MILITARY MEDALS. No 58203 Sergt. BATTERSBY. S.	
			58336 L/Cpl. BURBIDGE. J.	
			56267 Pte TURNER. G. C.	
			58308 " WORSWICK. H.	
			57995 " SCOTT. D.	
			69252 " MILLINGTON. W. G.	
			M2/272217 " OTTLEY. P. D. ASC (MT)	
			The General who was accompanied by an ADC. and Col. ENSOR. the ADMS. spoke of the good work the unit had done and after the presentation inspected the Camp.	
	5th		Lt. BINGER was evacuated to 49 CCS. with P.U.O. – full regret that he had been sick during the whole of his time with the unit & had been unable to see anything of its work.	
	6th		A special order of appreciation from Gen. Sir H. de la Gough and the G.O.C 3rd Division was published for information –	
	7th		Lt. V. C. PENNELL was posted for duty.	

(A7092). Wt. W12839/M1293. 750,000. 1/17. D. D. & L., Ltd. Forms/C.2118/14.

Instructions regarding War Diaries and Intelligence Summaries are contained in F. S. Regs., Part II. and the Staff Manual respectively. Title pages will be prepared in manuscript.

WAR DIARY
or
INTELLIGENCE SUMMARY.
(Erase heading not required.)

Army Form C. 2118.

Place	Date	Hour	Summary of Events and Information	Remarks and references to Appendices
FAVREUIL	Nov 7th	1917.	The 9th Brigade moved into the left sector of the line and having expressed a wish for their own ambulance to clear them in exchange with No 7. F.A. and took over the A.D.S. at ECOUST. Capt MANN and Lt PENNELL in charge. On the way up Capt MANN fell out of the car and injured his shoulder - so Capt MARTIN was sent to relieve him. An advanced aid post was under construction in Railway Reserve Trench	
			Capt DOWLING returned from leave.	
	10th		Lt HARPER posted for temporary duty with 8th K.O.R.L. Regt.	
	13th		D.D.M.S. VI Corps visited ECOUST and railway reserve post also inspected a Hot air apparatus getting into the chamber himself - The apparatus was the one in construction at ARRAS and used at the RED FARM main Dressing Station in the YPRES sector.	
	18th		Lt HOLMES and 17 ORs to 49 CCS. - 3 clerks to 49 CCS & 3 clerks to 29 CCS 1 NCO to 29 CCS (Achiet) to report arrival of trains to the OC, CCS.	
	20		Capt MARTIN & Lt PENNELL to Railway Reserve Trench with bearers of B & C sections - Capt WALLACE to ECOUST. Ambulance Cars pooled under Capt HACKETT - The Horsed Ambulance was posted at the Sugar Factory at 24.D.7.7. for the collection of walking wounded from ECOUST. - The attack of the 3rd Div. took place at 6.20 on the morning of the 20th and was quite successful there being very few casualties.	
	24		Lt PENNELL. 2 NCOs & 30 men returned to HQ	

(A7092). Wt. W12839/M1293. 750,000. 1/17. D. D. & L., Ltd. Forms/C.2118/14.

Instructions regarding War Diaries and Intelligence Summaries are contained in F. S. Regs., Part II. and the Staff Manual respectively. Title pages will be prepared in manuscript.

WAR DIARY
or
INTELLIGENCE SUMMARY.
(Erase heading not required.)

Army Form C. 2118.

Place	Date	Hour	Summary of Events and Information	Remarks and references to Appendices
FAVREUIL	Nov 25th 1917		Lt HARPER rejoined from the 8 K.O.R.L.R	
	27		Capt MARTIN and 22 O.R.s returned to H.Q.	
			During the month sick and wounded have been collected from the 9. 11 Brigade in the line and out. also from units of other brigades when in our area. From the line cases were carried from the R.A.Ps across the open at night & along the trench by day to Railway Reserve trench whence they were carried down the BULLECOURT-ECOUST road to ECOUST. On the morning of the offensive the light railway from railway reserve trench to ECOUST was used, the wounded being taken by hand trolley. As this was shelled continuously wheeled stretchers were used down the road as before. The road was visible to the Huns and was liable to occasional shelling & machine gun fire but no bearers were wounded. The A.D.S. received some shells also - several falling into the courtyard. The 16th Div. on our left had an A.D.S. in the same yard & by arrangement the work was pooled.	
			Prior to the 20th all wounded from the sector came through H.Q. of the Ambulance and we kept about 100 sick in NISSEN HUTS. We also ran the gas centre admitting about 15 cases. 12 of which came in in 2 days. All cases were bled & given oxygen but 3 of them including an officer died.	
			A great deal of construction work was done at H.Q. Hospital Tents were struck and NISSEN HUTS were [illegible] - They were all painted and fitted with stoves.	

(A7092). Wt. W12839/M1293. 750,000. 1/17. D. D. & L., Ltd. Forms/C.2118/14.

Instructions regarding War Diaries and Intelligence Summaries are contained in F. S. Regs., Part II. and the Staff Manual respectively. Title pages will be prepared in manuscript.

WAR DIARY
or
INTELLIGENCE SUMMARY.
(Erase heading not required.)

Army Form C. 2118.

Place	Date	Hour	Summary of Events and Information	Remarks and references to Appendices
FAVREUIL			The officers mess was tastefully decorated and fitted with a brick fireplace which took the eye of the G.O.C. who desired us to build him one similar. An "Incinerator - drying-room - hot water - ablution - bench and disinfector" was built - all the heat being obtained from the incinerator. The apparatus was home made & was capable of disinfecting 40 blankets an hour, besides supplying hot water from a tank of 100 gallons and heating a drying room. To supply it with sufficient fuel ~~refuse~~ was collected from other units.	
			The Bluelights started performances again & an orchestra of ~~string~~ seven was raised within the unit. Shows were given to No 7. F.A. & the D.A.C. The Canteen has been open all the month & in addition to ordinary dry goods has supplied beer and hot coffee.	
	Nov 30		Two pigs were taken on the strength of the unit till Xmas and allotted billets near the horse lines. A meeting was held to ~~provide~~ ~~about~~ a Committee for the Xmas festivities.	
			R. A. Hubbard [?] Lieut Colonel RAMC Commanding 142 Field Ambulance	

(A7092). Wt. W12839/M1293. 750,000. 1/17. D. D. & L., Ltd. Forms/C.2118/14.

140/2618

No. 142. 7. a.

Instructions regarding War Diaries and Intelligence Summaries are contained in F. S. Regs., Part II. and the Staff Manual respectively. Title pages will be prepared in manuscript.

WAR DIARY
or
INTELLIGENCE SUMMARY.
(Erase heading not required.)

Army Form C. 2118.

Vol 29

Place	Date	Hour	Summary of Events and Information	Remarks and references to Appendices
FAVREUIL	Dec 1st/17		Lieut HARPER posted to the A.D.S. ECOUST	Sheet 57 C FRANCE 1/40,000 –
	2nd		Capt DOWLING took up B Section bearers and relieved Capt WALLACE at ECOUST	
	3rd		D.D.M.S. VI Corps visited HQ to inspect the incinerator.	
	4.		Lieut PENNELL posted temporarily to 1st North. Fus. vice Capt CLARKE on leave	
	8th		Lieut HARPER returned to H.Q. sick. Capt DOWLING was relieved for 24 hrs by Capt MARTIN and went to ALBERT for an interview with D.M.S. Third Army with reference to a regular commission. An attempted robbery was made on the canteen till, the cash box being removed by a hand through the side of the wall. It was spotted by Sergt CHANDLER who raised a hue and cry and the box was dropped outside the Canteen – The police are active. The Camp Commandant + A.P.M came to investigate.	
	9.		The clerks returned from 29th + 49 C.C.S.	
			Crime and [illegible] to tea	
	10.		Capts DOWLING and MANN took over at A.D.S. – A little breeze arose over an expected attack by the HUNS on the left sector, following an attack this morning on the R. sector. S.O.S. all along the line. Several shells in vicinity of A.D.S.	
	12		Heavy shelling all day – B.C.P. in Railway Reserve was whitewashed and on the ECOUST Road –	
	13.		Whole Division ordered to "stand to" every morning at 6.30. am. Rose accordingly.	
	14.		No 77 F.A. billeted upon us. Gave up tent huts and discharged all patients. Two clerks and party at C.C.S. Two clerks ordered to march to BIENVILLERS less 2 officers + Bearers and party up the line. Remainder + car orders were sent to C.C.S. Capts DOWLING and MANN and party up the line to march with No 7. F.A. to their new location. Remainder of bearers to march with No 7. F.A. orders of O.C. No 7. F.A.	

. Instructions regarding War Diaries and Intelligence Summaries are contained in F. S. Regs., Part II. and the Staff Manual respectively. Title pages will be prepared in manuscript.

WAR DIARY
or
INTELLIGENCE SUMMARY.
(Erase heading not required.)

Army Form C. 2118.

142nd FIELD AMBULANCE No. .... Date .... R.A.M.C.

Place	Date	Hour	Summary of Events and Information	Remarks and references to Appendices
FAVREUIL BIENVILLERS	Dec	15th –	Rose shortly after dawn – handed over camp to O.C. No 77 F.A. Marched to BIENVILLERS a semi-destroyed village – with fairly good accommodation. Our total marching in strength 6 officers and 80 ORs – Our disposition is as follows. 1 Off. 19 ORs at 49 CCS. 4 ORs at the Batt's MORY, 5 ORs with Town Major FAVREUIL, 2 ORs at 3rd Division Depot Batt's 1 Off with 1st North Fus. 1 officer with 10 RWF. 2 officers and 81 ORs with No 7. F Amb 26 ORs on leave.	
	–	19	Lt. Col Halgood granted leave to U.K. from 20/12/17 to 19/1/18 Capt A. G. S. WALLACE takes over command of the Ambulance in absence of Lt Col Halford	
	–	20	The bearers & tent subdivisions were relieved in the line by No 4 F.A. and proceeded to BIENVILLERS by motor lorry. The Bearers who were at No 4 headquarters marched over.	
	–	25	Lt V. C. PENNELL rejoined from temporary Duty with 1st Northum. Fus. The ambulance sat down to a splendid dinner of Roast Pork, Boiled Ham mashed potatoes & cabbage followed by Plum Pudding & various fruits. The Evening was spent at a Smoking Concert.	
	–	26	Boxing Day. The men of the ambulance enjoyed a very successful Whist drive. Lt V. C. PENNELL Proceeded to VI Corps School at GIVENCHY-LE-NOBLE for temporary duty as M.O. i/c	

Alex. G. S. Wallace
Capt. RAMC
, R.A.M.C.
COMDG. 142ND FIELD AMBULANCE

(A7092). Wt. W12839/M1293. 750,000. 1/17. D. D. & L., Ltd. Forms/C.2118/14.

3RD DIVISION
MEDICAL

NO. 142 FIELD AMBULANCE

1918

Jan. 1918 7 140/2696 Vol 30

SECRET

WAR DIARY

OF

No 142 FIELD AMBULANCE

From 1.1.18 To 31.1.18

Instructions regarding War Diaries and Intelligence Summaries are contained in F. S. Regs., Part II. and the Staff Manual respectively. Title pages will be prepared in manuscript.

WAR DIARY
or
INTELLIGENCE SUMMARY.
(*Erase heading not required.*)

Army Form 2118.

142 Field Ambulance

Place	Date	Hour	Summary of Events and Information	Remarks and references to Appendices
BIENVILLERS	1918 Jan 1		CAPT H. L. MANN proceeded on leave to England AGSW	Sheet 11 LENS 1/100,000
"	" 2		Extract from London Gazette :- Mentioned in despatches - LIEUT COL A. H. HABGOOD & LIEUT & Q.M. E. S. BOWEN AGSW	
	" 3		One Tent (?) Subdivision (16 O.R.) proceeded to 20 C.C.S. for temporary duty. AGSW	
"	" 5		LT COL A. H. HABGOOD'S name appeared in the New Years Honours list as having been awarded the D.S.O. A Telegram was sent to Col Habgood congratulating him and a letter of congratulation was sent to Col. ENSOR, the A.D.M.S. to which he replied - "Very many thanks for the kind congratulations of the officers & other ranks of the 142 Field Amb. Please inform them how sensible I am that it is very largely due to the good work carried out in action by the R.A.M.C. that the C.M.G. has been given to me as the O.C. R.A.M.C. of the division." AGSW	
	" 6		Fatigue Parties of 12 to 15 O.R. are supplied daily to the Town Major for salvage work in the neighbourhood AGSW	
"			A reply to the telegram of congratulation was received from LT COL HABGOOD thanking all ranks AGSW	
	" 15		A Working Party of 1 NCO & 12 men proceeded for temporary duty at LA COUCHIE under instructions from the Area Commandant AGSW	
	" 21		The working Party of 1 NCO & 12 men returned from GAUDIEMPRE. AGSW	
	" 21		CAPT H. L. MANN rejoined from leave	
	" 23		LIEUT V. C. PENNELL rejoined from temporary duty as M.O. i/c VI Corps School at GIVENCHY-LE-NOBLE (?) AGSW	
FICHEUX	" 27		Marched from BIENVILLERS & took over the M.D.S. from 104 Field Ambulance and an A.D.S. at CROISILLES from 102 Field Amb AGSW	
			LIEUT COL HABGOOD rejoined from leave & takes over Command AGSW	

Alex G. S. Wallace
Capt RAMC

(A7092). Wt. W12839/M1293. 750,000. 1/17. D. D. & L., Ltd. Forms/C.2118/14.

Instructions regarding War Diaries and Intelligence Summaries are contained in F. S. Regs., Part II. and the Staff Manual respectively. Title pages will be prepared in manuscript.

WAR DIARY
or
INTELLIGENCE SUMMARY.
(Erase heading not required.)

Army Form C. 2118.

142 Field Ambulance

Place	Date	Hour	Summary of Events and Information	Remarks and references to Appendices
FICHEUX	Jan	28th	Visited the A.D.S. CROISELLES and the Quarry T.18 b 9.4 – Decided that the Quarry should become the A.D.S. & that the M.O. i/c R.A.P. should find an R.A.P. nearer the Battn H.Q. AGH	51 B. 1/40,000 S.2.6.7.4 AGH
		29	Assumed duties as acting A.D.M.S. in absence of Lt Col. Ross Taylor on leave & visited the Office daily. Went to 8th Brigade H.Q. with reference to change of A.D.S.	AGH
		30	Spent all day in connection with duties at A.D.M.S. Office.	AGH
		31	Duties at A.D.M.S. Office – Conference of O.C.'s ambulances in the afternoon at which [illegible] was [illegible] to O.C. No. 7 F.A.	AGH
			During the last month up to the 27th the Ambulance was closed for the reception of sick and the unit was split into numerous sections working at different places at 2 C.C.S.'s, baths, salvage and general duties. Billets were prepared & [illegible] for the area commandant and town major. For civilians rebuilt – an improvised disinfector was built ([illegible]).	
			Since the 27th a Main Dressing Station & Divisional Rest Station has been opened. Dental, Eye, Nasal & Aural cases are dealt with and an Officers class has been started under Capt. MARTIN M.C. for junior officers & American M.O.'s.	AGH

[signature]
Officer Commanding 142 Field Ambulance

SECRET

7

Medical
WR 31

WAR DIARY

OF

No 142 FIELD AMBULANCE

Feb 1918

140/2849

From 1 Feb 1918 To 28 Feb 1918

Instructions regarding War Diaries and Intelligence Summaries are contained in F. S. Regs., Part II. and the Staff Manual respectively. Title pages will be prepared in manuscript.

WAR DIARY
or
~~INTELLIGENCE SUMMARY.~~
(Erase heading not required.)

Army Form C. 2118.

142nd Field Ambulance

Place	Date	Hour	Summary of Events and Information	Remarks and references to Appendices
FISCHEUX	Feb 1st		Lieut HOLMES – MORC USA – wounded + at duty.	FRANCE
S.26.7.4	5th		G.O.C. 3rd Division visited HQ and inspected the trench walked dug under the huts. Suggested that it be covered to convert a Lewis Gun for protection purposes against aeroplanes. Issue [illegible] Capt MARTIN – proceeded on leave – Capt DOWLING rejoined from 13th Kings. Lt HOLMES from 1st GORDONS	Sheet 51B 1/40000
	6th		DADMS VI Corps visited HQ. I visited the ADS and 8th Bgde HQ again with reference to a change of ADS.	
	7.		Capt WALLACE relieved Lt PENNELL at ADS – marked out a Govt Garden Plot No 103 and salved two civilian derelict ploughs.	
	10		Lt HOLMES to U.K on leave with letters of introduction to Dons at Oxford + Cambridge. Driver PRATT – ASC an expert Norfolk ploughman busy ploughing the plot. The pair of Suffolk punches very bucked with their new role – probably think they are on leave + back at the farm.	
	12.		Reconnoitred a W.W.C.P. and selected the ADS at St LEGER by arrangement with Division on our right – Informed the ADMS of this	
	13.		Capt DOWLING to U.K on leave. Pancakes for dinner – being Shrove Tuesday	
	17.		Capt MANN relieved Capt WALLACE at ADS – Lecture on the 14th on Ordnance by ADOS VI Corps on 15th on Discipline by Commandant Officer VI Corps – On 16th by DADVS 34th Div. on Horses On 17th by ADMS 3rd Div – FA in Offensive operations.	
	21		Capt WALLACE on leave to UK. Capt MARTIN rejoined.	
	24th		Lecture by Col [illegible] ADMS on "FA in Defensive Warfare."	

(A7092). Wt. W12839/M1293. 750,000. 1/17. D. D. & L., Ltd. Forms/C.2118/14.

Instructions regarding War Diaries and Intelligence Summaries are contained in F. S. Regs., Part II. and the Staff Manual respectively. Title pages will be prepared in manuscript.

WAR DIARY
or
INTELLIGENCE SUMMARY.
(Erase heading not required.)

Army Form C. 2118.

France Sheet 51B
1/40000

Place	Date	Hour	Summary of Events and Information	Remarks and references to Appendices
FISCHEUX	Feb 25th		Col. BLISS – D.D.M.S. VI Corps visited + inspected new Gas Centre under construction.	A.A.H
S26.74	26		Lt HOLMES returned from leave.	A.A.H
	28		The Division has been in the line throughout the month on a three brigade front. Sick and wounded have been collected from the 8th Brigade through the A.D.S. at CROISILLES and from the surrounding district. Nominally the H.Q. has been an M.D.S. but actually the wounded have been evacuated direct to either 20 or 43 CCS situated just across the road. The M.D.S. has been kept for sick – the average number in hospital being 130 including special cases Skin & Eye, Nasal and Dental cases – No 1 Mobile Dental Unit being attached to the M.D.S. Evacuations from the A.D.S. took place daily by Light Railway – Serious cases & wounded by car. The patients were made as comfortable as possible the majority being accommodated with Red Cross beds. One Nissen Hut with 4 beds was reserved for officers + one with 9 beds for W.O.s + Senior NCOs.	
			The Blacklights mobilised and gave entertainments to 20 CCS 43 CCS + the patients in Hospital –	
			Two courses of instruction of the VI Corps School were conducted on the premises by Capt W.S. MARTIN – M.C. who was detached for this purpose.	
			A Gas Centre on the Thiago principle is under construction – Two MEAULTE Huts are being sunk into the ground – the first divided into 4 compartments for diagnosis, bath, dressing + treatment rooms, the second as a Ward for Gassed cases. A great deal of work was done in sinking these huts to the roof as a protection against aircraft.	
			Other measures of protection have been to open trap doors in the floors of the NISSEN Huts and dig trenches under the huts – these trenches are being connected up with each other.	

(A7092). Wt. W12839/M1293. 750,000. 1/17. D. D. & L., Ltd. Forms/C.2118/14.

Army Form C. 2118.

Instructions regarding War Diaries and Intelligence Summaries are contained in F. S. Regs., Part II. and the Staff Manual respectively. Title pages will be prepared in manuscript.

WAR DIARY
or
INTELLIGENCE SUMMARY.
(Erase heading not required.)

Place	Date	Hour	Summary of Events and Information	Remarks and references to Appendices
FISCHEUX	Feb. 28th 1918		A long trench has been dug down the ADRIAN hut entrance being effected by 3 trapdoors in the floor at intervals down the hut. Ramparts have also been constructed. A paddock has been constructed with a sand bath for the mules and outside horse lines for the heavy draught in fine weather. A garden plot of one acre has been ploughed & prepared for vegetables. No 103 Some dugouts were discovered in the Hun old front line near by and two of these were reopened and the timber removed - About 2000 feet were salved when a G.R.O was issued forbidding the removal of dug out timber without leave. Permission was sought from the Corps as the dugouts had all fallen in and the wood was in urgent need of but this was not granted. salvage and badly needed for the construction of other dug outs. is being constructed with the timber A large dug out 15 feet deep under a bank if it can be completed. and is intended as sleeping quarters for the personnel several G.S. wagon loads of [illegible] for fodder, Much salvage has been collected, and odds & ends of all sorts. ammunition, boots, zinc, dripping in several matches & games of matches The football team has been successful are played every Saturday & Sunday afternoons The Canteen is in full swing & since July 1917 has handed over about frs 3000 to the unit Fund. About frs 1000 was spent on Xmas festivities including prizes for whist drives - The football team has been fitted out with jerseys, boots and stockings, visiting teams have been entertained. The Bernafleights have been supplied with music and a [illegible] - A War Savings scheme has been started and for an expenditure of frs 325 - 15/6 War Savings Certificates to the number of 173 have been bought since Xmas by the NCOs, & men of the unit. C. A. [illegible] Lieut Col. RAMC Commanding 142 Field Ambulance	

(A7092). Wt. W12839/M1293. 750,000. 1/17. D. D. & L., Ltd. Forms/C.2118/14.

140/2849.

March 1918

142 Field Ambulance

WAR DIARY
or
~~INTELLIGENCE~~ SUMMARY.

(Erase heading not required.)

Army Form C. 2118.

Instructions regarding War Diaries and Intelligence Summaries are contained in F. S. Regs., Part II. and the Staff Manual respectively. Title pages will be prepared in manuscript.

142 Field Ambulance

Vol 32

Place	Date	Hour	Summary of Events and Information	Remarks and references to Appendices
FISCHEUX S.26.7.4	March 1st/18		The A.D.S. CROISILLES and bearers in the line were relieved by an ambulance of the 34th Division. Capt MANN and staff returned to HQ. Permission was given to Capts WALLACE and MARTIN to wear the badges of acting rank of Major under G.R.O. 3448 d/20/2/18 pending ratification by publication of names in London Gazette.	Sheet 51B FRANCE 1/40000
	2		Went round the 9th Brigade front and visited A.D.S. HENIN with O.C. 8th F.A. Conference of O.C.s F.A. to discuss recommended decrease in equipment. Combined recommendation submitted.	
	3		O.C. No 1 Mobile Dental Unit and caravan returned to GREVILLERS	
	4		1 NCO + 25 men supplied to 20 CCS as working party. Capt DOWLING proceeded to 3rd S.W. Machine Gun Battn as M.O. i/c. Lt HOLMES appointed O i/c Gas Centre	
	5		Officers ward closed, and arrangements made for reception of men requiring inoculation.	
	6		Inoculations cancelled. Officers ward remains open. D.D.M.S. VI Corps visited	
	7		Operation Orders of Defence Scheme from D.D.M.S. and A.D.M.S. Arrangements made to evacuate sick [illegible] and to form M.D.S. [illegible] Centre and Walking Wounded Dressing Station. Conference at office of A.D.M.S. of O.C.s F.As	
	8		A.D.M.S. visited. Large surgical ward cleared at farther end & dressing room of 3 tables formed. Various alterations made in accordance with O.O. of 6th & 7th.	
	9		Two reinforcements arrived yesterday from BLACKPOOL. One B1 and the rest B.2!! Report sent in to A.D.M.S.	
	10		Corps Commander accompanied by D.D.M.S. inspected the ambulance	
	11		Beautiful summer day. Rode to ADS HENIN and reconnoitred bearer routes in line. Visited by G.S.O. 1, AA&QMG, 3rd Div. accompanied by A.D.M.S.	

(A7092). Wt. W12839/M1293. 750,000. 1/17. D. D. & L., Ltd. Forms/C.2118/14.

Instructions regarding War Diaries and Intelligence Summaries are contained in F. S. Regs., Part II. and the Staff Manual respectively. Title pages will be prepared in manuscript.

WAR DIARY
or
INTELLIGENCE SUMMARY.

(Erase heading not required.)

Army Form C. 2118.

Place	Date	Hour	Summary of Events and Information	Remarks and references to Appendices
FISCHEUX	March 12th 1918		Orders last night to have everything in readiness by night of 12/13 for reception of Stretcher Cases walking wounded, sick + gassed cases. Bearers with exception of 3 squads returned from line & whole bearer Division under Major MARTIN – M.C. held in reserve. All clerical work to be done at M.D.S. Fifty sick remain in hospital to be used as hospital personnel. Visited by D.D.M.S., A.D.M.S. 34th Div. – A.D.M.S. 3rd Div. – Capt. GRANT-MORRIN attached for duty.	[illegible]
			Heavy bombardment during the night by our Corps artillery – No Hun attack – No casualties.	[illegible]
		13th	Began to fill up the medical ward with sick cases.	[illegible]
			Calm continues.	[illegible]
		14	Ditto – rumours of an attack expected on the morrow – Visit from A.A.Q.M.G. and A.D.M.S.	[illegible]
		15	No attack – take in more sick – have a game of Badminton.	[illegible]
		16	Begin to fill up the surgical & reception ward – with sick. VI Corps School to reopen	[illegible]
		17	on 18th under Major MARTIN. M.C. Scholars begin training.	[illegible]
		18	Deserters bring rumours of an attack on the 19th –	[illegible]
		19th	No attack – continues as before. Rain fell today – the first time for weeks. I think	
		20	weather better – Heavy bombardment at night.	
		21	Hun attack from MONCHY LE PREUX to six miles South – Cleared all sick from M.D.S. and opened for wounded – stretcher lying walking wounded and gassed. 3rd Division withstood all attacks but HUNS broke through 34th – 59th Div. capturing CROISILLES, ECOUST, NOREUIL VAUX – large number of 34th Div. wounded – and about 100 gassed cases – No mustard gas – apparently chloropicrin + phosgene mixed. 20 CCS being closed cases were sent to 43 CCS and the Division attached 4 clerks, 2 officers + 24 ORs. Walking wounded first evacuated by Light Railway from SOUTHAMPTON – then by motor lorry – 8 being attached to the M.D.S. for this purpose	
		22		

(A7092). Wt. W12839/M1293. 750,000. 1/17. D. D. & L., Ltd. Forms/C.2118/14.

Instructions regarding War Diaries and Intelligence Summaries are contained in F. S. Regs., Part II. and the Staff Manual respectively. Title pages will be prepared in manuscript.

WAR DIARY
or
INTELLIGENCE SUMMARY.
(Erase heading not required.)

Army Form C. 2118.

Place	Date	Hour	Summary of Events and Information	Remarks and references to Appendices
FISCHEUX	March 22		Seven men of 70th Sanitary Section + 28 T.U. from Scabies Station attached for duty. DADMS Guards Division called asking for billets – O.C. 93 F.A. called reporting to take over the M.D.S. with his whole ambulance + transport – On enquiry found it was intended that he should take over BLAIREVILLE and form a M.D.S. Fed them + sent them off. – ADMS called later in the evening + informed us that the line was to be withdrawn to the 3rd System and that the M.D.S. was to become the A.D.S. Transport packed and a portion of it sent to join transport of No 7 F.A. at WAILLY. Division moving its Corps HQ – Vague rumours of a break through at ERVILLERS, St LEGER and that HENIN Hill had been captured. Except for a flanking movement made necessary by the retirement of the Div on our Right the 3rd Div. stood held its own during 3 attacks. Line was withdrawn by 5 am.	[illegible]
	23		About 60 men of 9th F.A. arrived at 2 am + were billeted. Awakened by Signal Officer 3rd Div at 5 am + told that 9th I Brigade were taking over our dug out. Brigadier Gen POTTER and Bdge HQ arrived at 5.30 am – there in possession of our right flank – a school of TANKS on our left front parking in our mules' paddock – Had thirteen visitors to breakfast – ADMS + DADMS – an officer of 9 F.A. the 9th Inf. Bgde Staff + 3 Tank Officers. Wagons were sent to WAILLY in the morning – and 14 lorry loads of hospital equipment were sent to CCS + M.D.S. – Bearers were stationed at dug out building + continued in shifts of 8 hours – Brigade departed for BOISLEUX AU MONT and ADMS then for BRETENCOURT – tanks for the valley behind us. There were very few casualties during the day. Day full of rumours, roads full of troops – new divisions arriving.	[illegible]

(A7092). Wt. W12839/M1293. 750,000. 1/17. D. D. & L., Ltd. Forms/C.2118/14.

Instructions regarding War Diaries and Intelligence Summaries are contained in F. S. Regs., Part II. and the Staff Manual respectively. Title pages will be prepared in manuscript.

WAR DIARY
or
INTELLIGENCE SUMMARY.
(Erase heading not required.)

Army Form C. 2118.

Place	Date	Hour	Summary of Events and Information	Remarks and references to Appendices
FISCHEUX S 26.7.4	March 24th		Very fierce SOS bombardment at 9.45 continuing for an hour. Slept uninterrupted till 7.30 am [illegible] around steadily but not in great numbers. News arrived that the Huns had broken through the Fifth Army but French reinforcements were holding them back in front of SAILLY- SAILLYSEL. Frequent attacks on 3rd Div. Wounded report that masses came on and were annihilated. Asked GUARDS Div. called and arranged a mixed dressing station here but this was cancelled later. 9 FA lorry [illegible] [illegible] to 43 CCS.	[illegible]
	25th		The Hun [illegible] weather continues. The Division which still held its own against repeated attacks has withdrawn on the night of the 23/24 to the 3rd System the line running across the forward slopes of the hill in front of the ARRAS – BAPAUME road. The 3rd Div with the 4th Guards Brigade and the Guards Division on R. flank and the 15th Div. on the left. Shelling of BOISLEAU AU MONT increases. 9 FA moved to BLAIREVILLE to open a MDS. [illegible] Continue to [illegible] evacuating cases from No 7 & 8 who have dressing stations at NEUVILLE VITASSE and on the MERCATEL road respectively.	[illegible]
	26th		Am ordered to reconnoitre roads etc Rumours of a further retirement to conform to line on right. Line being hastily dug by [illegible] [illegible] prepared to open an ADS – BRETENCOURT if necessary. [illegible] cancelled [illegible] about 3/4 mile behind [illegible]. Continue to [illegible] material [illegible] [illegible] [illegible] MAT on the [illegible] [illegible] as 43 CCS had closed & retired [illegible] [illegible] [illegible] [illegible] [illegible] [illegible] Saw Major WALLACE & 4 ORs. As the Div. is retiring [illegible] the MERCATEL – FISCHEUX road direct line of [illegible] which should be [illegible] [illegible] [illegible] bearer post in that road Confer with OCs FA 7 & 8 and report to ADMS. Was ordered [illegible] camp at very low altitude [illegible] and retire from S.26.7.4. Two HUN aeroplanes [illegible] the camp [illegible] ARRAS later in the evening. One HUN machine gun. One was brought down near by & the [illegible] [illegible]. Shelling was [illegible] during the night [illegible] brought in practically dead, [illegible] [illegible] buried.	

(A7092). Wt. W12839/M1293. 750,000. 1/17. D. D. & L., Ltd. Forms/C.2118/14.

Instructions regarding War Diaries and Intelligence Summaries are contained in F. S. Regs., Part II. and the Staff Manual respectively. Title pages will be prepared in manuscript.

WAR DIARY
or
INTELLIGENCE SUMMARY.

(Erase heading not required.)

Army Form C. 2118.

Place	Date	Hour	Summary of Events and Information	Remarks and references to Appendices
FISCHEUX (BOISLEAU AU MONT)	March	27	Several of the huts being struck by H.E. shrapnel – no casualties. The men left at the dressing station were accommodated in the large dug out. Lt HOLMES Capt MORROW and the Padre with 40 O.R. departed at 1 am for BEAUMETZ the new M.D.S. (43 CCS site). Lorries returned for stores etc. and car post formed in MERCATEL–FISCHEUX road just behind No 7 & 8 and during the day the lorries were busy removing stores etc. When this had been done the whole party left for the new M.D.S. near BEAUMETZ – Major MARTIN – the bearers and myself remaining at the post on the FISCHEUX road. The line had retired on the flanks & on the shelling of the BOISLEAU cross roads had increased – our front line now running through BOIRY-BECQUERELLE. Major MARTIN and returned to M.D.S. in the afternoon. Massed attacks were still being made against the 3rd Divn – which held out & repulsed them all.	
	–	28	A day of terrible rumours. Very cold & windy. We have always thrown one. Large numbers of wounded passed through including 64, 3rd Division (34 officers). M.D.S. under command of O.C. 7 F.A. Joined by transport which had been sent to GOUY. Capt MANN reported that an Army [illegible] was shown him by an O.C. battery of guns which said that HUNS had broken through at HEBUTERNE so he set off with several [illegible] in a lorry to rescue the dumps and personnel in Armoured Cars. Rained very heavily during the afternoon & evening – 3rd Division had a lift at BERNAVILLE. The site of the M.D.S. is a deplorable sight – Kit, stores & half finished huts lying in all directions. Transport of 7 & 142, 93, 9, FAs together –	Above
		29	Heard this morning that Sergt BATTERSBY – Name on probation with the 4th R.F.s for a commission – had been recommended for V.C. [redacted] – No 7 & 8 F.A. moved to WAILLY but our car post was still left on the MERCATEL road & cars ran through MERCATEL. Lt DEODATI MORC.USA taken on strength from 27th. Owing to the confusion in DOULLENS he had set off on his own to meet the Division & joined at Divl HQ after 2 days on the road. Division to be relieved by 2nd Canadians. I went up the line to see Major MARTIN and found him in the R.F.s Aid Post. Arranged for relief. Sending horsed ambulance to follow troops out –	Above

(A7092). Wt. W12839/M1293. 750,000. 1/17. D. D. & L., Ltd. Forms/C.2118/14.

Instructions regarding War Diaries and Intelligence Summaries are contained in F. S. Regs., Part II. and the Staff Manual respectively. Title pages will be prepared in manuscript.

WAR DIARY
or
INTELLIGENCE SUMMARY.

(Erase heading not required.)

Army Form C. 2118.

Place	Date	Hour	Summary of Events and Information	Remarks and references to Appendices
BAC DE SUD	March 29		Roads from the line being congested – by transport of both divisions – blocked on the road by a G.S. wagon overturned by a 9.2 gun – a lorry run into by a train at the level crossing & by running into a limber & stopping my car. Bearers stopped at BEAUMETZ for the night. Transport & bearers under Majors WALLACE and MARTIN. Capt MANN	
		30th	Ambulance moved off with 9th Bgde. sent ahead to billet in IVERGNY	
IVERGNY ~~IVERGNY~~	Mar. 31st ~~April 1st~~		~~Completely billeted – IVERGNY.~~ ~~[illegible]~~ – Ambulance billeted – Church Parade this morning.	

[illegible]

Lt Col [illegible]

Commanding 142 Field Ambulance

(A7092). Wt. W12839/M1293. 750,000. 1/17. D. D. & L., Ltd. Forms/C.2118/14.

SECRET

Vol 33

6

WAR DIARY

OF

No 142 FIELD AMBULANCE 140/2900

Apr. 1918

From 1 April 1918 To 30 April 1918

Instructions regarding War Diaries and Intelligence Summaries are contained in F. S. Regs., Part II. and the Staff Manual respectively. Title pages will be prepared in manuscript.

WAR DIARY
or
INTELLIGENCE SUMMARY.
(Erase heading not required.)

Army Form C. 2118.

142 Field Ambulance

Place	Date	Hour	Summary of Events and Information	Remarks and references to Appendices
IVERGNY	April 1/18		Proceeded under orders G.O.C. 9th Brigade to I Corps Reserve Area First Army personnel by bus, transport by road, billeted in Chateaux to VIELFORT.	LENS Sheet 11 1/100,000
LE VIELFORT	"	2nd	Settled in new quarters – Kit inspections – clothing parade. Improvements to billets	[illegible]
		3rd	Schedule of training devised – lectures to nursing orderlies commenced	[illegible]
		4th	Training continued – Warning order from 9th Bgde to move to HERSIN area	
		5th	O.O. [illegible] + 9th Bgde to move to BRAQUEMONT – cancelled during night. Capt BREEN. T F P joined for duty. Pte OTTLEY – ASC motor despatch rider collided with lorry near BRUAY + brought in with concussion.	[illegible]
		6.	Warning order to move to new area in a few days	[illegible]
BRAQUEMONT		7	Proceeded by route march to BRAQUEMONT S.E. of NOEUX LES MINES. Billeted in site of No 7 CCS. Unpacked wagons + opened for sick of Brigade	[illegible]
		8.	Training continued – Made plans for M.A.S. Attack made on XI Corps. 8th + 9th Brigades moved north in support. Warning order to move at a moment's notice. Loaded wagons	[illegible]
		9.	Moved in afternoon to OBLINGHEM but before reaching objective – order cancelled so returned [illegible]	[illegible]
		9.	Orders to move at once arrived in the afternoon – Marched	
		10	unloaded wagons + prepared hospital – Orders to move at once [illegible] and opened a M.D.S. Two other ambulances [illegible] to CHATEAU L'ABBAYE N.W. BETHUNE – and opened a M.D.S. [illegible] Arranged with 2/1 WESSEX F.A. to take all stretcher cases. [illegible] No 1 CCS moving material. Arranged with [illegible] during the night – also transport of No 8 to look after Walking sitting cases. No 7 moved in during [illegible] Orders to clear the 11th Brigade 4th Division Transport ordered to move to a spot near LAPUGNOY – [illegible] Major MARTIN and Capt BREEN reconnoitring [illegible]	[illegible]
		11.	the 9th Brigade being [illegible] with the 5th Div. [illegible] clearing from the canal	[illegible]
		12.	arranged bearer [illegible] posts [illegible] through the dressing station About 360 [illegible] wounded and a dozen Hun prisoners	

(A7092). Wt. W12839/M1293. 750,000. 1/17. D. D. & L., Ltd. Forms/C.2118/14.

Instructions regarding War Diaries and Intelligence Summaries are contained in F. S. Regs., Part II. and the Staff Manual respectively. Title pages will be prepared in manuscript.

WAR DIARY
or
INTELLIGENCE SUMMARY.
(Erase heading not required.)

Army Form C. 2118.

Place	Date	Hour	Summary of Events and Information	Remarks and references to Appendices
CHATEAU L'ABBAYE	April	13th	4th Division (11th Brigade) had no casualties to clear.	~~[illegible]~~
		14th	The 10th Field Ambulance arranged to take over the clearing of the 11th Brigade - Major Mar	~~[illegible]~~
			tin & party returned to H.Q. which completed by 6 pm	~~[illegible]~~
			The line between X.22.a.9.2 and PONT TOURNANT taken over by 9th Brigade.	BETHUNE
			Major MARTIN Capt BREEN and 2 squads of bearers relieved the 2/1 WESSEX F.A. 55th Div.	1/40,000
			There were no casualties – the line being very quiet.	
			An A.D.S. was formed in a cellar on the LE HAMEL road and a car post in the	
		15th	outskirts of the village. squads of bearers were left with the 12th Kings. 1st N.F. The	
			4th N.F. had an aid post quite close to the car post. Work was done filling these	
			places ready and helping refugees to collect their belongings. The M.D.S. had very	
			little loss. of valuable stores left by the C.C.S.	
			Quiet day occupied chiefly in removing the large quantity	
		16	with Salvage dumps. No 7. took over the walking wounded	
		17	Ambulances of the 55th Division moved out of the area.	
			section. Transport was moved to a sandpit near FOUQUEREIL	
			Relieved in the line by No 8 F.A. Two motor ambulances attached to No 8 at ANNEZIN to	
		18	collect from 9th Brigade.	
			Quiet day. Casualties mostly from back areas.	
		19.	Transport moved to Chinese Camp near LAPUGNOY	
		20.	Church parades – Some shelling in vicinity of chateau	
		21.	Joined A.1. men reinforcements from Base Hospitals. Military medals were awarded to 55919 Pte E	
		22.	PRICE 88521 Pte G. CHIFFINCE DM2/134644 Pte H. OGDEN. ASC MT att.	
			attached 142 F.A. & M2 115657 Pte A.D. BARROW - ASC. MT att: 142 F. Amb	

Instructions regarding War Diaries and Intelligence Summaries are contained in F. S. Regs., Part II. and the Staff Manual respectively. Title pages will be prepared in manuscript.

WAR DIARY
or
INTELLIGENCE SUMMARY.
(Erase heading not required.)

Army Form C. 2118.

Place	Date	Hour	Summary of Events and Information	Remarks and references to Appendices
CHATEAU L'ABBAYE			Ten thousand rounds of SAA were salved.	ACE
	April	22	Relieved No 7. FA. in the line. One NCO and six squads were sent to the Transport lines.	ACE
		23	Operations to clear the chateau cellar and dig a dug-out were commenced.	
			2 NCOs and 13 men of B. Sect. Tent subdivision sent to Transport Lines. Capt. A. C. ELLIOTT	ACE
		24	RAMC joined for duty. Came under orders of XIII Corps at 12 noon.	
			Sick & wounded from 46th Division received into Dressing Station. Cellar was cleared of contents	ACE
		25	and construction of the dug out proceeded with.	
			DDMS XIII Corps visited MDS and forward posts. Chateau is being put in a	ACE
		26	state of defence	
			Uneventful day – Few wounded coming in. Weather fine – both 7 & 8 FA are in the grounds	ACE
		27	of the Chateau and in fore fields in the evening. A Ring tennis court provides exercise	
			Five Nissen Huts were removed during the day by the 3 Ambulances & conveyed to our new MDS site	ACE
		28	in G.S. Wagons. Several shell fell in the grounds during the evening. Wounded from the line few – but several from	ACE
			Three large Adrian Huts pulled down & removed – moved to Transport Lines & new MDS	
		29	CHOQUES. No 8. FA.	
			Day and night work was put in on the cellar and dug out. The entrance sandbagged. DDMS XIII Corps visited	ACE
		30	and a new way made through the terrace in front of the house.	
			About 100 G.S. Wagon loads of salvage of all descriptions were sent in during the month.	
			R.B. Hartford Lieut Col. RAMC Commanding 2/2 Field Ambulance	

6

SECRET

Vol 34

May 1918

140/2983.

WAR DIARY

OF

No 142 FIELD AMBULANCE

From 1 May 1918 To 31 May 1918

Instructions regarding War Diaries and Intelligence Summaries are contained in F. S. Regs., Part II. and the Staff Manual respectively. Title pages will be prepared in manuscript.

WAR DIARY
or
INTELLIGENCE SUMMARY.
(Erase heading not required.)

142 Field Ambulance

Army Form C. 2118.

Place	Date	Hour	Summary of Events and Information	Remarks and references to Appendices
CHATEAU L'ABBAYE			A large number of gassed cases were reported from ANNEZIN and extra cars had to be requisitioned -	BETHUNE
	May 1st /18		over 100 were admitted during the day. They were all bathed + put into pyjamas before	1/40000
			evacuation - and their eyes were [illegible] out with Sod. Bic. solution. The Red Cross flag was taken	
			down this morning as two companies of the 1st Gordons, & Coy of 13th Kings were billeted in the	[illegible]
			grounds. Corps Commander, DDMS, CR. Corps + Staff officers 3rd Div. visited the chateau.	
	2nd		76th Brigade HQ took over chateau leaving us the cellars + one room as ADS. The 7th Field	[illegible]
			Ambulance took over the ADS. We moved to D.22 central adjacent to the MDS at	
			D.22. b.9.5 which was being run by No. 7. FA. L/Corp R. SHIEL 58199 severely wounded	
			A great deal of work is being done at the MDS. In 3 days each Ambulance had put up	
LAPUGNOY	3.	•	one large double Nissen and 2 Nissen huts - besides camp improvements.	[illegible]
			Capt A.E. ELLIOTT and one Tent subdivision to CRS. (30 CCS) - Relieved No. 7. FA in the line	[illegible]
	4.		Capt MANN with Tent subdivision + Major MARTIN with bearers.	[illegible]
			Measures were taken to improve the camp site. Old horselines were dug up and salvaged. Seed	
	5.		potatoes planted. Deep latrines, cookhouse, QM stores + orderly room built.	[illegible]
			Subscribed £18 to the Rame POW + Comforts Fund	
	6.		Conference of OS + FA at No 7. Measures in case of enemy attack decided - Two shelters one	[illegible]
	8		large + one small ordered for bearer posts.	[illegible]
			Visited the RAP. and ADS 1 NCO + 24 men to Chateau L'ABBAYE. Also Lt HOLMES	
	9		and 1 NCO + 6 men to ADS. Posts in the line doubled. Fine sunny afternoon	[illegible]
			No 58199 L/Corpl SHIEL R awarded the Military Medal. Capt MANN returned to HQ	
	10		Lt HOLMES to HQ Major WALLACE to ADS	
	11		Cold + dull morning - but M. des CATS visible - Lt HOLMES to CRS Capt ELLIOTT to HQ. Relieved	[illegible]
	12		in the line by No 8 FA	

(A7092). Wt. W12839/M1293. 750,000. 1/17. D. D. & L., Ltd. Forms/C.2118/14.

Instructions regarding War Diaries and Intelligence Summaries are contained in F. S. Regs., Part II. and the Staff Manual respectively. Title pages will be prepared in manuscript.

WAR DIARY
or
INTELLIGENCE SUMMARY.
(Erase heading not required.)

Army Form C. 2118.

Place	Date	Hour	Summary of Events and Information	Remarks and references to Appendices
LAPUGNOY	May	14th/18	To help drain the land a part of it was dug up and planted with potatoes & cabbages. The transport was overhauled and the wagons washed down	[illegible]
		16	Relieved No 7 FA in the line - taking over ADS at ANNEZIN replacing squads in car posts R.A.P.s Capt ELLIOTT sent to ADS & Capt BREEN for duty with bearers.	[illegible]
		17	Lectures on Gas and its treatment by Col HUME RMS Consulting Physician First Army under orders of G.O.C. the motor ambulances were withdrawn from the car posts during the day time & allowed to proceed as far as these posts at night only. The car post at W. 23.c.7.6 was turned into a relay post - two extra squads of bearers were detailed for them and the new car post was formed at LEVERTANNOY - W 15.a.6.9.	[illegible]
		18	Visited the R.A.P.s bearer posts & ADS with ADMS. Very hot day. Considerable shelling of back areas - a piece of the base of a 12" shell fell close to the HQ. A series of trenches have been dug by Portuguese troops right through the camp & through the potato patch. Bomb protection walls in process of erection in Horse lines and round huts & tents.	[illegible]
		19	Tents protected by the [illegible] type of emplacement which improves the tent space & comfort at the same time affording the best possible protection.	
		20	A large number of gas cases from the left sector necessitated the use of all our cars & horsed ambulances to assist No 8 FA.	
		21	The DMS First Army inspected the ADS & bearer posts visiting the R.A.P.s also.	
		22	Three ORs gassed (W)	

(A7092). Wt. W12839/M1293. 750,000. 1/17. D. D. & L., Ltd. Forms/C.2118/14.

Instructions regarding War Diaries and Intelligence Summaries are contained in F. S. Regs., Part II. and the Staff Manual respectively. Title pages will be prepared in manuscript.

WAR DIARY
or
INTELLIGENCE SUMMARY.
(Erase heading not required.)

Army Form C. 2118.

Place	Date	Hour	Summary of Events and Information	Remarks and references to Appendices
LAPUGNOY	May	24th	Empire Day. Heavy rain. Under instructions from ADMS. a cabinet or anti gas sealing box was put under construction.	[illegible]
		25	Capt MANN to ADS in relief of Capt ELLIOTT.	[illegible]
		26	Registration Cards under Representation of People Act filled in. Huns shelled LAPUGNOY.	[illegible]
		27	Forty one men inoculated T A B. Huns shelled as before. Two enemy aeroplanes seen,	
		28	a rare occurrence by day. Several shells fell around the Horse lines killing one of our HD horses. Lines shifted.	[illegible]
		29	Capt ELLIOTT to CRS for temporary duty. Some shelling round the camp. L/Corpl READ wounded.	[illegible]
		30	No 8 FA relieved us at ANNEZIN and at Bearer post. More inoculation. Demolition party sent to transfer hut from AUCHELLE to FERFAY. GOC [illegible] Div.	[illegible]
		31	inspected gas cabinet yesterday. Full [illegible] for Brigade in reserve. During the month a considerable amount of salvage, building and bomb protective work was done. Work was done at the ADS of better shelters & shelters [illegible] of the bearer & relay posts.	

[signature illegible]
for Lt Col [illegible]
Commanding 142 Field Amb

(A7092). Wt. W12839/M1293. 750,000. 1/17. D. D. & L., Ltd. Forms/C.2118/14.

7

SECRET

Vol 35

June 1918.

WAR DIARY

OF

No 142 FIELD AMBULANCE

140/3070

From 1/6/18 To 30/6/18

Instructions regarding War Diaries and Intelligence Summaries are contained in F. S. Regs., Part II. and the Staff Manual respectively. Title pages will be prepared in manuscript.

WAR DIARY
or
INTELLIGENCE SUMMARY.
(Erase heading not required.)

Army Form C. 2118.

142 Field Ambulance

Place	Date	Hour	Summary of Events and Information	Remarks and references to Appendices
LAPUGNOY	June	1st 1918	Capt H. L. MANN departed upon special contract leave to UK. The inoculation of men continued. G.O.C 3rd Div. inspected transport lines.	Bethune 1/40000 Combined Sheet 44B
		2nd	Sunday - fine and hot. Services as usual. In the afternoon a Divisional Dog Show was held under distinguished patronage. The Huns stopped shelling LEBUVRIERE for the afternoon.	[illegible]
		3rd	Inoculations as before. G.O.C 3rd Div. inspected gas cabinet.	
		4	No. 7 FA relieved in the L. Sector. Majors WALLACE and MARTIN took over the ADS at CHATEAU L'ABBAYE	[illegible]
		5	A new gas proof cabinet was constructed in the trench. Major PARDIE G.S.O. U.S.A. visited.	[illegible]
		6	G.O.C 3rd [illegible] inspected gas cabinet shelter and approved. An extra squad of bearers went up the line. Lt HOLMES & 16 ORs rejoined from CRS (30 C.C.S.) Capt ELLIOTT remained.	[illegible]
		7.	Fine sunny day.	[illegible]
		8.	Sanitary improvements were made at the Transport Lines.	
		9.	Major WALLACE relieved at A.D.S by Lt HOLMES. G.O.C. 9th Bgde, G.O.C 76th Bgde inspected the gas shelters. Capt BREEN for temporary duty with 8th Kings.	[illegible]
		10.	Conference of O.C.s FA with ADMS.	
		11.	ADVS XIIIth Corps inspected Transport Lines. A large number of cases of P.U.O. from the line. Very infectious and virulent but short lasting attack.	
		12	Capt BREEN rejoined.	

D. D. & L., London, E.C.
(A8004) Wt W1771/M2031 750,000 5/17 Sch. 52 Forms/C2118/14

Instructions regarding War Diaries and Intelligence Summaries are contained in F. S. Regs., Part II. and the Staff Manual respectively. Title pages will be prepared in manuscript.

WAR DIARY
or
INTELLIGENCE SUMMARY.

(*Erase heading not required.*)

Army Form C. 2118.

Place	Date	Hour	Summary of Events and Information	Remarks and references to Appendices
LAPUGNOY	June	13/6/18	Major MARTIN left with Cpl ENSOR for temporary duty at ETAPLES – Capt GREEN takes over charge of Bearers and Lt. R.F. JOHNSON – MORC USA arrived as reinforcement.	[illegible]
		14th	Major WALLACE assumed command of ADS CHATEAU LABBAYE. The squads of bearers were spread in preparation for the evening stunt. Squads were located in LE PLOUY FARM (aid post of 1st N.F.) PERTH TRENCH aid post of 4th R.F. and at Relay & Car posts near the canal bank. Zero hour was at 11.45 pm and the infantry advanced under a creeping barrage of 2 Brigades RFA on the front of 3,500 yds and H.A. of I XI + XIII Corps. The line was advanced in depth to 450 yds on an average and considerable numbers of prisoners were captured. A slight drizzle came down just after midnight but the weather cleared later.	[illegible]
		15	Quiet morning – fine windy & sunny – Major WALLACE returned to HQ. Lt JOHNSON went to ADS. 2 NCOs + 11 bearers returned to HQ. Capt MANN rejoined from leave.	[illegible]
		16	Capt & QM BOWEN on leave to Ireland – Lt RF JOHNSON to 8 MORL permanent duty. Bearers take over the left sector from No. 7. Aid post of 2nd Suffolks in canal bank E 4 HINGES. Relay post in HINGES. Capt GREEN returned to HQ sick with the three days fever which is very prevalent throughout the Division. Capt MANN takes over the command of bearers.	
		17	Bearers interrelief	[illegible]
		18	L. R.A.P. returned to HINGES – Our relay post given up & one squad left at the new RAP. 2 squads returned to HQ.	[illegible]
		19	Evacuated the large hut in ADS owing to the large numbers of P.U.O. Personnel bivouacked in the wood.	[illegible]

D. D. & L., London, E.C.
(A8c04) Wt W1771/M2031 750,000 5/17 Sch. 52 Forms/C2118/14

Army Form C. 2118.

Instructions regarding War Diaries and Intelligence Summaries are contained in F. S. Regs., Part II. and the Staff Manual respectively. Title pages will be prepared in manuscript.

WAR DIARY
or
INTELLIGENCE SUMMARY.
(Erase heading not required.)

Place	Date	Hour	Summary of Events and Information	Remarks and references to Appendices
LAPUGNOY	June	22	Bearers & personnel at ADS changed over. Very showery weather.	[illegible]
		23	Capt A F L SHIELDS taken on strength but remains at HQ 3rd Div. for instruction in duties of DADMS. New ADMS arrive Col. McCLELLAND.	[illegible]
		25	The Car Post at LE VERTANNOY shifted to a farm house down the hill W. 15 a Central owing to the continuous shelling of the cross roads. The house was hit twice and the car post not position. We have now 3 large cars in the workshops.	[illegible]
			Major WALLACE and Capt BREEN relieved Capt MANN and Lt HOLMES at ADS.	[illegible]
		26	Efficiency of the Box Respirator changed for Tissot Glass. Sergt SHARP (M2-019310) G.H., ASC MT awarded the Military Medal. Authority XIII Corps R.O. 1774 d/ 25/6/18.	[illegible]
			No 56602 QMS EVANS E. awarded the Meritorious Service Medal (Supplement to London Gazette d/17/6/18).	[illegible]
		27	No 58908 Corpl. ALMOND G. 51241 Pte WILDE F.T. (since died) 528359 Pte NORTH J F wounded by a shell in the new car post at LE VERTANNOY. Shelter work getting on well. ADMS visited the HQ.	[illegible]
		28	Lt HOLMES visit the sick of 3rd DAC and 40 Bgde RFA (temporary duty). ADMS visited the advanced post.	
		29	Arrangements in train for opening a hospital for P.U.O. cases in LE BOURIERE Capt MANN in charge.	
		30	Hospital opened. War Saving Certificates purchased in June 86 – since initiation of scheme ([illegible] months) 454	

[illegible]
Cmdg 142 Field Ambulance
Lt Col RAMC

D. D. & L., London, E.C.
(A8c64) Wt W1771/M2031 750,000 5/17 Sch. 52 Forms/C2118/14

6

July 1918

Vol 36

SECRET

WAR DIARY

OF

No 142 FIELD AMBULANCE

140/3131.

From 1/7/18 To 31/7/18

Army Form C. 2118.

Instructions regarding War Diaries and Intelligence Summaries are contained in F. S. Regs., Part II. and the Staff Manual respectively. Title pages will be prepared in manuscript.

WAR DIARY
or
~~INTELLIGENCE SUMMARY.~~

(Erase heading not required.) 142 Field Ambulance

Place	Date	Hour	Summary of Events and Information	Remarks and references to Appendices
LAPUGNOY	July 1st 1918		Instructions to open a hospital for cases of P.U.O on the site of the Corps Rest Station at LEBUVRIERE. Five wards opened - holding 130 pts. Incinerator rebuilt latrines dug and cookhouse erected.	
	2nd		100 patients admitted - Capt MANN in charge. Packstore built -	
	3rd		Hospital full - Capt & QM BOWEN returned from leave	
	4th		Bearers at work on bombing protection at the P.U.O hospital	
	5th		Work continued - Lieut. elected Sergeant ROWE as 3rd Div War Savings Campaign Committee	
	6		Wagons overhauled and cleaned - Brass on watercarts scraped & polished	
	8		Lt WILHOIT joined for duty (MORC USA) Bearers relieved from the line	
	9		Transport inspected by Corps Commander. War Savings Certificates sold during the afternoon to NCOs & men of the unit 242 making a total of 696 since Xmas	
	10		Lt HOLMES proceeded on relief to Casual Officers Depot SOS USArmy & struck off the strength of the unit. Very hot & dusty	
	11		Rain fell during the day	
	12		Ditto -	
	13		Lt WILHOIT joined Major WALLACE at ADS.	
	14		The Fifth Summary report on Money, Men & Material submitted through the usual channels. Nett result since the reports were required - an increase of 2 field officers in the establishment. The purposes of previous reports were substantiated -	

D. D. & L., London, E.C.
(A8c04) Wt W1771/M2031 750,000 5/17 Sch. 52 Forms/C2118/14

Instructions regarding War Diaries and Intelligence Summaries are contained in F. S. Regs., Part II. and the Staff Manual respectively. Title pages will be prepared in manuscript.

WAR DIARY
or
INTELLIGENCE SUMMARY.
(Erase heading not required.)

Army Form C. 2118.

Place	Date	Hour	Summary of Events and Information	Remarks and references to Appendices
LEBOUVRIERE	July	16	P.U.O. Hospital visited by Consulting Physician 1st Army Col. [illegible] [illegible] [illegible] in the line of [illegible]	[illegible]
		17	Wet day.	[illegible]
		18	Ditto.	[illegible]
		19	Major Wallace went to H.Q. – Visited the ADS & posts	[illegible]
		20	Staff of ADS changed over with P.U.O. Hospital Staff	[illegible]
		22.	Cookhouse inspection – Ambulance Hospl. cookhouse placed fourth. –	[illegible]
		23	Rained a lot –	[illegible]
		24	R.A.M.C. Horse Show in the morning – One GS & 3 limbers selected for Divisional show.	
		25.	Wet day.	[illegible]
		26	Showery. DDMS visited – but not the P.U.O. Hospital. I visited the posts in the line. ADMS visited the P.U.O. Hospital	
		27	It was decided that a team should be shown in the Divisional Eliminating Show for the Corps Horse Show.	
		29	Fifth Army Concert party at LEBOUVRIERE under Lt. LESLIE HENSON of the Gaiety Theatre. Hun shelled the village during the evening. Numbers in hospital reduced.	
		31.	Defensive work – cleaning work etc. continued. War Savings Certificates. Total number since beginning of Branch Scheme 2170; " " June 1st 430; July 1st 313.	

[illegible] Lt. Col. RAMC
Commanding 1/2 Field Ambulance

D. D. & L., London, E.C.
(A8c04) Wt W1771/M2031 750,000 5/17 Sch. 52 Forms/C2118/14

11 CONFIDENTIAL

Aug. 1918

VR 37

WAR DIARY

OF

No 142 FIELD AMBULANCE

160/3200.

From 1/8/18 To 31/8/18

Army Form C. 2118.

Instructions regarding War Diaries and Intelligence Summaries are contained in F. S. Regs., Part II. and the Staff Manual respectively. Title pages will be prepared in manuscript.

WAR DIARY
or
~~INTELLIGENCE SUMMARY.~~
(Erase heading not required.)

142nd Field Ambulance

Place	Date	Hour	Summary of Events and Information	Remarks and references to Appendices
LEBUVRIERE	Aug	1st	D.M.S. Fifth Army visited the A.D.S.	5a Hazebrouck
		2nd	Heavy rain.	[illegible]
		3	Divisional Horse Show. The first and second prizes for mules were won by the unit. It rained a good deal during the day.	[illegible]
		4.	Anniversary day.	[illegible]
		5.	The wagons were packed according to a new scheme – an A.D.S. & M.D.S. limber made up and the tentage confined to one G.S. Wagon.	[illegible]
		6.	Lebuvriere shelled – two hospital huts damaged. Handed over the P.V.O. Hospital to 57 F.A. The A.D.S. & bearers were relieved by 58 F.A. during the afternoon.	[illegible]
		7	Unit marched to AUCHEL under Brigade orders.	
AUCHEL		8	Billets improved.	
		9	–Ditto– a considerable number of civilian sick were seen.	[illegible]
		10.	3rd Anniversary of embarkation of unit. H.M. The KING visited the XIII Corps area. The unit turned out & cheered spontaneously. Beat the Norfolk Fus. by 1 goal to nil at football.	
		11.	Church parade under Rev. MELLISH on football ground.	[illegible]
		12	Corps Horse Show. Won the mule stripped championship. Silver cup and medal.	
		13	Personnel by train to BREVILLERS. Transport by road to ANVIN thence to the LUCHEUX area.	J.J. Green
BREVILLERS		14	At Brevillers routine duties. Submitted scheme for water cart petrol tin carrier ~~and con~~ convertible into meat safe.	J.J.G.
"		15	Horse transport arrived from ANVIN area 4.30 AM.	

D. D. & L., London, E.C. (A8c04) Wt W1771/M2031 750,000 5/17 Sch. 52 Forms/C2118/14

Instructions regarding War Diaries and Intelligence Summaries are contained in F. S. Regs., Part II. and the Staff Manual respectively. Title pages will be prepared in manuscript.

WAR DIARY
or
INTELLIGENCE SUMMARY.
(*Erase heading not required.*)

Army Form C. 2118.

Place	Date	Hour	Summary of Events and Information	Remarks and references to Appendices
BREVILLERS	16		Division placed in GHQ reserve and to be prepared to move at 24 hours notice -	JJPR
			Submitted first days programme of training scheme while in rest area -	JJPR
			Routine duties - Two NCOs sent to attend a gas course -	
"	17		Recreational training proceeded with - Arrangements made for Sports on 21st	JJPR
"	18		Prize draw for War Savings Certificates under Divisional War Savings Scheme	
"	19 (corrected)		The Unit has now invested £2504-0-6 in these certificates.	JJPR
"	19		Conference at ADMS Office. Division to go into line in AYETTE area - Unit to move on night of 19th-20th to BIENVILLERS. Transport not actually needed for front line work to be parked near LA CAUCHIE.	
			Arranged to send advanced party in cars to BIENVILLERS - Personnel to march	JJPR
BIENVILLERS	20		Unit arrived at BIENVILLERS at 5.30 A.M. men very much exhausted. accomodation in dugouts. Orders received that 3rd Division would move into assembly positions behind 2nd Division on night of 20-21. 2nd Division to attack at 4.55 AM. 3rd Division to go through and attack at ZERO + 90 i.e. 6.25 A.M.	
			Unit attached to 9th Brigade. 13th Kings Liverpools and 1st Northumberland Fus. to attack supported by 4th Royal Fusiliers - Assembly positions along roads in F16 b and d - and F 15 b and d (BUCQUOY Combined 1/40000)	
			Four bearer squads attached to the two attacking battalions and one squad to battalion in support - eight squads with sixteen stretchers and a wheeled stretcher carrier to assemble in BADEN AVENUE about F15 c 5.3 under CAPT. T F P BREEN - and follow up advancing battalions - Motor ambulances	

D. D. & L., London, E.C. (A8c64) Wt W1771/M2031 750,000 5/17 Sch. 52 Forms/C2118/14

Instructions regarding War Diaries and Intelligence Summaries are contained in F. S. Regs., Part II. and the Staff Manual respectively. Title pages will be prepared in manuscript.

WAR DIARY
or
INTELLIGENCE SUMMARY.
(Erase heading not required.)

Army Form C. 2118.

Place	Date	Hour	Summary of Events and Information	Remarks and references to Appendices
BIENVILLERS	20th		to work forward to road junction at F20b 5.7 until zero + 90 and then to be withdrawn and work forward to AYETTE where the first ADS would be formed. Evacuation to be carried out to 2nd Div Dressing Station at MONCHY-AU-BOIS and from there to Corps Main Dressing Station at BAC DU SUD staffed by the Guards Division.	J.F.B
AYETTE	21st		LT. COL. HABGOOD D.S.O. and MAJOR WALLACE M.C. wounded about A12 d 5.8. while reconnoitring site for ADS on AYETTE - COURCELLES road. CAPT T.P.P. BREEN assumed command of unit. ADS formed with No. 8 Field Ambulance in sunken road at F11 b 5.2. bearers sent forward under LT. WILHOIT MORC USA to AERODROME TRENCH at A14 a 5.4. about 8 AM ordered to get in touch with battalions and evacuate along AYETTE COURCELLES road. Cars brought forward to AERODROME TRENCH about mid-day. CAPT BALLINGALL from No 7 Field Amb. attached for temporary duty in command of bearers. The Divisional objective was the railway embankment running through A28 cent on the 9th Bde front this had not been attained by the afternoon. Aid Posts at A14 d 3.5 and along along road in A20 b and c. Weather extremely hot. carrying very exhausting. 76th Bde in action in 9th Bde area in afternoon. bearers very tired. large numbers of stretcher cases. All available bearers sent forward at 10 AM assistance asked for and obtained from No 7 Field Ambulance Cars brought forward to A15 a 3.1. CAPT BALLINGALL relieved LT WILHOIT in AERODROME TRENCH.	

D. D. & L., London, E.C. (A8064) Wt W1771/M2031 750,000 5/17 Sch. 52 Forms/C2118/14

Instructions regarding War Diaries and Intelligence Summaries are contained in F. S. Regs., Part II. and the Staff Manual respectively. Title pages will be prepared in manuscript.

WAR DIARY
or
INTELLIGENCE SUMMARY.
(Erase heading not required.)

Army Form C. 2118.

Place	Date	Hour	Summary of Events and Information	Remarks and references to Appendices
AYETTE	22		Evacuation continued all day weather extremely hot - Aid posts moved forward touch maintained - HQrs moved back to ADINFER DOUCHY ROAD F4 a 5.4 - CAPT DOWLING RAMC reported for temporary duty - LT WILHOIT relieved CAPT BALLINGALL in AERODROME TRENCH - CAPT J POTTER MC reported for duty	JJPR
F4 a 54 [BOCUOY COMB 1/40.000]	23		Evacuation continued - Capt DOWLING relieved LT WILHOIT in AERODROME trench. LT WILHOIT to post at AYETTE Aid posts near west side RAILWAY embankment - weather still very hot bearers very tired - some shortage of stretchers. CAPT DOWLING moved forward to A14 d cent. not possible to get motor ambulances through COURCELLES -	JJPR
"	24		Aid posts now as follows - Northumberland Fusiliers at G5 d 2.8. Kings Liverpools G4 a. cent Royal Fusiliers A27 b 10.2 - Bearer post established by Capt DOWLING - at A28 C 10.3 - in old German hospital - This very elaborately fitted with tanks for giving gas and oxygen and lit with electric light &c - Cars brought through COURCELLES to west side of railway embankment at this place - Orders sent to transport and to HQ details to rejoin unit at F4 a 5.4 - Orders received that division would move into Corps reserve in Purple Line Area - Bearers withdrawn from line - arrived at HQ 8 P.M. accomodated under canvas -	JJPR

D. D. & L., London, E.C.
(A8064) Wt W1771/M2031 750,000 5/17 Sch. 52 Forms/C2118/14

Instructions regarding War Diaries and Intelligence Summaries are contained in F. S. Regs., Part II. and the Staff Manual respectively. Title pages will be prepared in manuscript.

WAR DIARY
or
INTELLIGENCE SUMMARY.
(Erase heading not required.)

Army Form C. 2118.

Place	Date	Hour	Summary of Events and Information	Remarks and references to Appendices
F4a54	25		Bearers resting - Foot and kit inspections - Orders received at 2 PM to open a Divisional Rest Station at LA CAUCHIE with CAPT. MANN and one tent Subdivision - by 6 A.M. Sick to be sent by rail to HUMBERCAMP and thence by car to LA CAUCHIE - Order complied with - Site consisted of five hospital huts with stores and offices &c. Roof in bad repair - Heavy rain at night -	J.F.P.B.
"	26		Visited LA CAUCHIE and ADMS Office - Car withdrawn from HUMBERCAMP Station as sick are now being detrained at V5 d 7.0. under arrangements made by ADMS. Guards Division - JFPB	
	27		F.M. Commanding-in-Chief visited unit and expressed his thanks for good work done by unit. JFPB	
	28		Order received at 1 AM that 76th Bde might take over at any time from Guards forward Brigade and that 3rd Division would probably relieve Guards Division in course of 24 hours. Visited 9th Brigade and also O.C. Guards Field Amb clearing the line and obtained map references of various posts &c. Routine duties.	
T25 c 5.8.	29		RAMC Operation Order No. 110 - received - Walking wounded post estab- as instructed - H.Q. moved to T25 c 5.8. Only a few casualties received. 9th Bde O.O. No 15 received - JFPB	Appendix I Appendix II

D. D. & L., London, E.C. (A8064) Wt W1771/M2031 750,000 5/17 Sch. 52 Forms/C2118/14

Instructions regarding War Diaries and Intelligence Summaries are contained in F. S. Regs., Part II. and the Staff Manual respectively. Title pages will be prepared in manuscript.

WAR DIARY
or
INTELLIGENCE SUMMARY.
(Erase heading not required.)

Army Form C. 2118.

Place	Date	Hour	Summary of Events and Information	Remarks and references to Appendices
T25 c 5.8.	30 -		Learned that 9th Brigade would probably go into line in relief of 76th Bde night of 30-31st Roads leading from ECOUST reconnoitred - Decided to clear through ST-LEGER when Brigade should go in. 9th Brigade OO No 17 received 8.30 PM. Car Post for Ford cars established at B5 c 8.9 - for large cars at B17. a. 8. 8 - Bearer H.Q. under CAPT. DOWLING RAMC. in BANKS TRENCH - in B10 b. Two squads with 1 L/cpl attached to each battalion - 1 Sgt placed in charge of each evacuation route - Horsed ambulances ordered to Quarry at B 8. a. 35 at 6.15 AM to collect walking wounded - JJPB	Appendix III
T25 c 6.8.	31		ADMS RAMC O.O. Received 1.30 A.M - Arrangements worked very satisfactorily RAPs as follows - Northumberland Fusiliers B5 c 9.9. Kings Liverpools B6 a 9.8 - Royal Fusiliers B17 b 8.7 - Most of ECOUST village taken casualties especially heavy among Kings Liverpools and right company Royal Fusiliers - 193 Walking wounded treated at MAISON ROUGE - Wire received at 11.30 PM that 76th Bde would take over front from right Divisional Boundary to C7 d 8.2. JJPBrown Capt RAMC	Appendix IV

A/OC 1/4 27 FA

Appendix I

S E C R E T.

3rd DIVISION R.A.M.C. OPERATION ORDER No. 110.

August 2[illegible]h, 1918.

1. (a) The 9th Infantry Brigade will move to the Support Brigade Area between ACHIET-LE-GRAND - ARRAS Railway and ARRAS-BAPAUME Road today: leading troops to cross railway at 12 noon.

(b) The 8th Infantry Brigade will move to Reserve Brigade Area between BOIRY and MOYENNEVILLE as soon as this area is vacated by 9th Infantry Brigade.

(c) The 56th Division on our left will attack BULLECOURT today at 1 p.m. The 76th Infantry Brigade will keep in touch with the 56th Division, and will take advantage of any weakening of the enemy owing to the advance of the 56th Division, to push on towards ECOUST and afterwards NOREUIL. The 76th Infantry Brigade will make as much ground as possible before 1 p.m. without becoming seriously engaged.

2. O.C., No. 142 Field Ambulance will move his Headquarters to a convenient spot near the MAISON ROUGE in T.25.c. where he will establish a Divisional Walking Wounded Collecting Post by 1 p.m. today.

Records will be kept and A.T.S. given.

The O.C., Bearer Division No. 142 Field Ambulance will keep in touch with the Infantry.

3. O.C., No. 8 Field Ambulance will close down the Main Dressing Station at AYETTE and open a Divisional Main Dressing Station at S.23.c.7.3. by 1 p.m. today.

4. O.C., No. 7 Field Ambulance will hand over the Walking Wounded Collecting Station at RANSART to a Field Ambulance of the Guards Division and will move his Headquarters to a convenient place near the ARRAS-BAPAUME Road; location to be notified to this office and 76th Infantry Brigade as soon as it is fixed.

5. Stretcher cases will be cleared to the Main Dressing Station at S.23.c.7.3. and thence by Motor Ambulance Convoy to C.C.S. at BAILLEULVAL.

6. Walking Wounded will be directed to the Walking Wounded Collecting Post at the MAISON ROUGE, and conveyed thence by motor lorry to the Walking Wounded Entraining Station at RANSART.

Six motor lorries are provided by 3rd Division "Q" for the purpose of clearing from the forward area from convenient places on the roads to the Walking Wounded Collecting Post at MAISON ROUGE.

The evacuation thence to the Entraining Station, RANSART, will be undertaken by the O.C., 30 M.A.C.

7. The Horsed Ambulances of the three Field Ambulances will be pooled at the Walking Wounded Collecting Post, MAISON ROUGE, and utilized for clearing of Walking Wounded as required. They will be at the disposal of O.C., No. 7 Field Ambulance.

8. O.C., No. 7 Field Ambulance will notify this office of location of his Advanced Dressing Station as soon as possible.

9. The Divisional Rest Station will remain at LA CAUCHIE. All sick will be collected at the Main Dressing Station where records of sick will be kept. Lying sick will be sent to C.C.S. by M.A.C. Slight cases for the Rest Station will be sent by motor lorry to the Entraining Station at RANSART. Nominal Rolls will accompany the patients, and they will be shown as transfers to No. 142 Field Ambulance.

10. O.C., No. 7 Field Ambulance will detail two clerks to report to O.C., No. 8 Field Ambulance for duty at the Main Dressing Station.

11. Field Ambulances to acknowledge.

D. C. Macdonald Major
~~Lieut-Colonel,~~
A.D.M.S., 3rd Division.

Copies to :-

3rd Division "G".
" " "Q".
8th Inf:Bde.
9th " "
76th " "
No. 7 Field Ambulance.
No. 8 " "
No. 142 " "
O.i/c D.R.Station.
C.R.A.
C.R.E.
D.A.D.V.S.
3rd Btn.M.G.C.
20th K.R.R.C.
3rd Div.Train.
D.D.M.S., VI Corps.
D.M.S., Third Army.
A.D.M.S., Guards Division.
A.D.M.S., 2nd Division.
A.D.M.S., 56th "
A.D.M.S., 62nd "
No. 30 M.A.C.
War Diary.
" "
File.

Appendix II

SECRET

9th INF. BDE. OPERATION ORDER No. 15. Copy No. 9

24th Aug 418

****

1. G.O.C. 3rd Division has assumed command of Left Div. Sector, VI Corps.

2. 9th Inf. Bde. (plus "B" Coy. M.G.Bn) will move to the 3rd Div. Support Brigade Area. to-day 24th Aug

3. Areas are allotted as follows:-

4th ROYAL FUS.	MORY SWITCH in B .9.a., b & d. (H.Q. B.9.b.0.8.)
13th KINGS.	HAMEL SWITCH in A .6.a. & b. (H.Q. A.6.b.5.3.)
1st NORTHD.FUS.	HAMERVILLE Trench in A.5.c. & d. (H.Q. A.5.d.6.0.)
T.M.Bty.	Trenches about A.11.a.5.6. to A.11.b.8.0.
"B" Coy. 3rd M.G.Bn.	Remainder of trenches in A.11.a. & c.

4. Movement will take place as follows:-

Unit	Starting point.	Time.	Route.
4th R.Fus.	S.22.c.9.2.	11-45 a.m.	Via HAMLINCOURT.
13th Kings.	do.	12-30 p.m.	do.
1st N.Fus.	Entrance of MOYENNVILLE.	11-45 a.m.	Via MOYENNE-VILLE.
"B" Coy.MGC	do.	12-30 p.m.	do.
9th T.M.Bty.	do.	12-40 p.m.	do.

5. A distance of 200 yards will be maintained between platoons on the march.

6. Units will report completion of move to Bde. H.Qrs.

7. 9th Bde. H.Qrs. remains at A.4.d.9.0.

8. ACKNOWLEDGE.

Issued at 9-45 a.m.

[signature]
Capt.,
Brigade Major, 9th Inf.Bde.

Copy No. 1 - G.O.C.
2 - 1/N.Fus.
3 - 4/R.Fus.
4 - 13/K.L.R.
5 - 9th T.M.Bty.
6 - "B"Coy.M.G.C.
7 - Sigs.
8 - Section of Fld.Coy.
9 - 142nd [illegible]
10 - B.T.O.
11 - Staff Capt.
12 - 76th Inf.Bde.
13 - 8th do.
14 - 3rd Div.
15 - do.
16 - File.
17 - War Diary
18 - do

Appendix III

9th INFANTRY BRIGADE OPERATION ORDER NO. 17.

****

Copy No. 18

Ref. maps 51B S.W.} 57C N.W.} 1/20,000.
Map "Z" (issued to Bns.only)

1. 9th Inf. Bde. (plus 1st GORDON HIGHRS.) will capture ECOUST and LONGATTE and will consolidate on the line VRAUCOURT RESERVE - NOREUIL SWITCH - LONGATTE TRENCH - LONGATTE SUPPORT - BULLECOURT AVENUE between C.20.a.7.8. and C.3.a.8.8. on the morning of Aug. 31st. Zero hour will be notified later.

2. Seven or more Tanks of "A" Coy. 12th Tank Bn. will co-operate and are allotted as follows:-

3 Tanks - Station REDOUBT.
3 " - ECOUST VILLAGE.
1 " - LONGATTE TRENCH.
1 " - NOREUIL SWITCH.

3. (a) The attack will be carried out by:-
1st GORDON HIGHRS. on the right.
4th ROYAL FUS. in the centre.
13th KINGS. on the left.
1st NORTHD.FUS. will be in reserve.

(b) "B" Coy. 3rd M.G.C. will move in support of the attacking battalions.

(c) 1 Stokes Mortar each will move in support of 4th ROYAL FUS. and 13th KINGS.

4. Boundaries between Battalions are as stated in para. 3 Operation Order No. 15 (Maps shewing their boundaries have been issued to Bns. only)

5. Artillery. An artillery barrage will be put down 300 yards from our present front line at Zero which will commence to creep forward at Zero plus 5 minutes at the rate of 100 yds. in 4 minutes. On reaching 400 yds. East of the objective it will form a protective barrage.

6.(a) The Infantry attack will be carried out in depth, that is to say each battalion will keep troops in hand to deal with situations arising from weakness or the non-arrival of troops on flanks on their objective.

(b) If the advance across the open is held up, the alternative method of gaining the objective by means of strong bombing attacks up VRAUCOURT RESERVE and NOREUIL SWITCH, LONGATTE TRENCH will be borne in mind by ~~Commanding~~ Officers Commanding 1st GORDON HIGHRS. and 4th ROYAL FUS. It is useless to bomb up a trench without troops following to hold the trench gained.

7. Company Commanders will endeavour to effect liaison with tank commanders on assembly positions before Zero.

8.(a) "D" Coy. 3rd M.G.Bn. is remaining in positions holding the line, and is arranging to cover the advance of the tanks to assembly by firing bursts.

(b) B Coy. 3rd M.G.Bn. is advancing in support of the attacking Bns. and will bring covering fire to bear wherever possible. Also M.G's will be prepared to fire an S.O.S. barrage in case of necessity after the objective is gained.

For this purpose the Coy. will be divided into 4 batteries, one battery moving in support of each battalion and one being kept in reserve.

9.(a) A Stokes Mortar will similarly follow in rear of 4th ROYAL FUS. and 13th KINGS.

(b) Attached R.E. and Tunnellers will remain in BANKS TRENCH, B.11.a., prepared to move forward on receipt of orders from Bde. H.Qrs.

10. (a) All units are specially warned against the enemy's gas tactics.

(b) Battalions are reminded that bombing fights are almost certain to ensue at the junction of the objective with trenches running towards the enemy. Provision of bombs will therefore be made to deal with this.

11. Brigade H.Qrs. will remain at MONY COPSE, B.18.a.1.1.

12. ACKNOWLEDGE.

Capt.,

Issued at 7-30 p.m. Brigade Major, 9th Inf.Bde.

Copies to;-

No.1.G.O.C.
2.1/North Fus.
3.4/Royal Fus.
4.13/Kings.
5.1st Gordon Hgdrs. per 76th Infy.Bde.
6.9th T.M.B.
7."B"Coy.M.G.Battn.
8."D"Coy.M.G.Battn.
9.76th.Infy.Bde.
10.8th Infy Bde.
11.Section 56th Field Coy.
12.Section of Tunnellers(via C.R.E)
13.Col.VICKERY'S Group.R.F.A.
14."B" Coy.12 Bn. Tanks.
15.3rd Division.
16.Staff Captain.
17.B.T.O.
18.142 Field.Amb.
19.War Diary.
20. -do-

11 Confidential

VR 38

Sept 1918

WAR DIARY

OF

140/3259

142nd Field Ambulance

From 1/9/18 To 30/9/18

Instructions regarding War Diaries and Intelligence Summaries are contained in F. S. Regs., Part II. and the Staff Manual respectively. Title pages will be prepared in manuscript.

Army Form C. 2118.

WAR DIARY
or
INTELLIGENCE SUMMARY.
(Erase heading not required.)

Place	Date	Hour	Summary of Events and Information	Remarks and references to Appendices
T25C 5.8 (MAISON ROUGE)	1		ECOUST and LONGATTE cleared of enemy - evacuation arrangements working smoothly - 9th Bde OO No 19 received* 3.30 AM 9th Brigade OO No 20° received 9.0 AM. RAMC O.O. 112+ received 11 AM. OC No 8 Field Ambulance did not get in touch with me before going into the line and some confusion resulted from his impression that the 9th Brigade would have no casualties and not be involved in the action. I ordered Capt Dowling to maintain all my bearers in the line and to keep in touch with the regimental MOs if and when they should move forward. I ordered him if possible to utilise the cars of No 8 Field Ambulance for the route through MORT HOMME and to keep the Ford cars as before on the ECOUST - ST LEGER road - JJ R Brown.	* App I ° App II + App III
"	2		First lorry load of walking wounded arrived 7.3 AM two hours after zero. lorries continued to arrive steadily until 12.30 PM when most of the walking wounded seemed to have been cleared. I arranged the triage so as to obtain the maximum speed in getting the wounded through in accordance with the	

(A7092). Wt. W12839/M1293. 750,000. 1/17. D. D. & L., Ltd. Forms/C.2118/14.

Instructions regarding War Diaries and Intelligence Summaries are contained in F. S. Regs., Part II. and the Staff Manual respectively. Title pages will be prepared in manuscript.

WAR DIARY
or
INTELLIGENCE SUMMARY.
(Erase heading not required.)

Army Form C. 2118.

Place	Date	Hour	Summary of Events and Information	Remarks and references to Appendices
T25 c 5.8. MAISON ROUGE	2		scheme shown 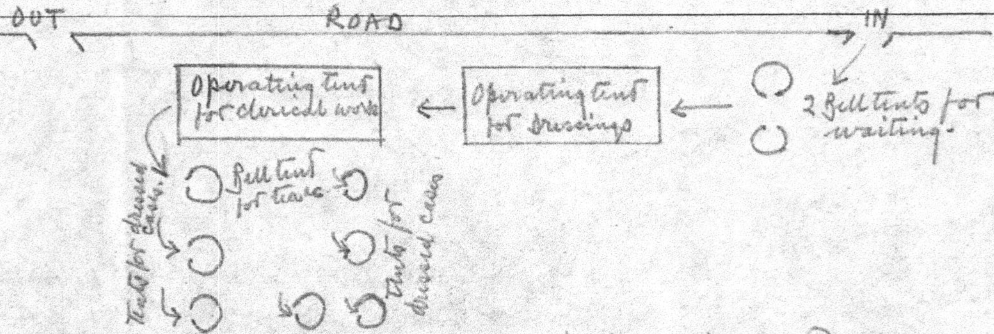 Total number of cases treated Officers 13 O.R. 324	
			Visited line in afternoon. Found that Royal Fusiliers Aid Post had moved to C 8 a 24. Northumberland Fusiliers to C 7 a 7.8 – The whole of NOREUIL had been taken but not LAGNICOURT. 9th Brigade OO No 21 received 11.15 PM. RAMC O.O. 113 received + arrangements made to withdraw bearers from the line – CAPT DOWLING and all bearers returned to Headquarters by 2 AM 3rd. JJPB	° APP IV + APP V
	3.		Bearers resting. Ammunition dump being established in rear of camp – Two bombs dropped near camp about 10 AM. JJPB	
	4		CAPTAIN C.S.E. WRIGHT RAMC (TC) and CAPT J.B. LEIGH RAMC (SR) reported their arrival for duty CAPT DOWLING RAMC (SR) reported his departure to rejoin the Machine Gun Battalion. Verbal instructions received from ADMS to close down the Rest Station at LA CAUCHIE as soon as possible tentage to be transferred to No 8 Field Ambulance. JJPB	
	5		Verbal instructions received from DADMS that unit would move on 6th to LA CAUCHIE. RAMC OO 114 received. JJPB	APP VI

(A7092). Wt. W12839/M1293. 750,000. 1/17. D. D. & L., Ltd. Forms/C.2118/14.

Army Form C. 2118.

Instructions regarding War Diaries and Intelligence Summaries are contained in F. S. Regs., Part II. and the Staff Manual respectively. Title pages will be prepared in manuscript.

Sept 1917

WAR DIARY
or
~~INTELLIGENCE~~ SUMMARY.
(Erase heading not required.)

142 Field Ambulance

Sheet iii

Place	Date	Hour	Summary of Events and Information	Remarks and references to Appendices
LA CAUCHIE (V17d 78)	6/9	A.M.	Bright morning. Thunderstorm with some rain later. O.O. Route No 114 received. Major D.C. MACDONALD M.C. DADMS 3 Division took over command (Authority - 3 Div a/21/38 dated 4.9.18). Unit moved to LA CAUCHIE. Took over the site vacated by the Guards Division, as a D.R.S.	BUCQUOY Combined Sheet.
	~~7/9~~	P.M.	Called on the 76th Inf Bde to which the unit is attached for duty and received the location of units. Arranged for horsed ambulances to collect the sick daily from all units in the area. Called on A.D.M.S. at HUMBERCAMP and reported arrival at LA CAUCHIE. Gave orders for equipment to be overhauled and deficiencies made good	
	7/9.	A.M.	Bright dry day. Windy. Rain threatening. Removed all patients from the old 3rd D.R.S. to the site vacated by the Guards and utilised the old site as a billet for personnel. Erected four marquees and received three extra from No 8 Field Ambulance. Put up 8 bell tents for scabies patients & ordered tent bottoms for them. A.D.M.S. called and inspected the camp. Satisfied with the arrangements made.	
		P.M.	10 Scabies cases dumped on us from No 45 C.C.S. at 7.30 pm. These men arrived without kits. They are shown by 45 C.C.S. as transfers to VI Corps Scabies Stn. This was the first intimation that the D.D.M.S. intended this to become a Scabies Station. The present accommodation will not allow of this. Visited the A.D.M.S. for orders & telephoned the D.D.M.S.	
	8/9	A.M.	Very wet day. Heavy showers of rain and hailstones. Proceeded with the constructional work of the camp. Held Kit inspection at 9 am. The D.D.M.S. VI Corps called and enquired about the accommodation of scabies cases. Have made arrangements for reception & treatment of 70 cases.	

(A7092). Wt. W12839/M1293. 750,000. 1/17. D. D. & L., Ltd. Forms/C.2118/14.

Instructions regarding War Diaries and Intelligence Summaries are contained in F. S. Regs., Part II. and the Staff Manual respectively. Title pages will be prepared in manuscript.

September 1918. **WAR DIARY** *or* ~~**INTELLIGENCE SUMMARY.**~~ Sheet IV.

142nd F.A.

(Erase heading not required.)

Army Form C. 2118.

Place	Date	Hour	Summary of Events and Information Refce Map. BUCQUOY Combined Sheet 1/40,000	Remarks and references to Appendices
LA CAUCHIE (V17d7.8)	9.9.18.		Lecture in Gas Defence. Average number of patients in hospital – 150. Orders received that unit will move with 76th Bde Group to DOUCHY area.	
"	10.9.18.		76th Brigade O.O. re move, and RAMC O.O. No115 received.	
DOUCHY	11.9.18.		Unit moved to DOUCHY. Orders received for move to FAVREUIL. 1 Tent sub-division remains at LA CAUCHIE.	
FAVREUIL (H10a.25)	12.9.18.		Unit moved to FAVREUIL and formed a D.R.S. on the site of an old hutted camp. Captain (A/Lieut. Col.) G.O. CHAMBERS RAMC reported for duty as O.C. 142nd F.A. from Cavalry Corps.	
"	13.9.18.		Lieut. Col. G.O. CHAMBERS RAMC. takes over duties of O.C. this day. Reported at ADMS 3rd Division Office at TRIANGULAR COPSE near GOMIECOURT this morning. Inspected all equipment of F.A. many articles are unserviceable and deficient. Indents for new issue to replace are being prepared. Organised the construction of the Div. Rest Station and improved the road for traffic. ADMS visited camp in afternoon. Weather improving wind N.W.	G.O. Chambers. Lieut. Col. RAMC
"	14.9.18.		Construction of the camp, salving of material, continued to-day. The D.R.S. opened at 10 a.m. for the reception of Divisional sick. Special arrangements made for Diarrhoea, and Scabies Cases. The DRS at LA CAUCHIE still open but has ceased admitting. Available accommodation for patients – 100. 64 Patients in hospital.	G.O.C.

D. D. & L., London, E.C. (A8094) Wt W1771/M2031 750,000 5/17 Sch. 52 Forms/C2118/14

Instructions regarding War Diaries and Intelligence Summaries are contained in F. S. Regs., Part II. and the Staff Manual respectively. Title pages will be prepared in manuscript.

WAR DIARY
or
~~INTELLIGENCE SUMMARY.~~
(*Erase heading not required.*)

Army Form C. 2118.

Sheet V.

O.C. 142nd F.A. [illegible]

Place	Date	Hour	Summary of Events and Information Refer Map. BUCQUOY England Sheet 1/40.000 & 57 C	Remarks and references to Appendices
FAVREUIL (H10 a.2.5)	15.9.18.		ADMS 3rd Div. O.O. No 116. Received at 3.30 a.m. detailing orders for Bearer Division of this F.A. to accompany 9th Brigade into the line. O.C. Bearer Division sent forward to reconnoitre this morning. Visited ADMS this morning. DADMS called and necessary arrangements were made re the move into the line and taking over from 62nd Division. On night 15/16. 3rd Division relieved 62nd Div. in the line (HAVRINCOURT Sector). Bearers of 142nd F.A. relieved bearers of 62nd Div. in the Sector. Posts taken over K32 b 4.5½, K33 b central, K27a central. Ambulance Car Post at J35b 9.0. Trolley loading Post at K32a central, Yorkshire Bank K31.B. Evacuation is by hand carriage to K32a central, thence by trolley to J35b.90. Thence by Ambulance car to ADS at ROYAULCOURT and on by ambul. cars of 7th F.A. to M.D.S. N. of BEUGNY (7th F.A.). Bearer Reserve Post and park for Horse Ambul. wagons is at BERTINCOURT. Weather fine & warm.	[illegible]
"	16.9.18.		O.C. visited Bearer Reserve Post at BERTINCOURT under Capt. WRIGHT. RAMC. and then went on to 9th Brig. H.Q. at V36b2.1. along Canal du NORD. where he met G.O.C. 9th Brig. and O.C. Bearer Division Major BREEN. RAMC. Medical arrangts were discussed. Weather hot & sultry.	[illegible]

(A8604) Wt W1771/M2031 750,000 5/17 D. D. & L., London, E.C. Sch. 52 Forms/C2118/14

Instructions regarding War Diaries and Intelligence Summaries are contained in F. S. Regs., Part II. and the Staff Manual respectively. Title pages will be prepared in manuscript.

WAR DIARY
or
~~INTELLIGENCE SUMMARY.~~
(Erase heading not required.)

Army Form C. 2118.

Sheet VI.

O.C. 142nd F. Amb^ce

Place	Date	Hour	Summary of Events and Information Ref. Map 57/C 1/40.000.	Remarks and references to Appendices
FAVREUIL (H10a 2.5)	17.9.18.		The work of improving site of Div. Rest Station and extending its construction is in progress. The site is very dirty and much labour will be required to improve it. Accommodation for patients 150. C.O. visited ADMS this morning at MARICOURT WOOD (14 central) and was instructed to reconnoitre a site for HQ in the locality of BEUGNY. This was done and the site selected is at I16c 3.5. Visited O.C. No 7 F.A. at I9d 5.5. and O.C. No 8 F.A. (M.D.S.) at BEAUMETZ (J 3 b 1.1.) thence to Reserve Bearer Section at BERTINCOURT; took Capt. WRIGHT RAMC forward to reconnoitre roads in Canal du Nord area. P 4 a.b., J 35 c.d.; thence to 9th Bde HQ and met Major BREEN, RAMC and then inspected R.A.Ps and line of evacuation from HAVRINCOURT to Car Post in J35d 6.9. Weather fine and fresh. Wind S.W.	[illegible]
"	18.9.18		Capt. MANN RAMC arrived at 3 a.m. from LA CAUCHIE bringing with him the tent subdivision, medical equipment, 3 Hospital marquees by lorries together with 23 patients. Instructions sent to Capt. WRIGHT RAMC that HQ will be established at BEUGNY this afternoon and that he will proceed there with his personnel and transport this afternoon. Weather fine. Wind W.	[illegible]
BEUGNY (I16c 3.5)	19.9.18		Informed this morning that Capt (A/major) BREEN RAMC was killed in action last evening when searching for wounded.	

Instructions regarding War Diaries and Intelligence Summaries are contained in F. S. Regs., Part II. and the Staff Manual respectively. Title pages will be prepared in manuscript.

WAR DIARY
or
~~INTELLIGENCE SUMMARY.~~
(Erase heading not required.)

Army Form C. 2118.

Sheet VII

O.C. 142nd F. Amb^ce

Place	Date	Hour	Summary of Events and Information Ref^ce Map Sheet 57C 1/40,000	Remarks and references to Appendices
BEUGNY (1.16c 3.5)	19.9.18		This occurred during a hostile barrage whilst the enemy made an attack on our front at HAVRINCOURT. The whole bearer personnel were working under great pressure and though shelling was most severe, all casualties were evacuated by them to the car collecting post at J36c1.9. I detailed Captain WRIGHT RAMC to take command of the Bearers and to report to Brig. H.Q. forthwith. During the afternoon I made a reconnaissance of the road through HAVRINCOURT Wood to CLAYTON CROSS with Captain WRIGHT, Major WILLIS (OC Bearers 77 F.A.) and another officer of 77 FA. I decided to evacuate through this route from YORKSHIRE POST and give up the route via the Canal. A Post will be continued for Walking wounded at J36c1.9 and for casualties occurring along the canal. 3 ambulance cars will be kept at CLAYTON CROSS Q2c.2.2. Report sent to ADMS re the above. Reconnoitred roads thro' HERMIES and DOIGNIES. Cooler. Wind fresh N.W.	[initials]
"	20.9.18		Owing to continued shelling last night in and around my HQ. I have moved 500 yards to north of village of BEUGNY to I.15b 9.1. Visited DRS to-day. Much improvement has been made. Capt [illegible] RAMC rejoined to-day. Weather fine. Wind SW.	[initials]

D. D. & L., London, E.C. (A8094) Wt W1771/M2034 750,000 5/17 Sch. 52 Forms/C2118/14

Instructions regarding War Diaries and Intelligence Summaries are contained in F. S. Regs., Part II. and the Staff Manual respectively. Title pages will be prepared in manuscript.

WAR DIARY
or
~~INTELLIGENCE SUMMARY.~~
(Erase heading not required.)

Army Form C. 2118.

Sheet VIII
O.C. 142nd F. Amb^ce

Place	Date	Hour	Summary of Events and Information Sheet 57/C.	Remarks and references to Appendices
BEUGNY I15b9.1	21.9.18.		Inspected D.R.S. much improvement has been made. 8 hospital marquees in groups of 2 have been erected. Total accomodation 200. Weather unsettled. Wind S.W.	(initials)
"	22.9.18		Visited line and collecting posts this afternoon with Capt. POTTER. The Car Post is now 400 yards S.W. of CLAPTON CROSS at Q7b6.4. There is good accomodation here for 12 lying cases and 30-40 walking wounded. Visited Brig. H.Q. and saw Staff Captain. Visited Yorkshire Bank and saw Capt. WRIGHT. Reconnoitred area near old Car Post at J 35 d.2.2. for a new site. Weather very wet, wind S.W.	(initials)
"	23.9.18		Visited DRS and met ADMS who inspected the camp. He expressed great satisfaction with all he saw and with the general arrangements of organisation. Sent Capt. POTTER with a small working party to J 35 d.2.2. to make the new site for W.W.C.Post. Weather improving wind S.W. Capt. SHIELDS RAMC joined for duty.	(initials)
"	24.9.18		Visited Car Post at Q7b6.4. and selected a site for Dump of Stretchers & blankets. Met O.C. Bearers there and attended a Conference later at ADMS office (6P.M). Taking O.C. Bearers to attend. General outline of operations discussed and medical arrangements of evacuation made. Capt. SHIELDS reconnoitred the forward area. Weather fine wind W.	(initials)
"	25.9.18		Arrangements being made for making Dump at Q7b6.4. and sending up necessary supplies there in view of forthcoming active operations. Weather unsettled much rain	(initials)

D. D. & L., London, E.C.
(A8004) Wt W1771/M2031 750,000 5/17 Sch. 52 Forms/C2118/14

Instructions regarding War Diaries and Intelligence Summaries are contained in F. S. Regs., Part II. and the Staff Manual respectively. Title pages will be prepared in manuscript.

WAR DIARY
or
~~INTELLIGENCE SUMMARY.~~
(Erase heading not required.)

Army Form C. 2118.

Sheet IX.

O.C. 142nd F. Ambce

Place	Date	Hour	Summary of Events and Information Refce Map. Sheet 57 C.	Remarks and references to Appendices
BEUGNY (I 15 b 9.1)	26.9.18.		Attended conference at ADMS office this afternoon. Informed that Zero hour will be 5.20 am tomorrow. At 6 P.M. moved my H.Q. to YORKSHIRE BANK. K 32 b 4.5. where Bearers and W.W.C.P. are located. Another W.W.C.P. with H. amb. cars under Lieut. WILHOIT. M.O.R.C. is located at J 35 d 3.6. Ambulance Car Post and Dump under Capt. SHIELDS. RAMC. are located at Q 7 b 6.4. All reserve bearers under Capt. WRIGHT and Capt POTTER RAMC are situated at YORKSHIRE POST. By 9 P.M. all arrangements were completed for operations tomorrow. Weather unsettled. Wind S.W.	
YORKSHIRE BANK (K 32 b 4.5)	27.9.18.	5.20 AM.	Attack by VI Corps on enemy positions E of HAVRINCOURT begins. Casualties began to arrive at K 32 b 4.5. within 2 hours - these came in steadily for several hours. Evacuation worked smoothly and all 9th Brig. wounded were reported cleared by 11 am. after 1st and 2nd objectives had been gained. In the afternoon 9th Brigade took RIBECOURT. Casualties from this action were not heavy and were cleared by 5 P.M. Many wounded from other brigades and divisions were dealt with at K 32 b 4.5 also at J 35 d.3.6. The former post had to be made an ADS early in afternoon. These posts were taken over by 62nd Div (2/1st 2/3 W Riding F. Ambces) at 5 P.M. also R.A.P's as were required. 9th Brigade were withdrawn from the line the [Same evening. 6 P.M.	

D. D. & L., London, E.C.
(A8604) Wt W1771/M2031 750,000 5/17 Sch. 52 Forms/C2118/14

Instructions regarding War Diaries and Intelligence Summaries are contained in F. S. Regs., Part II. and the Staff Manual respectively. Title pages will be prepared in manuscript.

WAR DIARY
or
~~INTELLIGENCE SUMMARY.~~
(*Erase heading not required.*)

Army Form C. 2118.

Sheet X.

O.C. 142nd F. Amb.ce

Place	Date	Hour	Summary of Events and Information Ref Map Sheet 57 C.	Remarks and references to Appendices
YORKSHIRE BANK (K32 b4.5).	28.9.18.		All wounded were evacuated quickly, the route for ambulances being via Canal du NORD to J35d.3.6 thence to ADS at RUYAULCOURT, returning empty to K32b4.5 via log road and Q7b6.4. Number of casualties collected and passed through 142nd F.A. from 5 am to 5 P.M. were:- 253 - lying cases, 400 - sitting, 581 walking. Total - 1239. (of which 71 were gassed cases). Weather fine.	
"	28.9.18.		9th Brig. & 142nd F.A. in Support in HAVRINCOURT area. Bearers are resting at K32b4.5 and Q7b6.4. Weather unsettled.	
"	29.9.18.		9th Brig. withdrawn to rest (but in reserve) around area E of HERMIES and Canal du NORD. 142nd F.A. Bearers and HQ. returned to BEUGNY. Conference at ADMS office 7.15 P.M. re forward move. Weather unsettled.	
BEUGNY (I.15 b9.1.)	30.9.18.		Arrangements made during the night 29/30th for concentration of whole F Amb.ce less 1 officer and 2 tent subdivisions remaining at D.R.S. at BEUGNY in view of impending move forward. Concentration completed by 9 a.m. The whole ambulance is now ready to move off at 2 hours notice. Weather fair. Wind N.W. DRS closed down for admissions. Ambulance moved at 10 P.M. to HERMIES area at J36 b3.3. Capt. LEIGH RAMC. proceeded to 13/King's Liverpool Regt. on permanent duty.	

G.O. Chambers
Lieut. Col. O.C. 142nd F. Amb.ce

D. D. & L., London, E.C.
(A8094) Wt W1771/M2031 750,000 5/17 Sch. 52 Forms/C2118/14

S E C R E T.

Copy No.....5

3rd DIVISION R.A.M.C. OPERATION ORDER No. 114.

5th September 1918.

Reference BUCQUOY Combined Sheet 1/40,000.

1. 3rd Division, less artillery, will move into the VI Corps Reserve Area tomorrow September 6th; to be clear of present area by 6 p.m.

2. No. 7 Field Ambulance will move to 9th Infantry Brigade Area round MONCHY au BOIS.

3. No. 8 Field Ambulance will move to the 8th Infantry Brigade Area South of RANSART.

4. No. 142 Field Ambulance will move to Field Ambulance site at LA CAUCHIE.

5. O.C.,No. 8 Field Ambulance will leave one Tent Sub-division less 1 Officer at the Divisional Rest Station at S.23.c.7.4. until further orders.

6. O.C.,No. 7 Field Ambulance will be responsible for the collection of sick from 9th Infantry Brigade, 3rd Divnl. Artillery, and 3rd Btn.M.G.C.

7. O.C.,No. 142 Field Ambulance will be responsible for collection of sick from 76th Infantry Brigade, 3rd Divnl.R.E., and 20th K.R.R.C.

8. A.D.M.S. Office will close at present location at 3 p.m. September 6th and open at HUMBERCAMP at same hour.

9. Field Ambulances to acknowledge.

F. McLennan
Lieut-Colonel,
A.D.M.S.,3rd Division.

Copies to :-

1. 3rd Divn "G".
2. " " "Q".
3. No. 7 Fld Ambce.
4. No. 8 " "
✓5. No. 142" "
6. 8th Inf:Bde.
7. 9th " "
8. 76th " "
9. C.R.A.
10. C.R.E.
11. 3rd Btn.M.G.C.
12. 20th K.R.R.C.
13. 3rd Div.Train.
14. D.A.D.V.S.
15. D.D.M.S.,VI Corps.
16. D.M.S.,Third Army.
17. A.D.M.S.,2nd Divn.
18. A.D.M.S.,62nd "
19. A.D.M.S.,Guards Divn.
20. War Diary.
21. " "
22. File.

S E C R E T.

3rd DIVISION R.A.M.C. OPERATION ORDER No. 113.

September 2nd, 1918.

Reference BUCQUOY Combined Sheet 1/40,000.

1. 3rd Division, less Artillery, will be relieved in the line by the Guards Division tonight 2nd/3rd September.

2. (a) On relief the 8th Infantry Brigade will move to the Area South of St. LEGER with Brigade Headquarters as below.
(b) 9th Infantry Brigade will move to Area "B" with Brigade Headquarters at A.5.c.0.3.
(c) 76th Infantry Brigade will move to Area "C" with Brigade Headquarters at BOIRY St. MARTIN (S.30.a.).
(d) 8th Infantry Brigade will move tomorrow afternoon September 3rd to Area "A". (H.Q. at T.25.a.)

3. Os.C.,Field Ambulances will get into touch with their affiliated Brigades, where the Areas "A", "B", and "C" will be explained to them.

4. No's. 7 and 142 Field Ambulances will remain in their present locations.
No. 8 Field Ambulance will move to the 8th Brigade Area.

5. Bearer Divisions will be relieved in the line tonight, and will rejoin their Units.

6. O.C.,No. 7 Field Ambulance will hand over the Walking Wounded Collecting Post at B.21.a.0.6. to O.C.,No. 9 Field Ambulance at dawn tomorrow; relief to be completed by 10-0 a.m.

7. O.C.,No. 8 Field Ambulance will hand over the Main Dressing Station at S.23.c.5.2. to O.C.,No. [illegible] Field Ambulance; relief to be completed by 10-0 a.m. tomorrow.

8. Walking Wounded Collecting Post at T.25.c.2.8. will close at 10-0 a.m. tomorrow. Any walking wounded who may arrive there after that hour will be directed to the Main Dressing Station at S.23.c.5.2.

9. The six motor lorries supplied by 3rd Division "Q" for Walking Wounded will be sent to rejoin the M.T.Column by noon tomorrow.

10. The Office of the A.D.M.S. will close at BOIRY St. MARTIN at 8-0 a.m. tomorrow, and open at the same hour at X.13.b.8.4.

11. Field Ambulances to acknowledge.

F. M. Lennan

Lieut-Colonel,
A.D.M.S.,3rd Division.

Copies to all recipients of O.O. 111.

SECRET.

9th INFANTRY BRIGADE OPERATION ORDER No. 21. Copy No. 14.

****

Ref. map, 57C N.W. 1/20.000. 2nd Sept. 1918

1. The 3rd Division (less artillery) will be relieved in the line by the Guards Division to-night Sept. 2nd/3rd.
2. The 3rd Guards Brigade are relieving all troops North of line:- C.16.b.4.2. - C.16.a.4.5. - C.9.d.3.3. - C.8.c.0.3. - C.12.b.9.0.
3. After relief, units of 9th Inf. Bde. will move to area A.11, A.12, A.18 : a & b, parts of A.5.c. & d., square B.7 and B.13.a. & b., exact details of which have been shown on special maps issued to units concerned.
4. On completion of relief "B" Coy. 3rd M.G.C. will move to area just W. of MOYENNEVILLE in A.3 and parts of A.2 and 8, where they will rejoin M.G.Bn.
5. The attached section of 56th Fld. Coy. will join its company on Sept. 3rd in area just W. of ARRAS - ACHIET Railway. It will move to-day to A.4.d.9.0.
6. Arrival in new area and location of H.Qrs. will be notified to Bde. H.Qrs.
7. Reference paras. 1, 2 and 3, the units of 3rd Guards Brigade will not actually relieve unit for unit of 9th Bde., but are moving into their own dispositions.

   All 9th Bde. units will commence to withdraw at 1-0 a.m. Sept. 3rd.
8. (a) Bde. H.Qrs. will close at MORY COPSE at 1-0 a.m. and will open at A.4.d.9.0. on arrival.

   (b) 3rd Guards Brigade have opened at MORT L'HOMME.
9. ACKNOWLEDGE.

[signature]
Capt.,
Brigade Major, 9th Inf.Bde.

Issued at 10-45 p.m.

Copy No. 1 - G.O.C.
2 - 1/N.Fus.
3 - 4/R.Fus.
4 - 13/K.L.R.
5 - 9/T.M.Bty.
6 - Bde. Sigs.
7 - B Coy. 3rd M.G.C.
8 - 76th Inf.Bde.
9 - 8th do.
10 - 3rd Guards Bde.
11 - 3rd Div.
12 - do.
13 - Sect.56th Fld.Coy.
14 - 142nd Fld.Amb.
15 - B.T.O.
16 - S.C.
17 - War Diary
18 - do.
19 - File.

S E C R E T.

3rd DIVISION R.A.M.C. OPERATION ORDER No. 112.

1st September, 1918.

1. The VI Corps is to advance tomorrow in conjunction with the XVII Corps on the left.
The attack on the 3rd Division front will be carried out by the 8th Infantry Brigade, which will pass through the 9th and 76th Infantry Brigades at Zero hour.

2. The 8th Infantry Brigade will move forward tonight and will be formed up in its battle positions in rear of the front line of the 9th and 76th Infantry Brigades prior to Zero hour.

3. One Battalion each of the 76th Infantry Brigade and the 9th Infantry Brigade will come under the orders of the G.O.C., 8th Infantry Brigade, and will move forward in support to the 8th Infantry Brigade.

4. Os.C., Nos. 7 and 142 Field Ambulances will be responsible for the evacuation of wounded from the 76th and 9th Infantry Brigades respectively.

5. O.C., No. 8 Field Ambulance will be responsible for the evacuation of wounded from the 8th Infantry Brigade, and, after Zero hour, from the Battalions of the 76th and 9th Infantry Brigades in support to the 8th Infantry Brigade, in addition.

6. Os.C., No. 7 and No. 142 Field Ambulances will be prepared to place two large Motor Ambulance Cars each, at the disposal of O.C., No. 8 Field Ambulance on demand, if assistance is required by him in the clearing of wounded.

7. The Bearer Divisions of No. 7 and No. 142 Field Ambulances, with the exception of the squads required for clearing the wounded of the 76th and 9th Infantry Brigades, will be kept in readiness to assist the Bearers of No. 8 Field Ambulance, if necessary.
Orders will be issued from this office.

8. The evacuation of stretcher cases will be carried out as at present.

9. Walking Wounded will be directed to L'HOMME MORT, where motor lorries will meet them and take them to the Walking Wounded Collecting Post at the MAISON ROUGE.

10. The six motor lorries supplied by 3rd Division "Q" for walking wounded will come under the orders of O.C., No. 8 Field Ambulance from Zero hour. They will be parked at the Walking Wounded Collecting Post, MAISON ROUGE.

11. As the action developes the route of evacuation will be changed, at the discretion of O.C., No. 8 Field Ambulance, from L'HOMME MORT - ST. LEGER route to Sugar Factory - MORY - ERVILLERS route.

12. Zero hour will be notified later.

13. Field Ambulances to acknowledge.

D. C. Macdonald

Major, D.A.D.M.S.,
for A.D.M.S., 3rd Division.

Copies to all recipients of O.O. 111.

SECRET. Copy No. ... 15

9th INFANTRY BRIGADE OPERATION ORDER NO. 20.

Reference maps 51B S.W.) 1/20.000. Sept. 1st 1918.
57C N.W.)

1. The VI Corps is to advance to-morrow, Sept. 2nd in conjunction with XVII Corps on the left.
The objectives are MORCHIES and LAGNICOURT.

2. The attack on the 3rd Division front is to be carried out by the 8th Inf. Bde. which will pass through the 9th and 76th Inf. Bdes. at Zero hour.

3. The 8th Inf. Bde. are moving forward to-night and are forming up on battle positions in rear of the front line prior to Zero hour.

4. The 1st NORTHD. FUS. will come under the orders of G.O.C. 8th Inf. Bde. and will move forward in support to 8th Inf. Bde.
1 Battalion 76th Inf. Bde. is to act similarly.

5. The attack of 8th Inf. Bde. will be made under a creeping barrage in co-operation with tanks.

6. The M.G.Coys. in the line are forming a creeping barrage to cover the advance of the infantry.

7. Zero hour will be notified later.

8. Headquarters of 8th Inf. Bde. are being established at L'HOMME MORT, B.17.a.6.8.

9.(a) On the situation being cleared up after our attack this evening on NOREUIL SWITCH - 4th ROYAL FUS. and 13th KINGS will reorganise between the 9th Bde. boundaries:-
South Boundary - line running through C.8.c.0.2. and C.9.d.3.2.
North Boundary - line joining U.26.d.0.0. and C.5.d.0.0.

(b) This re-organisation will be in depth as far back as the line C.8.c.8.2. - C.8.b.4.5. - BULLECOURT Av.

(c) The inter-battalion boundary will be a straight line joining C.8.b.8.8. and C.10.a.2.8.

10. Headquarters of Battalions will remain as follows:-

1st Northd.Fus.	C.7.a.~~2x~~.78
4th Royal Fus.	C.8.a.2.4.
13th Kings.	U.26.c.5.1.

11. ACKNOWLEDGE.

T.L.Malone
Capt.,
Brigade Major, 9th Inf.Bde.

Issued at 8-0 p.m.

Copy No. 1 - G.O.C.
2 - 1/N.Fus.
3 - 4/R.Fus.
4 - 13/K.L.R.
5 - 9/T.M.Bty.
6 - 9th Bde.Sigs.
7 - Lt.Col.VICKERY.
8 - 76th Inf.Bde.
9 - 8th Inf.Bde.
10 - 3rd Div.
11 - 3rd Div.
12 - B.T.O.
13 - Sect.56th Fld.Coy.
14 - Sect. Tunnellers.
15 - Staff Capt.
16 - 142nd Fld.Amb.
17 - File.
18 - War Diary.
19 - do.

SECRET.

9th INF. BDE. OPERATION ORDER NO. 19. Copy No. 1

****

Ref. map 57C N.W. 1/20.000. 1st Sept. 1918.

1. The following objective has to be taken by to-night by 9th Inf. Bde.:- NOREUIL SWITCH between C.9.d.3.2. and C.5.c.5.2.

2. 4th ROYAL FUS. and 13th KINGS will at once endeavour to get as much of this as possible, by infiltration, 4th ROYAL FUS. on right and 13th KINGS on left, as explained verbally by Brigadier this morning.

The exact positions gained must be accurately and very rapidly communicated to Bde. H.Qrs.

3. Should any of the objective remain uncaptured at 6-0 p.m. to-night, that portion will be attacked at that hour by 2 Coys. 4th ROYAL FUS. on right and 2 Coys. 13th KINGS on left, as explained by B.G.C. this morning. This will be done in conjunction with 52nd Div. on our left.

4. In order to arrange a barrage for this 6-0 p.m. attack, it is absolutely essential to know the exact positions captured by infiltration by 4-45 p.m. to-day at Bde. H.Q.

5. Patrols of 4th ROYAL FUS. have already found NOREUIL SWITCH clear as far East as C.9.d.8.4. The frontage of the attack (if no ground is gained meanwhile) will be C.9.d.8.4. (road inclusive) to Div. left boundary C.5.c.5.2. where touch will be gained with 52nd Div.

6. Whatever frontage remains to be attacked will be halved between 4th ROYAL FUS. and 13th KINGS by a straight line running from the centre of the jumping off line to the centre of the objective.

7. The jumping off line will be LONGATTE SUPPORT and BULLECOURT AVENUE between C.3.c.0.2. and C.3.a.8.3. The length of the objective depends on the success of the infiltration but will be equally divided between the 2 Battns.

8. A map is attached to Battns. showing boundaries and objective should the situation be as at present.

9. Barrage arrangements for 6-0 p.m. attack will be communicated later.

10. Bns. will at once demand what amn., flares, etc. are required.

11. ACKNOWLEDGE.

[signature]
Capt.,
Brigade Major, 9th Inf. Bde.

Issued at 2-30 p.m.

Copy No.
1 - G.O.C.
2 - 1/N.Fus.
3 - 4/R.Fus.
4 - 13/K.L.R.
5 - 9/T.F.B.
6 - Sigs.
7 - 142nd Fld.Amb.
8 - B.T.O.
9 - 76th Inf.Bde.
10 - 8th do.
11 - Lt.Col.VICKERY.
12 - Sec.56th Fld.Coy.
13 - Sec. Tunnellers.
14 - C.Coy. 3rd M.G.C.
15 - 3rd Div.
16 - do.
17 - File.
18 - War Diary
19 - do.
20 - S.C.

Oct. 1918

140/3327

142nd F.A. Ambce

Confidential

6

WO 39

WAR DIARY

OF

No 142 FIELD AMBULANCE

From 1.10.18 To 31.10.18

Instructions regarding War Diaries and Intelligence Summaries are contained in F. S. Regs., Part II. and the Staff Manual respectively. Title pages will be prepared in manuscript.

WAR DIARY
or
~~INTELLIGENCE SUMMARY.~~
(Erase heading not required.)

O.C. 142nd F. Amb^ce

Army Form C. 2118.

Folio 1.

Place	Date	Hour	Summary of Events and Information Ref. Map. Sheet 57c 1/40,000; " 57b "	Remarks and references to Appendices
CANAL DU NORD. (J36 b 3.3)	1.10.18		142nd F.A. marched from BEUGNY to present site during the night 30th/1st on moving forward into 9th Brigade area. Weather very rainy during end of march.	
		1.00	~~Hour~~ of arrival.	E.D. Chambers Lieut. Col. OC. 142nd F.A.
	"	9.00	Unit moved forward to site in K29d. (near RIBECOURT)	
K29d 8.9.	"		HQ of 142nd F.A. established at this site. The 9th Brigade and 142nd F.A. are in reserve. The 7th and 8th Brigades are in the line around RUMILLY. ADMS located at L25 b 3.5 also site of M.D.S. (8th F.A.) Under instructions from ADMS. I sent Capt. POTTER MC RAMC. and Tent Sub-division personnel to MARCOING in afternoon to form an A.D.S. This order was cancelled later in day and personnel withdrawn to K29d 8.9. I visited 9th Brig. HQ at L27 b 1.3 and discussed medical arrangements with Staff Captain.	(EDC)
"	2.10.18		8th and 9th Brigs. attacked at 6 P.M. last night and took RUMILLY. ADS (8th FA) is at G19d 9.8. (MASNIERES) Line of evacuation along road from ADS to MARCOING thence to M.D.S. at (RIBECOURT) L25 b 3.5 57c. Heavy Ambul. cars have been pooled for evacuation purposes. R.A.Ps are situated as follows:- (KSLI) G20d.6.4. (57b) (R.S.F) G28 central. (R.Scots). G21 c 1.2. Bearer Relay Post (to avoid village) G20 b 9.7. A.D.S. G19.d.9.7. Ambulance Car Post G26 c 6.5. Lieut. S.E. WILHOIT MORC. U.S.A. proceeded to 7/K.S.L.I. as M.O. on temporary duty. Weather fine. Wind S.W.	(EDC)

*D. D. & L., London, E.C. (A8064) Wt W1771/M2031 750,000 5/17 Sch. 52 Forms/C2118/14

Instructions regarding War Diaries and Intelligence Summaries are contained in F. S. Regs., Part II. and the Staff Manual respectively. Title pages will be prepared in manuscript.

WAR DIARY
or
~~INTELLIGENCE SUMMARY.~~
(Erase heading not required.)

O.C. 142nd F. Ambce

Army Form C. 2118.

Folio 2.

Place	Date	Hour	Summary of Events and Information Ref Maps. 57 B., 57C. 1/40,000	Remarks and references to Appendices
K29 d.8.9. (57C).	3.10.18.		I visited 9th Brigade yesterday evening and again this afternoon. In view of impending operations the ambulance is under short notice to move (no definite time limit given). Further orders are awaited in view of the above. The forward area has been reconnoitred by myself and other officers yesterday. The Car Post at G26.c6.5 has been changed into an ADS for the Right Sector. Evacuation of this sector proceeds across the Canal at MASNIERES to this ADS thence to M.D.S at RIBECOURT. Orders received that D.R.S. is to remain open for reception of sick. Capt. MANN RAMC has been so informed. Inspected all equipment of 142 FA today and ordered it to be carried on vehicles assigned by M.E. No order had apparently been observed beforehand on this question, the result being that many vehicles were much overloaded at the expense of others. Transport is now loaded according to scale. Weather fine. Wind Westerly	(initials)
"	4.10.18.		Foot inspection made this morning at 9. AM. Iron Ration and First Field Dressing parade at 11. A.M. 1/Lieut. G.H. REDDICK MORC reported for temporary duty at D.R.S FAVREUIL yesterday. Weather changeable	(initials)
"	5.10.18.		In view of active operations in near future, I reconnoitred the present front of 3rd Divn. and sent 9 squads of Bearer Div. under Capt. WRIGHT. to be stationed at MASNIERES (in the same location as ADS of 7th FA — G26c.6.5 (57B) I visited 9th Brig. HQ. and discussed situation. Operations probably on morning of 6th/7th.	(initials)

D. D & L., London, E.C.
(A8064) Wt W1771/M2031 750,000 5/17 Sch. 52 Forms/C2118/14

Instructions regarding War Diaries and Intelligence Summaries are contained in F. S. Regs., Part II. and the Staff Manual respectively. Title pages will be prepared in manuscript.

WAR DIARY

or

~~INTELLIGENCE SUMMARY.~~ O.C. 142nd Field Ambulance

(Erase heading not required.)

Army Form C. 2118.

Folio 3

Place	Date	Hour	Summary of Events and Information Ref Maps 57B. 57C.	Remarks and references to Appendices
K29 d 8.9. 57C.	6.10.18.		Visited D.R.S. at FAVREUIL. 156 patients still in hospital. Difficulty in evacuating owing to MAC having moved forward. Informed ADMS accordingly. ADMS 3rd Div. Oper. Order No 119 received. Date of Op. postponed.	
"	7.10.18.		9th Brig. Op. Order No 33. received 0700 hours. Weather strong S.W. wind.	(initials)
			Attended Conference at ADMS office - RIBECOURT - about medical arrangements during forthcoming operations. OC Bearers was present. Sent remainder of Bearer Divn under Capt POTTER to join the party at G26 c 5.5 - the ambulance having moved into the Brewery 100 yards away from ADS 7th 7A. Visited 9th Brig. HQ. this afternoon selected site for Walking Wounded Collect. Station at L30 c 0.3. (57C). Where 3 Horse Amb. Wagons. 1 (ADS) Limber, 1 water cart. will proceed	
		17.00	this evening. Moved with Major SHIELDS up to Ambulance Site at G26 c 55. (Brewery). Remainder of Amb. will stay at K29 d 8.9. Weather cold strong SW wind.	(initials)
MASNIERES (G26 c.5.5)	"	18.00	Arrived at G26 c 55. - MASNIERES. Major WRIGHT is in charge of Bearers with Captain POTTER second in command of Bearers. MAJOR SHIELDS proceeded on leave to U.K.	

2353 Wt W2544/1454 700,000 5/15 D. D. & L. A.D.S.S./Forms/C. 2118.

Instructions regarding War Diaries and Intelligence Summaries are contained in F. S. Regs., Part II. and the Staff Manual respectively. Title pages will be prepared in manuscript.

WAR DIARY

or

~~INTELLIGENCE SUMMARY.~~

(Erase heading not required.)

O.C.
142nd Field Ambulance.

Army Form C. 2118.

Folio 4.

Place	Date	Hour	Summary of Events and Information — Refce Map. 57C. 57B.	Remarks and references to Appendices
MASNIERES (G26c55.	7.10.18	18.00	This evening HQ 9th Inf. Brig is located in CATACOMBES - MASNIERES (G20d7.2). Arrangements made thro' Staff Captain for Regimental MOs to send guides to my HQ. to take back 2 bearer squads each. This was done during the night 7th/8th with the exception of the Northumberland Fusiliers whose guide did not arrive till 0700 hours on the 8th. A Walking Wounded Collecting Stn has been formed by 142nd FA. at L30 c0.8. Capt. POTTER is in charge of evacuation through Left Sector, north of MASNIERES - through ADS (8th FA) at G19d9.7. Major WRIGHT is supervising evacuation of Right Sector thro' village to ADS (7th FA) at G26c6.5. Disposition of Bearer Squads is given in Appendix I.	
"	8.10.18	0430	– Zero Hour. 9th Inf. Brig. attacked SERANVILLERS. 1st and 2nd Objectives and this village were captured. R.A.P's reported clear by 11.00 hours. Casualties moderate; a larger proportion than usual of Stretcher cases was noted. Location of R.A.P's and Posts of 142nd FA sent to ADMS at 09.00 hours. ADMS, GUARDS Division and OCs 4th and 9th FAs called midday and decided to take over this site as a MDS later in the day. Reported to me by Capt. POTTER that 8th FA had closed their ADS at G19d9.7 - at 09.00 hours owing to shortage of officers. I detailed Capt. the Revd MACMAHON to superintend the Walking Wounded Post L30c0.8 which he conducted most successfully and expeditiously. No. of effective MOs in 142nd FA is 4 including C.O.	Appendix I.

2353 Wt. W2544/1454 700,000 5/15 D. D. & L. A.D.S.S./Forms/C. 2118.

Instructions regarding War Diaries and Intelligence Summaries are contained in F. S. Regs., Part II. and the Staff Manual respectively. Title pages will be prepared in manuscript.

WAR DIARY
or
~~INTELLIGENCE SUMMARY~~.
(Erase heading not required.)

Army Form C. 2118.

O.C.
142nd Field Ambulance

Folio 5.

Place	Date	Hour	Summary of Events and Information Refce Maps 57C. 57B.	Remarks and references to Appendices
MASNIERES (G26c55)	8.10.18.		Wounded from ~~Left~~ Sector are evacuated therefore direct to MDS at RIBECOURT. Approximate number of walking wounded passed thro. L30c0.8 to 5PM was 230. Visited Brig: HQ in afternoon. Brig: still in line, expecting to be relieved by GUARDS Divn during the night 7/8+1. (7th/9th) Very little hostile shelling during the day in this sector. Weather fine Wind S.W.	
"	9.10.18.	01.00	9th Inf. Brig O.O. No 35 received re withdrawal of Brigde from the line.	
		02.00	ADMS. No MS979 received re Taking over of line by GUARDS who will attack at 04.30 hours. The 9th Brigde will withdraw this morning into reserve to area K15, K16, K21b, K22a. Bearer Squads reported from R.A.Ps at 07.00 & 07.00 hours. All wounded cleared and 142nd FA withdrawn from line at 10.00 hours concentrated at L30c0.8. at 10.15. Marched back at 10.30 hrs. to previous site W of RIBECOURT in K29c.8.9. where it will remain.	
K29c.8.9	9.10.18	12.00 hrs.	Arrived and opened HQ at this site. Situation Report at 09 hrs sent to ADMS. Visited 9th Brig. HQ at K13d5.4 this afternoon and made arrangements with Staff Captain for collecting sick of Battalions between 10 and 11 hrs. daily. DRS at FAVREUIL to close down forthwith. All sick to be sent to BEAUMETZ. Weather Colder Wind N.W.	Appendix II

2353 Wt. W2544/1454 700,000 5/15 D. D. & L. A.D.S.S./Forms/C. 2118.

Instructions regarding War Diaries and Intelligence Summaries are contained in F. S. Regs., Part II. and the Staff Manual respectively. Title pages will be prepared in manuscript.

WAR DIARY
or
~~INTELLIGENCE SUMMARY.~~
(Erase heading not required.)

O.C. 142nd Field Ambulance.

Army Form C. 2118.

Folio 6.

Place	Date	Hour	Summary of Events and Information Refce Map. 57 C 57 B.	Remarks and references to Appendices
K29c89	10.10.18.		Visited ADMS at HERMIES and D.R.S at BEAUMETZ to arrange about moving Marquees and other equipment there from former DRS - FAVREUIL. Afterwards visited DRS at FAVREUIL. About 60 patients are left - the DRS is closed for admissions - Marquees are being struck and equipment packed. Pay Day.	(218)
"	11.10.18.		Ambulance passed day in clothing, Iron Ration, and Boot inspections. Ablution (hot baths improvised) is being carried out. Clean clothing issued. Transport has been overhauled and repaired. Weather cloudy, rain in evening	(219)
"	12.10.18.		Warning order for move of Brigade received from 9th Inf. Brig. (No. B.M. 296). Reconnoitred proposed area around NOYELLES and left holding party in site selected (L11 b2.0). Orders issued to Ambulance for preparation of move tomorrow.	(220)
NOYELLES (L11b2.0)	13.10.18.		Orders received from ADMS re move of 3rd Division - No M.S. 984. also Brigade Order No 36 re move into NOYELLES area. 142nd FA. moved at 10.30 hrs to L11 b.2.0. This is a good site, ample cellar accomodation and rooms for Office Stores etc. Horse Transport in open field good surface and grazing. Orders issued regarding Reception and Evacuation of Sick of Brigade. Cases will be detained only until further orders. Evacuation direct to C.C.S. DADMS called in afternoon. Weather fine though cloudy, wind W.	Appendix III (221)

Instructions regarding War Diaries and Intelligence Summaries are contained in F. S. Regs., Part II. and the Staff Manual respectively. Title pages will be prepared in manuscript.

WAR DIARY
or
~~INTELLIGENCE SUMMARY.~~
(Erase heading not required.)

O.C. 142nd Field Ambulance.

Army Form C. 2118.

Folio 7.

Place	Date	Hour	Summary of Events and Information Ref Maps 57 B. 57 C.	Remarks and references to Appendices
NOYELLES (L11 b2.0)	14.10.18		Equipment inspection this morning. Visited Brig HQ regarding any early move forward of Brigade. RAPs as follows:- No 4s. L14 b5.1, R 4s L11a 9.9, [illegible] L9c66. Brig. HQ are at L11 b7.8. The Divisional Commander, 3rd Division	
"			called at 142nd FA. this morning to enquire as to present medical arrangements for the Brigade, also, number of sick and wounded occurring during recent times, and as to casualties in the Ambulance. In conclusion, he expressed great satisfaction with the Ambulance in the way it had acquitted itself in the field. A Rest Station for the Brigade (i.e. sick requiring 4 days treatment) is now formed - evacuation direct to 20 and 46 CCSs near BEUGNY. Weather fine wind N.W.	280
"	15.10.18.		Div Rest Station at BEAUMETZ - closed. A Divisional Dump of medical equipt. formed to-day at this ambulance site - lorries transporting material from former dump at FAVREUIL. Med. arrangts. 3rd Div. no 55/247. received. Weather fair.	[illegible]
"	16.10.18		Medical (Scabies) inspection of unit carried out to-day. The Brigade Rest Station is now formed and can accomodate 50 patients. Weather fine and mild.	[illegible]
"	17.10.18		All medical equipment for the Dump has now arrived and a suitable site has [been selected for it.	

Instructions regarding War Diaries and Intelligence Summaries are contained in F. S. Regs., Part II. and the Staff Manual respectively. Title pages will be prepared in manuscript.

WAR DIARY
or
~~INTELLIGENCE SUMMARY.~~
(Erase heading not required.)

Army Form C. 2118.

O.C.
142nd Field Ambulance.

Folio 8.

Place	Date	Hour	Summary of Events and Information Refce Maps 57B. 57C.	Remarks and references to Appendices
NOYELLES (L11 b2.0)	17.10.18.		Orders re Fire, Patients, Orderly Officer and Orderly Sergeant have been revised and re-published. Visited ADMS at FLESQUIERES in afternoon re the return of personnel with E.M.O. and 1/Lieut. WILHOIT from 9th Brigade. Weather fine. Wind W.	[illegible]
"	18.10.18.		Captain POTTER M.C. RAMC. proceeded on 14 days leave to U.K. to-day. Visited D.A.D.O.S and 9th I. Brigade H.Q in the afternoon. Weather fine and dull.	[illegible]
"	19.10.18		Captain CLARK RAMC and Captain HARMINS RAMC reported for duty this morning and were taken on the strength accordingly. Capt. CLARK. proceeded in the evening for tempy duty at VI Corps P.O.W. cage at I 3c.2.8. (57B) under instructions from ADMS to that effect. Number of effective officers in the unit including C.O. is 4. Capt. BOWEN, Q.M, went sick to-day. Warning Order from 9th Inf. Brig. re forecast of move to-morrow received. Orders issued to Field Ambulance accordingly. Weather good, rain in the evening.	Appendix IV.
"	20.10.18		Order No 38 (copy No 7) received from 9th Inf. Brigde. Orders for the march issued. The unit proceeded by route march to BEVILLERS, starting at 1100 hrs from NOYELLES, arriving at BEVILLERS at 16.30 hrs. Owing to continuous rain	Appendix V.

2353 Wt. W2544/1454 700,000 5/15 D. D. & L. A.D.S.S./Forms/C. 2118.

Instructions regarding War Diaries and Intelligence Summaries are contained in F. S. Regs., Part II. and the Staff Manual respectively. Title pages will be prepared in manuscript.

WAR DIARY
or
~~INTELLIGENCE SUMMARY.~~
(Erase heading not required.)

O.C. 142nd Field Ambulance

Army Form C. 2118.

Folio 9

Place	Date	Hour	Summary of Events and Information Ref. Maps. Sheet 57B. 57C	Remarks and references to Appendices
BEVILLERS			and the bad state of the roads in some places, the march was made rather trying and difficult but it was carried out satisfactorily and to time.	
C22d 3.2	20.10.18	1630	HQ. F.A. are located at C 22 d 3.2. Billets for personnel are very dirty and there is much crowding. This cannot be helped as the village is packed with troops and there is consequently much congestion owing to some units of 62nd Div. keeping holding parties in many billets. Capt. BOWEN still on sick list. 1 N.C.O. and 2 men have been left behind at NOYELLES in charge of the dump. Weather: much rain all day	(20)
"	21.10.18.		Small Brigade Rest Station opened for Brigade sick as no Divl or Corps Rest Station has so far been opened. Visited O.C. 2/2 W. Riding F.A. (62nd Div). to ascertain locations of medical units & R.A.P.s in 62nd Div. Sector of line. Warning Order from 9th Inf. Brig. received. Weather: rain and cold.	(20)
"	22.10.18.		RAMC O.O. No 121 d/22.10.18 received. 9th Inf. Brig. O.O. No 40 received. In these orders active operations on Third Army Front tomorrow are outlined. The task of the 3rd Div will be to pass through 62nd Div and seize objectives as far as a line N.E. of ESCARMAIN. The Brigade will march to QUIEVY this	

Instructions regarding War Diaries and Intelligence Summaries are contained in F. S. Regs., Part II. and the Staff Manual respectively. Title pages will be prepared in manuscript.

WAR DIARY
or
~~INTELLIGENCE SUMMARY.~~
(Erase heading not required.)

O.C. 142nd Field Ambulance

Army Form C. 2118.

Folio 10.

Place	Date	Hour	Summary of Events and Information Ref. Map. Sheet 57B	Remarks and references to Appendices
BEVILLERS (C22d3.2)	22.10.18		evening. 142nd FA will accompany it to QUIEVY. Orders issued accordingly. Rest Station closed and unit ready to march at 17.00 hrs. Capt. HARMINS RATIE. ordered for temp. duty with 2/7 the Royal Scots. The number of effective officers with the unit is now 3 including C.O. Capt. BOWEN – Q.M. evacuated to hospital this morning. Proceeded with Staff Captain at 16.00 hrs to QUIEVY to find billets. Unit marched under Major WRIGHT	Appendix VI.
QUIÉVY D19b7.7.	22.10.18	17.00	at 19.05 hrs from BEVILLERS, arrived at QUIEVY 21.30 hrs. owing to congestion of traffic on the road. HQ. 142nd FA located at D19b7.7. from 18.00 hrs. Capt. CLARK rejoined for duty this evening. Z day is 23.10.18. Weather rainy & cold.	
"	23.10.18.		ADS (8th F.A) is now opened near HOTEL de VILLE in SOLESMES.	
			M.D.S (7th FA) is in the CHURCH in QUIEVY. All motor and horsed ambulances are pooled under O.C. 7th FA. Walking Wounded Posts are at D6a7.1, D6d7.1, D24a4.5.	
		03.20	Zero hour. 76th Brig on right and 8th Brig on left attacked thro' 62nd Division 9th Brig. in reserve, moved from QUIEVY between 07.00 and 07.40 hrs. Bearer	
		08.00	Div. under Major WRIGHT and Capt. CLARK marched at 08.00 hrs. in rear of 9th Inf. Brig. HQ. 142nd FA will remain for the present at QUIEVY: 2 Bearer Squads have been sent to each battalion in the Brigade. Weather this morning was fine.	

2353 Wt. W2544/1454 700,000 5/15 D. D. & L. A.D.S.S./Forms/C. 2118.

Army Form C. 2118.

Instructions regarding War Diaries and Intelligence Summaries are contained in F. S. Regs., Part II. and the Staff Manual respectively. Title pages will be prepared in manuscript.

WAR DIARY
or
~~INTELLIGENCE SUMMARY.~~
(Erase heading not required.)

O. C. 142nd Field Ambulance

Folio 11

Place	Date	Hour	Summary of Events and Information Refce Map Sheet 57B 51A.	Remarks and references to Appendices
QUIÉVY (D19.b7.7)	23.10.18		142nd F.A. moved to SOLESMES during afternoon - location D6d4.0 (57B). Visited Brigade in SOLESMES and then reconnoitred around ROMERIES and met Major WRIGHT there where he had located his bearers and had a Car Post. Wounded evacuated from here to MDS SOLESMES.	
SOLESMES (D6d.4.0)	"	1700hrs	Went up to Car Post in ROMERIES (W21c8.6) 51A. Owing to the bridge having been destroyed - wounded have to be transhipped from cars on E. side of stream hand-carried, and placed in cars on the west side. The site of this Exchange Post is W21d4.9. Cars have been taken round and run between ROMERIES and a Car Post established by Major WRIGHT at LE TROUSSE MINON. W17d0.7. Inspected this post with Major WRIGHT in the evening and visited 9th Inf Brigde HQ at the same location. All objectives were gained during the day's fighting. Casualties moderate; N. Fusiliers suffered most casualties, chiefly in officers. The line runs some 1500 yards South of RUESNES. An ADS has been opened by 8th FA at ESCARMAIN. The 9th Brig. will attack again to-morrow morning. Weather fine.	
"	24.10.18.		Went up to Car Post W17d0.7. where OC Bearers was also located, at 0500hrs.	

Instructions regarding War Diaries and Intelligence Summaries are contained in F. S. Regs., Part II. and the Staff Manual respectively. Title pages will be prepared in manuscript.

WAR DIARY
or
~~INTELLIGENCE~~ SUMMARY.
(Erase heading not required.)

O.C. 142nd Field Ambulance.

Army Form C. 2118.

Folio 12.

Place	Date	Hour	Summary of Events and Information Ref. Maps 57B. 51A.	Remarks and references to Appendices
SOLESMES (D6d.40)	24.10.18		Evacuation proceeded smoothly. R.A.P.s were established during the morning in valley between ESCARMAIN and PONT à PIERRES. They moved forward, as action progressed, to the valley 2500 yards N.E. in squares R.25, R26. Line held N.E. of RUESNES but railway objective had not been gained. 142nd F.A. Car Post was moved forward to R.31 b 4.0. evacuation by car thence to A.D.S. at ESCARMAIN. Orders received to open a M.D.S. at VERTAIN in the afternoon. necessary arrangements made accordingly. In afternoon this order was cancelled and 1?7th F.A was ordered to open a M.D.S. in ESCARMAIN. 142nd F.A. Post at W17d0.7. continued to function as a Walking Wounded Collect. Post throughout the day — evacuation by Horsed ambul. wagons to M.D.S. Received Orders to open an A.D.S in BEAUDIGNIES. This is only to be done when R.A.P.s move forward, as they are located at present in line and between BEAUDIGNIES and M.D.S. Visited O.C. Bearers again in afternoon also A.D.M.S. in SOLESMES.	(initials)
"	25.10.18		The Car Post at R31 b 4.0. which was formed yesterday afternoon was opened to-day as a small A.D.S. also as a Walking Wounded. C.P.	

2353 Wt. W2544/1454 700,000 5/15 D. D. & L. A.D.S.S./Forms/C. 2118.

Instructions regarding War Diaries and Intelligence Summaries are contained in F. S. Regs., Part II. and the Staff Manual respectively. Title pages will be prepared in manuscript.

WAR DIARY
or
~~INTELLIGENCE SUMMARY.~~
(Erase heading not required.)

Army Form C. 2118.

O.C.
142nd Field Ambulance.

Folio 13.

Place	Date	Hour	Summary of Events and Information Ref. Maps. 51A. 57B.	Remarks and references to Appendices
SOLESMES D6d.4.0	25.10.18		The route to MDS at ESCARMAIN has been well flagged. Patrols sent out to the Railway report no enemy there. 9th Inf Brig. are consolidating their line N.E. of RUESNES between that village and the Railway. 8th Inf. Brig. will attack in morning. 8th FA. have found a site for an ADS in RUESNES at same location as RAP 4th/R.F.s. in R20d.2.4. Major SHIELDS RAMC returned from leave to-day. Weather dull but fine.	See Appendix VII
"	26.10.18		9th Inf. Brig. is now in support - 8th Inf. Brig. in the line - 76th Brig. moving up. Inspected RAPS and ADS to-day which is combined with the Car Relay Post at R31 b 4.0 - 1 NCO. 3 nursing Orderlies under Capt. MANN RAMC (142nd FA) at this site. Orders received from ADMS to be prepared to move 142nd FA forward to LE TROUSSE MINON to-morrow - should 3rd Division move on across railway line - and to reconnoitre for an A.D.S. further forward. Weather fine.	
"	27.10.18.		3rd Div. RAMC. O.O. No124 received confirming the above order. At 1600 hrs. order was given for unit to move up the same evening to LE TROUSSE MINON, but this was afterwards postponed until early to-morrow morning. 9th Brig. is in reserve. An ADS has been opened by 8th FA. at RUESNES (R20 b1.1.)	

Instructions regarding War Diaries and Intelligence Summaries are contained in F. S. Regs., Part II. and the Staff Manual respectively. Title pages will be prepared in manuscript.

WAR DIARY
or
~~INTELLIGENCE SUMMARY.~~
(Erase heading not required.)

Army Form C. 2118.

Folio 14.

O.C.
142nd Field Ambulance.

Place	Date	Hour	Summary of Events and Information Ref. Map Sheets. 51A. 57B.	Remarks and references to Appendices
SOLESMES D6d.4.0	27.10.18		Arrangements made to open an ADS. beyond RUESNES, in the event of a withdrawal of the enemy, and to reconnoitre roads in that locality as suitable for motor amb. cars. Visited 9th Inf. Brig. HQ to-day. Weather very wet towards evening.	
LE TROUSSE MINON. W17d1.8 (Sheet 51A)	28.10.18		142nd F.A. moved to W17d1.8 at 07.30 hrs this morning. Owing to limited accommodation at this place, also to frequent shelling of the locality at nights, the Transport lines and bulk of personnel were encamped near the ESCARMAIN road at W11c8.2. The site at R31b4.0 is now used as a Car Relay Post for cars going up to Car Post at RUESNES (R20b.1.1); 1 N.C.O. & 3 men of Nursing Section and 4 Bearer Squads are located there. ADMS. called at W17d1.7 in morning. In the afternoon met ADMS at ROMERIES to arrange for medical attendance on numerous civilian refugees who were sick in the village. Capt. CLARK was detailed for this duty, and he formed an aid post for this purpose in the village. Weather fine & dry. Major SHIELDS RAMC has gone to ADMS office on temporary duty as DADMS whilst latter is on leave. Visited 9th Inf. Brig. HQ to-day.	
"	29.10.18		9th Inf. Brig. O.O. No 43 received re move of 9th Inf. Brig. to SOLESMES to-day on relief by a Brigade of 2nd Division. Orders for move of 142nd F.A. to SOLESMES issued and arrangements made for billetting the ambulance on its arrival. 142nd F.A. moved at 14.00 hrs to SOLESMES.	Appendix VIII
SOLESMES (E1c3.2) (Sheet 57B)	"	16.00 hrs.	HQ. 142nd FA opened at this site on arrival. Transport is billetted in Factory at D6d.4.0. 9th Inf. Brig. O.O. No 44 and 3rd Div RAMC O.O. No 125 received. These orders detail the 9th Inf. Brig. and 142nd FA to move on 31.10.18 to CATTENIERES and the whole Division will come into Corps Reserve on that date.	

Instructions regarding War Diaries and Intelligence Summaries are contained in F. S. Regs., Part II. and the Staff Manual respectively. Title pages will be prepared in manuscript.

WAR DIARY
or
~~INTELLIGENCE SUMMARY.~~
(*Erase heading not required.*)

O.C.
142nd Field Ambulance

Army Form C. 2118.

Folio 15.

Place	Date	Hour	Summary of Events and Information Ref. Sheets. 51A 57B.	Remarks and references to Appendices
SOLESMES (E1 c 3.2)	29.10.18.		Car Relay Post at R31 b 4.0 and billets in W17d 1.8 were closed down this morning as 2nd Division did not wish to take over these sites. Weather fine. Wind S.W.	
"	30.10.18		Inspected all transport this morning. Several cases of diarrhoea have suddenly occurred in the unit; none, however, very serious. The only cause that I can assign to it at present is that the men may have eaten vegetables contaminated with Mustard Gas. Many cabbages were growing in the fields where severe fighting has recently taken place and may thus contain some of the liquid on the leaves. Further investigations are being made. Orders issued for move to CATTENIERES tomorrow.	Appendix IX
CATTENIÈRES (H12 c 9.9.)	31.10.18.		142nd F.A. marched at 08.14 hrs this morning to CATTENIERES under 9th Infy Brig. arrangements. HQ opened here at 1200 hrs. Rest Station for Brigade Sick opened at same site during afternoon. Weather fair, rather cold.	
			~~Summary of operations during the month.~~ During the month of October the 3rd Division has been almost continuously engaged in active operations. 142nd F. Amb. was in action from 5.10.18 to 9.10.18 in the MASNIERES-RUMILLY sector, affiliated to 9th Inf. Brig. during its attack on SERANVILLERS. Evacuation of wounded was carried out by Bearer Division under Major WRIGHT and Capt. POTTER, M.C. Early forward reconnaissance enabled cars to be pushed well ahead of MASNIERES - all wounded being promptly cleared. 142nd F.A. was then in rest at NOYELLES for a week. On 23.10.18. the unit went into action again in front of SOLESMES. Major WRIGHT and Capt. CLARKE were i/c of Bearers. An ADS under Capt. MANN was opened at R31 b 4.0 on 24.10.18. The unit was relieved in the line on 29.10.18.	

C. D. Chambers
Lieut. Colonel RAMC
O.C. 142nd F. Ambce

(A7092). Wt. W12839/M1293. 750,000. 1/17. D. D. & L., Ltd. Forms/C.2118/14.

Copy No 2

SECRET

App I

M.A. 55

A.D.M.S. 3rd Division

Ref Maps 57 B., 57 C.

8.10.18

SITUATION REPORT. 142 Field Ambulance

Time 09.00 hours.

1. 2 Bearer Squads with R.A.P's situated as follows:-

Northumberland Fusiliers	G.27.b.1.8.
Royal Fusiliers	G.22.c.8.5.
King's Liverpools	G.22.c.3.4.

2. Bearer Relay Post G.19.d.9.7.
(3 Squads, 2 wheeled stretchers)
Amb. Car Collect. Post. G.22.c.7.6.
(Capt POTTER & 1 squad)

3. H.Q. 142 Field Amb and 8 Bearers
Squads in reserve G.26.c.6.5

4. Walking Wounded Collecting Station, L 30.c.0.8.
(Tent Division personnel)
H. Amb. Wagons, A.D.S. Limber, Water Cart.
Lorries evacuate from here to M.D.S. RIBECOURT - Horse Ambulance Wagons supplement A.D.S. (7 FA) in evacuations.

5. Routes of Evacuation - Two.
(A) Left Sector - From R.A.P.s at G.22.c.8.5 where a Car Collecting Post (future ADS in event of R.A.P's moving forward) is stationed at G.22.c.7.6. Thence by Car through G.21 c & a, G 20 d and c, past (old) ADS, 8 FA, where a Car Relay Post has been formed, and on to M.D.S. RIBECOURT via MARCOING.
(B) Right Sector from R.A.P's at G.27 b.1.8. by hand carriage to Bearer Relay Post at G.27.a.2.8. Thence by wheeled Stretcher across Canal Bridge to ADS (7 FA) G.26.c.6.5. Road to this Relay Post is at present unfit for Ambulance Cars on account of debris lying about.

6. Evacuation has proceeded smoothly - No congestion reported from any post.

(Sd) G. O. Chambers
Lieut Colonel
OC 142 Field Amb.

E O Chambers
Lieut. Col.
, R.A.M.C.
COMDG: 142ND FIELD AMBULANCE

Copy No 2

SECRET App II

MA 56.

Ref Maps 57B, 57C

Staff Captain
9th Inf Bde

Time 11·00 hours
8·10·18.

SITUATION REPORT 142 Field Ambulance

1. H.Q. 142 F.A. — (Brewery) G.26.c.6.5

2. Bearer Relay Post G.19.d.9.7
(for Northumberland Fusiliers)

3. Ambulance Car Post G.22.c.7.6.
(for Kings + Royal Fusiliers)

4. Walking Wounded L.30.c.0.8.
Collecting Station

Adv. Dressing Station (7 FA.) G.26.c.5.5.
Main Dressing Station (8 FA) L.25.b.3.5.

(Sd) E O Chambers
Lieut Col
OC 142 FA.

E O Chambers
Lieut. Col.
.... R.A.M.C.
COMDG: 142ND FIELD AMBULANCE

MA/66 (no5) Appendix III Copy No 2

Orders by Lieut-Col. C.O.Chambers R.A.M.C.

Commanding No.142 Field Ambulance.

1. Reveille at 6.00 hours on 13/10/18.
Breakfast at 6.30 "

2. Tents will be struck and packed on their respective wagons by 9.00.hours.

3. Wagons will be loaded under the supervision of Capt.Potter,and loading will be completed by 9.30.hours.

4. Excess stores will be collected outside Qr.Mr's Stores,transport of which will be arranged by Capt.Potter.

5. Blankets surplus to those carried on G.S.Wagons and Limbers will be rolled in bundles of ten and placed in a Horsed Ambulance wagon.

6. Officers' Kits will be loaded on "A" and "B" Baggage Wagons.

7. The Unit will be ready to move by 10.00 hours in full marching order on receipt of further instructions.
Major Wright will be in charge of Bearer Division and Captain Mann in charge of Tent Division and Horse Transport on the march.

C.O. Chambers

Lieut-Col. R.A.M.C.
Comdg. 142 Field Ambulance.

12/10/18.

Secret.

App IV

Warning Order by Lieut-Col., G.O.CHAMBERS., R.A.M.C.
Commanding No. 142 Field Ambulance.

1. Reveille at 06-00 hours 20/10/18.
Breakfast at 06-30 hours "

2. No. 142 Field Ambulance with all transport will be prepared to move at 09-00 hours.

3. Patients in hospital will be evacuated to C.C.S. by 08-00 hours under arrangements to be made by Capt H.L.MANN., R.A.M.C.

4. Excess stores will be collected outside Q.M's Stores and placed in No. 142 Field Ambulance Section of the Divisional R.A.M.C. Dump. Major C.S.E.WRIGHT., R.A.M.C. will be responsible that this isdone by 08-30 hours.

5. All blankets issued under G.R.O.419 and Mobilization Equipment will be carried, rolled in bundles of ten,on G.S.Wagons, Limbers and Horsed Ambulance Wagons as heretofore.

6. Water Carts will be filled with chlorinated water by 08-00 hours.

7. Officers' Kits will be loaded on "A" & "B" Baggage Wagons by 08-30 hours.

8. Capt MANN will be responsible that all canvas is struck and loaded on wagons by 08-30 hours. He will also supervise the loading of the wagons generally which will be completed by the above hour.

9. One N.C.O. and 2 Men will remain behind in charge of the Divisional Dump, for the safe custody of which they will be responsible. They will be rationed from the 21st inst by the Area Commandant MARCOING.

10. Detailed orders for move will be issued later.

G.O.Chambers

Lieut-Colonel., R.A.M.C.
Comdg No. 142 Field Ambulance.

19/10/18.

Orders by Lieut-Colonel., G.O.CHAMBERS., R.A.M.C.
Commanding No. 142 Field Ambulance.

App V Secret

No 6.

1. No. 142 Field Ambulance will march to BEVILLERS at 10-45 hours to-day.

2. The Unit will be in full marching order, and will march in rear of 9th Bde H.Q. & 9th T.M.Bty arriving at cross-roads G.15.d.3.9. RUMILLY at 12-05 hours.

3. Capt MANN., R.A.M.C. will proceed by Ambulance Car at 10-30 hours to meet Staff Capt. at BEVILLERS Church at 12-00 hours. 1 N.C.O. & 3 men will form this Billeting party. Capt MANN will arrange for a guide to be left at this point to direct No. 142 Field Ambulance and Motor Ambulance Cars, which proceed independently to the Billeting site allotted by the Staff Captain.

4. Sgt SHARP. A.S.C.(M.T.) will remain at H.Q. NOYELLES to direct all motor ambulances to Church at BEVILLERS and will himself proceed by the last car returning from C.C.S.s. (Sick evacuation)

Issued at 09-50 hours
20/10/18.

G.O. Chambers
Lieut-Col., R.A.M.C.
Comdg No. 142 Field Ambulance.

Secret.

~~Operation~~ Orders by Lieut-Col. G.O.CHAMBERS., R.A.M.C.
No 6 A. Commanding No. 142 Field Ambulance.

Ref. Sheet 57B. 1/40000 22/10/18.

1. No 142 Field Ambulance will move this evening to QUIEVY under Brigade arrangements.

2. The usual distance will be maintained during the march, strictest attention being paid to march discipline.

3. A billetting party of 1 N.C.O. and 3 men under O.C. 142 Field Ambulance will leave H.Qrs. at 1630 hours by Amb. car.

4. All baggage, surgical and medical equipment will be packed on their respective wagons by 1700 hours.
Capt H.L.MANN., R.A.M.C. will supervise the loading and be responsible for its correct distribution.

5. Officers' Kits and Mess equipment will be packed and loaded on "A" & "B" Baggage Wagons by 1700 hours.

6. Sgt G.H.SHARP., A.S.C.(M.T.) will conduct the Heavy Amb. Cars to No 7 Field Ambulance M.D.S. at QUIEVY to form a pool, to arrive there by 1800hours. Sgt SHARP will remain there for temporary duty.

7. Major C.S.E.WRIGHT. R.A.M.C. with Capt H.L.MANN.,R.A.M.C will march the Field Ambulance to QUIEVY, following in rear of 56 Field Coy R.E. The starting point will be the cross-roads BEVILLERS C.22.d.3.1., time 1904 hours.

8. A guide will be posted at the Balloon site, western edge of QUIEVY to conduct the Field Ambulance to its billets.

G.O. Chambers.

Lieut-Colonel., R.A.M.C.
Comdg No. 142 Field Ambulance.

Secret. App VI

ADDENDUM TO ~~OPERATION ORDER~~ ORDERS No 6. BY LIEUT-COL. G.O.CHAMBERS., R.A.M.C.
COMMANDING NO 142 FIELD AMBULANCE.

---

1. The Horsed Ambulance Wagons will proceed to the M.D.S. QUIEVY (No 7 F.A.) to arrive there at 18-00 hours.

2. One Horsed Ambulance Wagon will proceed to the cemetery at the junction of the SOLESMES-BRIASTRE-QUIEVY Road to take Walking Wounded to the M.D.S. QUIEVY.

3. One R.A.M.C. man in addition to the Wagon Orderly, will be with this wagon.

4. Sgt MOORE will proceed with a mounted orderly this afternoon to locate the exact position of the cemetery referred to in para. 2.

G O Chambers

Lieut-Colonel., R.A.M.C.
Comdg No 142 Field Ambulance.

22/10/18.

Orders by Lieut-Colonel G.O.CHAMBERS., R.A.M.C. SECRET. Appendix VII.
(107) Comdg No. 142 Field Ambulance.

Ref Sheet 51A 25.10.18.

1. An Advanced Dressing Station will be opened forthwith at the present Bearer Post at R.31.b.4.0. One N.C.O. and 3 Nursing Orderlies with sufficient Medical and Surgical Equipment will proceed there forthwith. Capt H.L.MANN., R.A.M.C. will be in charge of A,D.S.
2. As soon as R.A.Ps. move forward to RUESNES an A.D.S. will be opened at BEAUDIGNIES near the RUESNES Road and the former A.D.S. will close down.
3. 1 Motor Ambulance Car will be stationed at the A.D.S.
4. The Bearer Post will still be located at the same site, R.31.b.4.0. One loading party (1 squad) will be kept there. Squads in reserve will remain at W.W.C.P. in W.17.d.1.8.
5. Walking Wounded C.P. One N.C.O. and 3 men will be detailed for this post. H.Qrs Bearers will remain at W.17.d.1.8. for the present, and H.Qrs 142 Field Ambulance will remain at SOLESMES (D.6.d.4.0.) (57B)

G.O.Chambers.

12-00 hours
25/10/18.

Lieut-Colonel., R.A.M.C.
Comdg No. 142 Field Ambulance.

-After Order

1. A Walking Wounded Collecting Post will be opened forthwith at R.31.b.4.0. Directing Boards will be placed at suitable points along road through R.31.b. & a., Q.26.d.c., Q.35.d. to M.D.S. ESCARMAIN.
2. Capt MANN., R.A.M.C. will be responsible that this is carried out.
3. The present W.W.C.P. will remain open for stragglers.

G.O.Chambers.

12-50 hours
25/10/18.

Lieut-Colonel., R.A.M.C.
Comdg No. 142 Field Ambulance.

Orders by Lieut-Col., G.O.CHAMBERS., R.A.M.C. SECRET. Appendix VIII
(408) Comdg No. 142 Field Ambulance.

1. 142 Field Ambulance will march to SOLESMES at 14-00 hours to-day.
2. Transport to be loaded by 13-00 hours. Capt MANN., R.A.M.C. will be responsible that this is correctly carried out.
3. A Billeting Party of 1 N.C.O. & 6 men will proceed at 12-00 hours punctually to SOLESMES and will meet O.C. opposite A.D.M.S. office on arrival. Out of this party a guide will be sent by O.C. to the junction of roads at PIGEON BLANC to await arrival of F.A. and conduct to the allotted billets.
4. The personnel (Bearers) - Car Relay Post, R.31.b.4.0. will be withdrawn this morning. The personnel (Nursing Section) will remain with Medical & Surgical Equipment ,also 2 stretchers, until relieved by personnel of a Field Ambulance of the 2nd Division.
A car of 142 F.A. will be sent there early this afternoon and convey this personnel and equipment on relief. The car will then proceed to SOLESMES and ask for location of 142 F.A. from A.D.M.S. office.
5. Major WRIGHT will be in charge of Unit on the march.

G.O. Chambers

11-30 hours
29/10/18.

Lieut-Colonel., R.A.M.C.
Comdg No. 142 Field Ambulance.

Appendix IX

~~OPERATION~~ ORDERS (No. 9) BY LIEUT-COL., G.O. CHAMBERS., R.A.M.C. **SECRET**
COMMANDING FIELD AMBULANCE.

Ref. Sheet 57B. 1/40000 30/10/18.

1. No. 142 Field Ambulance will march tomorrow, starting from the road junction outside present H.Qrs. at ~~XX-XX~~ 08-14 hours.
2. The strictest attention must be paid to march discipline and adherence to the time given for moving off. The Unit will halt at 10 minutes to the clock hour during the march. 300 yards distance between Units will be maintained.
3. Reveille will be at 06-00, Breakfast at ~~07-00~~ 06-30 hours.
4. All equipment will be packed on transport by 07-30. The Unit will be ready to move off at 08-00 from the starting point. Transport will march 100 yards im rear of Field Ambulance personnel, the head being stationed by 08-00 at the edge of the road where it is at present encamped, and ready to follow on in rear of the personnel when the latter passes this point. 50 yards section interval will be maintained between sections of transport.
5. Capt. H.L. MANN., R.A.M.C. will be responsible for the loading of transport and for its march discipline during the move.
6. Bearer and Tent Division personnel will parade in full marching order at 07-50 hours, under Major. C.S.E. WRIGHT., RA.M.C. and will be by the starting point at 08-00 hours ready to move off.
7. Motor transport will move in charge of Sgt SHARP. A.S.C.(M.T.) to the new location at 08-00 hours He will take 1 N.C.O. & 1 man as a holding party and will meet O.C. 142 Field Ambulance at the Church in CATTENIERES at 10-30 hours.

Issued at 18.00 hrs.

G.O. Chambers.

Lieut-Colonel., R.A.M.C.
Comdg No. 142 Field Ambulance.

14 Confidential VR40

Nov. 1918

14/3601

WAR DIARY

OF

No 142 FIELD AMBULANCE

From 1 Nov 1918 To 30 Nov 1918

Instructions regarding War Diaries and Intelligence Summaries are contained in F. S. Regs., Part II. and the Staff Manual respectively. Title pages will be prepared in manuscript.

WAR DIARY
or
~~INTELLIGENCE SUMMARY.~~
(Erase heading not required.)

Army Form C. 2118.

Folio 5.

O.C.
142nd Field Ambulance.

Place	Date	Hour	Summary of Events and Information Ref. Map. 57B	Remarks and references to Appendices
CATTENIÈRES (H12C.9.9)	1.11.18		Brigade Rest Station opened. All equipment unloaded and inspected to-day. 9th Inf. Brig. Order No 45 received. Weather fair. Wind S.W.	
"	2.11.18		Attended conference of OCs FAs at ADMS office this morning. The following was discussed: (1) Marquees at the Dump to be taken over by CCS at AWOINGT. (2) 4 CCS opens at SOLESMES tomorrow. (3) Oxygen cylinders to be carried by FAs. (4) Instructions re prevention of Trench Foot to be issued shortly and a mixture of Whale Oil and Mustard to be drawn from No 7 F.A. later on. (5) Bunion Ripley [illegible] 500 Calomel tubes to be drawn from ADD Dept M.S by each F.A. (6) Strict precautions to be taken against the spread of Influenza. In the afternoon I visited the 3rd Div. Medical Dump at NOYELLES to arrange about the marquees (re above) and called on SMO at AWOINGT to arrange for their collection. Amendments to 9th Inf. Brig. OO. No 45 received. Weather fine.	C.E. Chambers Lieut Col RAMC
"	3.11.18		9th Inf. Brig. Group moved by route march to QUIEVY to-day leaving CATTENIÈRES at 11.30 hours. Orders for the move attached.	(1) Appendix I
QUIEVY (D19 b6.6)	"	12.00	Arrived at QUIEVY – good billets – plenty of accommodation. Visited ADMS office & in the evening 8th Brigade HQ. Captain HARMAN'S RAMC proceeded to-day as MO. to 7/K.S.L.I. Some rain, otherwise fair. Wind S.W.	
"	4.11.18		ADMS called this morning. Moving of Fd Ambulances forward as M.D.S in the event of action & arrangements [illegible] for the carrying of extra supplies to be obtained [illegible]	(1)

(A7092). Wt. W12839/M1293. 75,050. 1/17. D. D. & L., Ltd. Forms/C.2118/14.

Instructions regarding War Diaries and Intelligence Summaries are contained in F. S. Regs., Part II. and the Staff Manual respectively. Title pages will be prepared in manuscript.

WAR DIARY
or
~~INTELLIGENCE SUMMARY.~~
(*Erase heading not required.*)

Army Form C. 2118.

Folio 2

O.C.
142nd Field Ambulance

Place	Date	Hour	Summary of Events and Information Ref. Map. 57 B 51 A	Remarks and references to Appendices
QUIÉVY (D19 b6.6)	4.11.18		A small Rest Station opened for reception of sick. Weather changeable.	(cd)
			An epidemic of P.U.O. has again arisen. Cases are isolated and those showing persistent symptoms, rise of temperature etc. are	
"	5.11.18.		transferred to Corps Rest Station at CARNIERES. Weather wet and dull.	(cd)
			Number of cases of P.U.O. to-day in unit was 7.	
"	6.11.18.		The outbreak of P.U.O. has extended to the 142nd FA, attacking chiefly the Horse Transport personnel - out of a total of 35 - 11 have gone down with this complaint and been transferred to C.R.S. - CARNIERES. Prompt measures of disinfection have been carried out (fumigation by formalin, washing floors with cresol) and arrangements made for a twice daily parade of the unit for gargling a disinfectant gargle. This gargle consists of Liq. Cresolis 1 dram. Chloroform 10 minims & Water 1 pint.	
			Number of cases reported with P.U.O. to-day in the unit was 5.	(cd)
"	7.11.18		Work of disinfection of all billets occupied by 142nd FA carried on. P.U.O. is not prevalent as far in the Infantry of 9th Brigade. There has been a marked decrease to-day in the P.U.O. outbreak. 1 case only (H.T personnel) reported with P.U.O. Weather cold - humid - rain. Unsettled weather continues.	(cd)
" ROMERIES (W21 b5.0)	8.11.18	1400 hrs	Brigade moved to ROMERIES to-day and 142nd FA opened a Rest Station at W22 c4.0. HQ at W21 b5.0. Orders for the March issued on leaving QUIÉVY.	Appendix II

(A7092). Wt. W12539/M1293. 75,000. 1/17. D. D. & L., Ltd. Forms/C.2118/14.

Instructions regarding War Diaries and Intelligence Summaries are contained in F. S. Regs., Part II. and the Staff Manual respectively. Title pages will be prepared in manuscript.

WAR DIARY
or
~~INTELLIGENCE SUMMARY.~~
(Erase heading not required.)

Army Form C. 2118.

O.C.
142nd Field Ambulance. Folio 3

Place	Date	Hour	Summary of Events and Information Sheet 57A 1/40.000 / " 51 "	Remarks and references to Appendices
ROMERIES (W21 b 5.0)	9.11.18		The outbreak of P.U.O. in the unit has subsided - Slight cases are being treated in the Rest Station - others are evacuated to C.C.S. SOLESMES. Sent car to NOYELLES to bring forward as much stores as possible to Dump at SOLESMES. A certain quantity of C.C.S. marquee material is still at former dump - S.M.O. C.C.S. AWOINGT group informed of this and asked to clear as early as possible. Orders received from 9th Inf. Brigade for march to FRASNOY tomorrow. Marching Orders for Ambulance issued accordingly at 22.00 hrs this evening. Weather fine, cold at night. Wind N.W.	Appendix III
FRASNOY (M10 b.6.6) Sheet 51	10.11.18		F.A. marched at 08.00 hrs to FRASNOY arriving there at 14.00 hrs. Delay was owing to heavy traffic on the line of march. Evacuated six sick (including one old S.I. wound) to 143 F.A. at ROMERIES for C.C.S. This was done under A.D.M.S. instructions. Billets here are very poor overcrowding is unavoidable and the place is very dirty. Orders received from the Brigade at about 18.00 hrs for continuance of the march tomorrow to LA LONGUEVALLE. Orders accordingly issued.	
"	11.11.18	06.30 08.30	Orders received at 06.00 hrs from Brigade cancelling all movement for to-day. Verbal news circulated that Armistice has been signed and that hostilities cease at 11.00 hrs to-day - confirmed by wire shortly afterwards. The 9th Inf. Brigade Group is remaining in FRASNOY for the present. Weather fine - cold.	

(A7092). Wt. W12839/M1293 75,000. 1/17. D. D. & L., Ltd. Forms/C.2118/14.

Instructions regarding War Diaries and Intelligence Summaries are contained in F. S. Regs., Part II. and the Staff Manual respectively. Title pages will be prepared in manuscript.

WAR DIARY
or
~~INTELLIGENCE SUMMARY.~~
(Erase heading not required.)

O.C. 142nd Field Ambulance

Army Form C. 2118.

Folio 4

Place	Date	Hour	Summary of Events and Information Sheet 51 1/40000	Remarks and references to Appendices
FRASNOY (M10 b.6.6.)	12.11.18.		Address given by G.O.C. 3rd Division to 9th Inf. Brigade Group this morning at which 142nd F.A. attended. The outline of demobilisation scheme and educational scheme were explained to the troops and the news that 3rd Division had been selected to march into GERMANY was given out: exact details as to location and date of march will be notified later. C.O's Parade of F. Amb. at 14.00 hrs – a short address followed by outline of work in training and general improvement of quarters etc. and the reasons for this being carried out in the next few days was explained to the men. Capt. CLARKE RAME sent to 34 CCS with P.U.O. Weather fine and cold at night. Wind N.	
"	13.11.18.		Attended Conference of O.C's F.A's at office of ADMS in FRASNOY. Points of discussion concerned future line of march and the work of training in march discipline and general turn-out of ambulances. Scheme of training for 142nd F. Amb. set out for the next 4 days. Visited No 8 F.A. Dump at SOLESMES with DADMS 3rd Division. Arranged with (1) OC 34 CCS to take in all medl and surgl stores from the dump; (2) R.O.O. SOLESMES to take over all Ordnance stores; (3) R.S.O to take over all ASC supplies. 142nd F.A. Dump at NOYELLES was finally cleared today. Receipt obtained for those stores handed into No 8 F.A. Dump. Weather fine and cold.	See Appendix IV

(A7092). Wt W12839/M1293 75,000. 1/17. D. D. & L., Ltd. Forms/C.2118/14.

Instructions regarding War Diaries and Intelligence Summaries are contained in F. S. Regs., Part II. and the Staff Manual respectively. Title pages will be prepared in manuscript.

WAR DIARY
or
~~INTELLIGENCE SUMMARY.~~
(Erase heading not required.)

O.C. 142nd Field Ambulance.

Army Form C. 2118.

Folio 5

Place	Date	Hour	Summary of Events and Information Sheet 51 1/40.000	Remarks and references to Appendices
FRASNOY (M.10 B6.6)	14.11.18		Programme of Training being carried out. All M.E on transport checked and re-loaded. 3rd Division is under orders to march on 16th inst. en route for COBLENZ to occupy the bridgehead on the RHINE during Peace Negotiations and period of Armistice. Roadspace of a F.A. compiled and sent to ADMS. Weather fine cold at night.	Appendix V (207)
"	15.11.18.		Training continued to-day, arrangements made for handing in surplus stores to DADOS and for sending other stores by lorry under Brigade arrangements. Orders 9th Inf. Brig. No 48 received for move of Brig group to-morrow. Orders - F. Amb. No 13. issued	Appendix VI (208)
"	16.11.18.		F.A. marched to LA LONGUEVILLE this morning, arriving at 1400 hrs. The weather was very cold but fine and the march was carried out in good time. The F.A. was well turned out, good march discipline maintained for which appreciation was received from B.G. and ADMS. 1 MAC car joined for temporary duty	
LA LONGUEVILLE (136 a6.3)	16.11.18	14.00 hrs.	to assist in evacuation along line of march. Orders received from Brigade for to-morrow's march - which was later cancelled. Weather continues cold and fine	(209)
"	17.11.18		F.A. is located in good billets. All horses are under cover. Clipping is being carried out. Brig. Group is not moving to-day. Wind N.E. Weather very cold. Wind N.	(210)

(A7092). Wt. W12839/M1293 75,0.0. 1/17. D. D. & L., Ltd. Forms/C.2118/14.

Instructions regarding War Diaries and Intelligence Summaries are contained in F. S. Regs., Part II. and the Staff Manual respectively. Title pages will be prepared in manuscript.

WAR DIARY
or
~~INTELLIGENCE SUMMARY.~~
(Erase heading not required.)

Army Form C. 2118.

O.C.
142nd Field Ambulance
Folio 6

Place	Date	Hour	Summary of Events and Information	Remarks and references to Appendices
			Ref. Maps. VALENCIENNES 1/100,000 NAMUR 1/100,000	
LA LONGUEVILLE	18.11.18.		142nd F.A. moved this afternoon at 14.00 hrs. to SOUS-LE-BOIS with "B" Group. Orders for the march issued, based on 9th Inf. Brig O.O. No 49. Standing orders for the march, regarding Dress, Discipline and loading of Transport issued to the unit.	Appendix VII Appendix VIII
HOSPICE " SOUS-LE-BOIS			Unit arrived in new destination at 16.30 hrs. Good billets and ample accomodation. Sick are evacuated to No 5 CCS in the same locality.	
			Weather. Milder. Rain in evening	(20)
"	19.11.18.		"B" Group did not move today. Capt. CLARKE RAMC. returned from 34 CCS - SOLESMES. Order No 50 (9th Inf. Brig.) received for the move tomorrow to COLLERET. F.A. orders issued accordingly.	Appendix IX
			Weather. dull. very foggy at night.	(20)
"	20.11.18		F. Amb. marched to COLLERET this morning. G.O.C. inspected "B" Group marching past & the march was carried out in good time, muddy underfoot - Unit arrived at new billets	
COLLERET. " (NAMUR) 3A.9.1		11.30	at 11.30 hrs leaving former place at 09.00 hrs. Visited ADMS at COUSOLRE re. duties as S.M.O. "B" group and facilities for carrying out disinfection and Sanitation. ADMS has detailed 1 NCO and 3 men of Sanitary Section - to 9th Inf. Brig. H.Q. and these men will be available for these duties.	
			Weather fine in morning very misty & rain at night	(20)
			There will be no move tomorrow. No further moves will take place pending improvement of Railway and Road Communications	

(A7092). Wt. W12839/M1293. 750,000. 1/17. D. D. & L., Ltd. Forms/C.2118/14.

Instructions regarding War Diaries and Intelligence Summaries are contained in F. S. Regs., Part II. and the Staff Manual respectively. Title pages will be prepared in manuscript.

WAR DIARY
or
~~INTELLIGENCE SUMMARY.~~
(Erase heading not required.)

Army Form C. 2118.

Folio 7

O.C.
142nd Field Ambulance.

Place	Date	Hour	Summary of Events and Information Ref: Map. NAMUR (8) 1/100,000.	Remarks and references to Appendices
COLLERET (3A9.1)	21.11.18.		Route march in the morning. ADMS visited ambulance mid-day. Recreation – football – in the afternoon. Weather fine – very cold at night.	(initials)
"	22.11.18		Squad and Section drill in the morning – recreation in the afternoon. The billets in this village are very good – ample and comfortable quarters for the men. Health of troops continues very good. Weather fine – frost throughout the day and night.	(initials)
"	23.11.18		9th Inf. Brig. Order No 51 detailing move of "B" group tomorrow. F.A. Transport has now been divided into First and Second Line Transport. In the former – all water carts, maltese cart and 3 L.G.S. wagons are included; in the latter – 5 G.S. wagons (Medical Store and Baggage) + L.G.S. wagon (Cook's Limber) and 3 Horse-Amb. wagons will accompany marching personnel of F. Ambce. F.A. Orders (No 16) issued re march.	Appendix X Appendix XI
BIERCÉE (3D.2.8)	24.11.18.		Weather continues fine and cold. 142nd F.A. marched to BIERCÉE today, arriving at 13.30. Wind N. The march was completed in very good time, weather was cold and dry. Billets not so good as before. Rain towards evening. Orders received for move to MARBAIX tomorrow. F.A. Orders issued	(initials) (initials) Appendix XII
MARBAIX (3E 45.90)	25.11.18		Arrived at MARBAIX at 14.00 hrs. good billets. orders received to move to GOUGNIES area. Weather drizzled – wet underfoot.	Appendix XIII (initials)

(A5092) Wt. W42839/M1293 75 4000 1/17 D. D. & L. Ltd. Forms/C2118/12.

Instructions regarding War Diaries and Intelligence Summaries are contained in F. S. Regs., Part II. and the Staff Manual respectively. Title pages will be prepared in manuscript.

WAR DIARY
or
INTELLIGENCE SUMMARY.
(Erase heading not required.)

Army Form C. 2118.

O.C. No 142 Field Ambulance

Place	Date	Hour	Summary of Events and Information	Remarks and references to Appendices
VILLERS -POTERIE	26/11	am	Showery & cold day	1/100,000 NAMUR
			Arrived at VILLERS-POTERIE at 14.00 hours.	
		P.m.	Lieut Col CHAMBERS RAMC. Officer Commanding proceeded on leave to U.K. Major A.F.L. Shields RAMC assumed temporary command during his absence.	A.F.L.S.
	27/11		Showery day.	
			Orders received to move to ST GERARD ~~tomorrow morning~~	Appendix XIV
ST GERARD	28/11		Very wet day	A.F.L.S.
			Ambulance moved to ST GERARD and arrived at 13.00 hours. Rained most of the march.	App. XV
			Billets good.	
			Orders received for move to PURNODE	A.F.L.S.
	29/11		Dry day.	
PURNODE			Ambulance arrived at PURNODE at 13.30 hours. Brigadier General complimented the unit on their appearance and good marching. Orders received for march to SKEUVRE	A.F.L.S. App. XVI
SKEUVRE	30/11		Dry day.	
			Ambulance marched to SKEUVRE and arrived at 12.00 No men fell out. Visited ADMS office	A.F.L. Shields Major OC No 142 Field Amb.

Appendix 1. SECRET

Orders (No.10.) by Lieut-Colonel. G.O.CHAMBERS., R.A.M.C.
Comdg No. 142 Field Ambulance.

Ref. Sheet 57B. 1/40,000. **3.11.18.**

1. No.142 Field Ambulance will march to QUIEVY to-day; starting point will be at C.25.c.5.1. at 15-06 hours.
2. The Field Ambulance will be prepared to move off at 14-30. in order to reach the starting point at the above hour.
3. Dress- Full marching order. Water bottles to be filled with chlorinated water before moving off.
The strictest march discipline will be maintained throughout the march. 300 yards will be maintained between units, 50 yards section interval between transport.
4. Capt E.R.CLARKE., R.A.M.C. will arrange for closing down hospital and disposal of sick.
5. Major C.S.E.WRIGHT., R.A.M.C. will be in charge of personnel on the march and Capt H.L MANN., R.A.M.C. in charge of transport and loading of wagons.
6. All transport will be loaded according to Mobilization scale Attention is to be paid to disposition of loads on wagons. The loading will be completed by 14-00 hours.
7. A holding party of 1 N.C.O. and 3 men will proceed to QUIEVY at 11-00 hours.
8. Motor transport will move independently this afternoon at 15-00 hours by the main road BEAUVOIS-BEVILLERS under Sgt SHARP A.S.C.

G.O.Chambers

Lieut-Colonel., R.A.M.C.
Comdg No. 142 Field Ambulance.

Appendix II

Orders (No.11.) by Lieut-Col., C.O.CHAMBERS., R.A.M.C.
Comdg No. 142 Field Ambulance.

SECRET

Ref. 57B & 51A., 1/40,000 7.11.18

1. No. 142 Field Ambulance will march from QUIEVY at 10-17 hours the 8th. inst.
2. Reveille will be at 06-30 hours, Breakfast at 07-00 hours.
3. The Field Ambulance will be ready to move off from present billets at 09-30 hours.
Dress-Full marching order. Water bottles will be filled before moving off.
4. Loading of wagons will be carried out under the supervision of Capt. H.L.MANN., R.A.M.C. Such M.D.S. equipment as cannot be carried on transport will be left behind in i/c of a N.C.O. to be brought on to SOLESMES Dump (No.8 F.A.) by lorry later in the day.
5. Officers' Mess Equipment and Kits will be loaded on wagons by 09-00 hours.
6. Capt E.R.CLARKE., R.A.M.C. will arrange for collection of Regimental sick at 08-00 hours and their evacuation together with those in the Ambulance to C.R.S. directly afterwards He will proceed independently with Motor Ambulance Cars later to ROMERIES.
7. Major. C.S.E.WRIGHT., R.A.M.C. will proceed with billeting party (2.O.R) to ROMERIES in the Ford Car at 08-15 hours to meet Staff Captain there at 09-00 hours.

C.O.Chambers

Lieut-Colonel., R.A.M.C.
Comdg. No. 142 Field Ambulance.

Orders (No.12.) by Lieut-Col., G.O.CHAMBERS., R.A.M.C. Appendix III SECRET
Comdg No. 142 Field Ambulance.

Ref. Sheets 51A & 51., 1/40,000. 9.11.18.

1. No. 142 Field Ambulance will march with 9th Infantry Brigade Group to FRASNOY to-morrow the 10th inst. and will be ready to move at 09-00 hours.
2. Reveille will be at 06-00 hours, Breakfast at 06-30 hours.
3. Dress -full marching order. Water bottles will be filled prior to movim g off.
4. Sick in the Brigade Rest Station will be evacuated to C.C.S. at SOLESMES by 08-00 hours. The Rest Station will then close down. This will be carried out by Capt.E.R.CLARKE.,R.A.M.C.
5 All equipment stores etc will be properly loaded on wagons by 08-30 hours under the supervision of Capt.H.L.MANN., R.A.M.C.
Such M.D.S. equipment as cannot be carried on transport of unit will be sent to No.8 Field Ambulance Dump at SOLESMES and a receipt obtained on handing over.
6. Major.C.S.E.WRIGHT., R.A.M.C. will be in charge of the Field Ambulance during line of march. Capt. H.L.MANN., R.A.M.C. will be in charge of transport. The usual distances between sections will be maintained and the strictest attention to march discipline observed during the march.

G.O.Chambers

Lieut-Colonel., R.A.M.C.
Comdg No. 142 Field Ambulance.

Appendix IV

Orders by Lieut-Colonel. G.O.CHAMBERS., R.A.M.C.
Comdg No. 142 Field Ambulance.

13.11.18.

1. The Field Ambulance will go into Sectional Training forthwith. Commands of Sections will be allotted as follows:-

"A" Section --- Capt.J.POTTER.,M.C.,R.A.M.C.(Acting.)

"B" Section --- Major.C.S.E.WRIGHT.,R.A.M.C.

"C" Section ---Capt.H.L.MANN.,R.A.M.C.

2. The following time-table will be adhered to during course of training:-

	09-00--10-00	10-00--12-00	14-00--15-00
14.11.18.	Physical Ex. Squad Drill Sect. "	Section Equip. & Transport Fatigues. Misc. Duties.	Inspection by C.O. at 14-00 hours. Sectional Football
16.11.18.	-ditto-	-ditto-	Inspection Route March.
17.11.18.	-ditto-	-ditto-	Inspection Football.

3. On Saturday at 14-00 hours there will be a competition for the best turned out Section of the Ambulance,Personnel & Transport. Points will be given for Drill, Smartness & General Turnout. The A.D.M.S. has kindly consented to act as Judge.

4. Orderly Officers' & Orderly Sergeants' Duties will be fully carried out in accordance with Standing Orders.

5. Capt.J.POTTER.,M.C.,R.A.M.C. will see local village sick at M.I. Room, No. 85 Billet at 10-00 hours. Those unable to attend will be visited at their billets and treated accordingly.

G.O.Chambers

Lieut-Colonel., R.A.M.C.
Comdg No. 142 Field Ambulance.

13.11.18.

Appendix V.

A.D.M.S., 3rd Division.

The following is the actual road space to be allowed for a Field Ambulance on line of march.

Formed up as in detail below, this formation has been always adopted by No. 142 Field Ambulance and found most satisfactory for march discipline.

DETAIL.	ROAD SPACE.
1. Personnel	80 yards
2. Interval between Personnel & Transport	100 "
3. 1st Section of Transport (3 Horsed Ambulances & 3 G.S. Wagons.)	55 "
4. Interval between 1st & 2nd Sections	50 "
5. 2nd Section of Transport (3 G.S. Wagons & 3 Limb. G.S. Wagons.)	55 "
6. Interval between 2nd & 3rd Sections	50 "
7. 3rd Section of Transport (1 Limb. G.S. Wagon, 5 Water Carts, 1 Maltese Cart & Spare animals pairs 2.)	45 "
TOTAL ROAD SPACE	415 "

If Motor Ambulance Cars are to be allowed for, additional road space will be as follows:-

5 Heavy Ambulance Cars	25 yards
2 Light " "	10 "
Interval of 5 yards between each.	30 "
" between Horse Transport & Motor Ambulances.	50 "
TOTAL ROAD SPACE	115 "
GRAND TOTAL ROAD SPACE	530 "

[signature]

Lieut-Colonel., R.A.M.C.
Comdg No. 142 Field Ambulance.

13.11.18.

SECRET

Orders (No.13.) by Lieut-Col., G.O.CHAMBERS., R.A.M.C.
Comdg No. 142 Field Ambulance.

Appendix VI

Ref. Sheet 51. 1/40,000 15.11.18.

1. No. 142 Field Ambulance will march with 9th Infantry Brigade Group to LA LONGUEVILLE tomorrow Nov. 16th.---Starting point will be at road junction M.11.c.0.0. at 10.23 hours.
2. Reveille will be at 06.00 hours, Breakfast at 06.30 hours.
3. The Field Ambulance will parade at road junction M.10.a.2.2. at 09.40 hours, to move off at 10.00 hours so as to pass the starting point at 10.23 hours.
4. Dress-Full marching order. Water bottles will be filled before marching off. Haversack ration will be carried.
The strictest attention will be paid to smartness in turnout and march discipline.
200 yards distance will be maintained between units- 50 yards in terval between the unit and its transport and between sections of transport .
5. Loading of wagons will be carried out by Section Commanders commencing punctually at 08.00 hours.
All blankets will be collected in bundles of 10 ready for loading on Medical Stores & L.G.S. Wagons by this hour.
All greatcoats and fur coats will be rolled and labelled by each man and ready for loading on Baggage Wagons by the same time.
6. Officers' Kits and Mess Equipment & Sergeants' Mess Equipment will be loaded on "A" Baggage Wagon by 08.30 hours.
7. Regimental sick will be collected by Motor Ambulance Cars at 08.30 hours and evacuated forthwith to 3rd Can. C.C.S., at LE QUESNOY. Capt.H.L.MANN will be responsible that this is done.
8. A holding party of 1 N.C.O. & 2 men will proceed at 09.00 hours by Ambulance Car to occupy the billets vacated by No.7 Field Amb. at LA LONGUEVILLE.
9. Motor Transport will move independently under Sgt SHARP.,A.S.C.
10. Cpl. PEDDAR.,R.A.M.C. will remain behind in charge of the stores to be taken forward by the Brigade lorry, in which he will travel to the new area.

G.O. Chambers

Lieut-Colonel.,R.A.M.C.
Comdg No. 142 Field Ambulance.

Appendix VII

Orders (No.14.) by Lieut-Colonel. G.O.CHAMBERS., R.A.M.C. **SECRET**
Comdg No. 142 Field Ambulance.

Ref. VALENCIENNES 1/100,000 17.11.18

1. No. 142 Field Ambulance will march with "B" Group to SOUS-LE-BOIS ~~xxxxx~~ tomorrow,Nov. 18th.
Starting point will be at cross roads 600 yards S. of L in LONGUEVILLE at 14.40 hours.
2. Reveille will be at 07.00 hours, Breakfast 07.30 hours, Dinner at 12.00 hours.
3. The Field Ambulance will parade onthe field in present billets at 14.00 hours,to move off at 14.20 hours, so as to pass the starting point at 14.40 hours.
4. Loading of wagons will be carried out under the supervision of Section Commanders commencing at 10.00 hours.
All blankets, greatcoats and fur coats will be collected near their respective wagons, and rolled ready for loading by 09.30 hours.
Officers' Kits will be loaded at the same time.
5. All cooking and mess equipment will be loaded by 13.30 hours.
6. Regimental sick will be collected by 09.00 hours and evacuated forthwith to C.C.S.
The Orderly Officer will be responsible that this is carried out.
7. A holding party consisting of 1 N.C.O. & 2 men will proceed on bicycles to occupy the billets allotted at SOUS-LE-BOIS leaving at 11.00 hours. They will report at the Town Major's Office for necessary instructions.
8. Motor Ambulance Cars will not move before 16.40 hours so as to allow 2 hours to elapse after the tail of the column has passed.
9. Attention is drawn to Standing Orders on Dress, March Discipline Transport etc issued under this Office No. S.O.5. dated 17.11.18.

G.O. Chambers

Lieut-Colonel., R.A.M.C.
Comdg No. 142 Field Ambulance.

Appendix VIII

-: MARCH DISCIPLINE :-

No. S.O.5.

1. The stristest attention is to be paid to march discipline. Dress- Full marching order. Caps to be worn and Steel Helmets to be strapped to back of Valises. Mess Tins to be slung below the Valise. Water Bottles to be filled before moving off.

2. On line of march the paying of proper compliments to superior officers is t o be strictly carried out. It is important that the greatest attention be given to this matter by all ranks.

3. 50 yards distance will be maintained between 142 Field Ambulance and the rear of the preceding Unit- 25 yards between the personnel of this Unit and its Transport, 25 yards between sections of Unit Transport.

4. Wagon Orderlies will not hang on to rear of vehicles but march behind.

5. The Advance Party will invariably be accompanied by 1 O.R. detailed for the special duty of disinfecting billets allotted.

6. Hay nets will be filled daily and carried on the sides of the wagons.

7. Greatcoats and fur coats ONLY will be rolled, labelled and packed on the Baggage Wagons of the respective sections. The loading will be carried out under the supervision of the Section Commanders.

8. All st ores ear-marked for transport by lorry will on no account be placed on the wagons, except under the direct instructions of the C.O.

9. Cooking utensils etc of the respective Messes must be cut down to the irreducible minimum. The scale allowed is as follows:-

"A" Officers' Mess
1 Pannier, 2 Boxes and 1 Bag containing Cooking utensils etc

"B" Sergeants' Mess
2 Boxes, and 1 Bag containing 3 Dixies, Saucepans etc.

"C" R.A.M.C.

1 Soyers Stove	7 Dixies	2 Boxes knives etc.	
5 Tins Frying	1 Broom	1 Axe	Salt
Cooks' Clothing	Cloths drying	Fuel when obtainable	

"D" A.S.C.(H.T.)
4 Dixies, 1 Pannier, 1 Case knives etc.

C.D. Chambers

Lieut-Colonel. ,R.A.M.C.
Comdg No. 142 Field Ambulance.

17/11/18.

Appendix IX

Orders (No 75) by Lieut-Colonel G. O. Chambers RAMC SECRET
Comdg No 142 Field Ambulance.

Ref Sheets VALENCIENNES & NAMUR 1/100000 19.11.18

1. No. 142 Field Ambulance will march with "B" Group to COLLERET to-morrow. Nov. 20th. Starting Point will be at Cross Roads 600 yds. N.E. of last S in SOUS LE BOIS at 09.02 ~~hours~~.

2. Reveille will be 05.30 hours. Breakfast 06.00 hours.

3. The Field Ambulance will parade outside present billets at 07.50 hours, ~~[illegible]~~ to move off at 08.20 hours so as to pass the starting point at 09.02 hours.

4. Loading of wagons will be carried out under the supervision of Section Commanders, commencing at 06.30 hours. Officers kits will be loaded at the same time.

5. Regimental Sick will be collected by 07.30 hrs and evacuated to No 5 CCS. SOUS-LE-BOIS. The Orderly Officer will be responsible for this being carried out.

6. Billetting party consisting of 1 N.C.O and 1 man will proceed on bicycles, leaving present billets at 07.30 hrs, to the road junction on MAUBEUGE ROAD to COLLERET so as to meet Staff Captain or his representative there at 08.30. Billets will be clearly marked.

8. Horses and mules will hook-in at 07.50 hrs.

9. Motor Ambulance Cars will not move before 11.30 hrs. so as to allow 2 hours to elapse after the tail of the Column has passed.

10. Attention is drawn to Standing Orders issued under this office No. S.O.5 dated 17.11.18.

11. Brigade lorry will be at HQ. at 08.00 hrs. to take on surplus stores. As much M.T. equipment as possible should be included. Cpl. PEDDER RAMC. will be in charge and travel in the lorry.

12. Wheeled Stretcher Carriages will be carried inside H.A. Wagons — 2 per wagon.

G. O. Chambers.
Lieut-Colonel
O.C. 142nd F. Amb.

Opera   Appendix XI

Orders (No.16.) by Lieut-Colonel G.O.CHAMBERS.,R.A.M.C.   SECRET
Comdg No. 142 Field Ambulance.

Ref. NAMUR 1/100,000   23.11.18.

1. No. 142 Field Ambulance will march to BIERCEE tomorrow Nov. 24th. --- Starting point will be at Road junction 900 yards S.E. of T. in COLLERET at 09.25 hours.
2. Reveille will be at 05.30---Breakfast 06.00 hours A haversack ration will be carried.
3. The Field Ambulance ,personnel and transport, will parade on the square at 08.25 to move off at 08.45 so as to pass the Starting point at the time above given. Transport will parade on the road adjoining the square---head opposite Q.M.Stores.
4. Disposal of H.T. & personnel will be as under:-
(A) S.S.M.HOLLOWAY.,A.S.C.(H.T.)will accompany the marching personnel with 3 Horsed Ambulances and Cooks' L.G.S.Wagon.
(B) Sgt CHANDLER.,R.A.M.C. will be N.C.O. i/c 1st Line Transport consisting of
3 L.G.S.Wagons
3 Water Carts
1 Maltese Cart
The whole will march in charge of Capt H.L.MANN.,R.A.M.C. who will make the necessary arrangements with the Brigade Group Transport Officer regarding time of moving off.
(C) Sgt MOORE.,A.S.C.(H.T.) will be N.C.O. i/c 2nd Line Transport consisting of
6 G.S.Wagons
He will report to O.C.,No.4 Coy A.S.C. at 09.00 hours regarding time of moving off.
5. Loading of Wagons will commence at 07.00 hours and will be completed by 08.00 hours. Section Commanders will be responsible for the correct loading of their wagons.
6. Sick will be collected by 07.30 hours and evacuated to No.5 C.C.S.,SOUS-LE-BOIS forthwith, under arrangements made by the Orderly Officer.
7. The Billeting Party, 1 N.C.O. & 2 Men, will proceed on bicycles at 08.00 hours to ~~LEERS.~~ (~~The Church LEERS.~~) BIERCEE Capt+CLARKE.,R.A.M.C. as Officer i/c Billeting Party will proceed at 08.00 hours in an Ambulance Car which will take light Mess utensils of Officers' & Sergeants' Messes and 6 dixies of Mens' Mess. 1 cook of each mess will accompany. This Ambulance Car will be used for taking urgent sick to hospital on arrival of troops in new area. Capt Clarke will ~~report to Staff Captain on arrival for billets in~~ proceed to BIERCEE.
8. The remainder of Ambulance Cars will proceed i/c Sgt SHARP., A.S.C.(M.T.) at 11.30 to BIERCEE
9. Officer i/c Billeting Party will detail 3 guides to be stationed at the Inn 900 yards N.E. of the U in FOSTEAU to conduct:-
(A) Marching personnel (under O.C.)
(B) 1st Line Transport ("   Capt MANN)
(C) 2nd Line Transport ("   Sgt MOORE)
to the Billetiing area. These guides should be at this point by 13.00 hours.
10. Surplus stores i/c Cpl PEDDER will be taken on by lorry. Orders will be issued later.
11. Horsed Ambulance Wagons will each carry 2 wheeled stretchers carriers and 3 two-gallon tins filled with chlorinated water in addition to their water tanks which will be also filled.
12. Attention is drawn to Standing Orders No.S.O.5. dated 17.11.18 No compliments will be paid on the march.

G.O.Chambers
Lieut-Colonel.,R.A.M.C.
Comdg No. 142 Field Ambulance.

+ to the same place

Appendix XII

Orders. (No.17.) by Lieut-Col. G.O.CHAMBERS.,R.A.M.C. **S E C R E T**
Commanding No.142 Field Ambulance.

Ref. Map NAMUR. 1/100.000 24/11/18.

1. No. 142 Field Ambulance will march to MARBAIX tomorrow, 25 inst. Starting point will be at cross roads 200 yds. South of L in LOCK at 11.02 hours.
2. Reveille will be at 06.30 hours. Breakfast at 07.00 hours.
3. The Fd. Amb. will parade on the road outside present billets; head opposite Orderly Room, at 09.20 hours to move off at 09.45 to the road junction 500 yards S.E. of S in BOIS DE VILLERS where it will join in the line of march after the 3rd.M.G.Btn. has passed.
4. Disposal of H.T. will be as laid down in Standing Orders No.S.O.5 1st.Line Transport will march directly behind that of the 3rd.M.G.Btn Capt. MANN. as officer in charge, will arrange.accordingly. Sergt.Moore A.S.C.-H.T., in charge of 2nd Line Transport, will receive orders from O.C. No.4.Coy A.S.C.regarding time of moving off and joining the Train.
5. Loading of wagons will commence at 08.00 hours and will be completed by 09.00 hours.
6. Sick will be collected by 09.00 hours and evacuated to No.56 C.C.S. CHARLEROI. Capt. CLARKE is detailed for this duty. He will afterwards proceed with Ambulance Cars to the new area at the time given in para.8.
7. The Billetting Party will proceed at 08.00 hours to the Church in MARBAIX where they will await the arrival of Capt.POTTER,M.C. R.A.M.C Oi/c Billetting Party, who will proceed by car at 08.30 hours. The mess equipments and personnel will proceed by this car, as laid down in S.O.
8. The remaining Ambulance Cars under Capt.CLARKE,R.A.M.C. will not leave present billets before 13.10 hours.
9. Officer i/c Billetting will detail 3 guides to be stationed at the cross roads 800 yards N. of the A in MARBAIX to conduct R.A.M.C. personnel, 1st Line Transport, & 2nd Line Transport to their Billets. The guides will be there by 12.00 hours.
10. Surplus stores i/c Cpl PEDDER.,R.A.M.C. will be taken on by lorry which will report at 08.00 hours.
    The extra 185 blankets will be carried in the G.S.Wagon from the 13th KINGS' LIVERPOOL REGT.

G.O. Chambers.

Lieut-Colonel.,R.A.M.C.
Comdg No. 142 Field Ambulance.

App XIII Orders (No 18) by LIEUT-COLONEL G.O. CHAMBERS RAMC **Secret**
Commanding No 142 Field Ambulance

Ref NAMUR 1/100000. 25.11.18

1. No 142 Field Ambulance will march to the GOUGNIES area tomorrow 26th inst. Starting Point will be at Road Junction 100 yds S of I in BERZEE STATION at 10.22 hours.
2. Reveille at 06.00 hours. Breakfast 06.30 hours Haversack Ration will be carried
3. The Field Ambulance will parade in front of present Billets, opposite Q.M. Stores - at 08.15, to move off at 08.30 hours so as to pass the starting point at the time above given
4. Disposal of H.T will continue as before, ~~Tide~~ ~~Sunt~~ and will be ready to move off at 08.30 hours
5. Loading of wagons will commence at 07.00 hours and will be completed by 08.00 hours.
6. Sick will be collected at 08.00 hours and evacuated under arrangements to be made by Capt CLARKE RAMC
7. Orders for Billeting Party and guides will be issued later
   Major SHIELDS RAMC will act as Officer i/c of Billeting Party and will proceed by Ambulance Car at 08.00 hours to the new area
8. The remaining Ambulance Cars under Capt CLARKE RAMC will not leave present billets before 12.30 hours
9. Surplus Stores and Blankets will be dealt with as before.
10. Major WRIGHT RAMC will inspect all billets before the Unit moves off.

G.O. Chambers

Lieut Colonel, R.A.M.C.
COMDG: 142ND FIELD AMBULANCE

App XIV

Orders (No 19) by MAJOR A.F.L. SHIELDS RAMC
Commanding No 142 Field Ambulance

Ref NAMUR 1/100 000 27.11.18

1. No 142 Field Ambulance will march to ST GERRARD tomorrow the 28th inst :- Starting Point will be Railway level crossing 300 yards E. of GOUGNIES Station at 09.38 hours

2. Reveille at 06.00 hours, Breakfast 06.30 hours. A haversack ration will be carried

3. The Field Ambulance will parade in front of the Church at 08.15 hours to move off at 08.30 hours so as to pass the starting point at the time above given.

4. Disposal of H.T. will be as before.
1st Line Transport will be ready to move at 08.30 hours
2nd Line Transport will move under orders of O.C. No 4 Coy 3rd Div Train.

5 Loading of wagons will commence at 07.00 hours & will be completed by 08.00 hours

6. Sick will be collected at 08.00 hours.
Capt CLARKE RAMC will arrange to inform O.C. No 30 M.A.C. by motor cyclist, the numbers of sitting & lying cases for evacuation to C.C.S. giving location. & will leave an orderly with the cases pending the arrival of the M.A.C. Cars

7. Orders for Billeting Party
Capt POTTER M.C, RAMC will act as O/c Billeting Party and will proceed at 08.00 hours and report to Communal Secretary ST GERRARD at 09.00 hours
Cpl INMAN & Pte TURNER will proceed at 07.45 hours on bicycles to report to Capt POTTER at ST GERRARD at 09.00 hours.

8. Instructions regarding surplus stores will be issued later

9. Major WRIGHT RAMC will inspect all billets before the Unit moves off.

A F L Shields
Major.

Appendix XV

Order (No 20) by Major A & L SHIELDS RAMC
commanding No 142 Field Ambulance

28.11.18

Ref NAMUR 1/100000

1. No 142 Field Ambulance will march tomorrow 29th inst to a destination to be notified later
Starting point will be Road Junction 800 yards S. of H in BOUCHAT at 09.35 hours

2 Reveille at 05.15 hours, Breakfast 05.45 hours
A Haversack Ration will be carried

3 Loading of wagons will commence at 06.15 hours and will be completed by 07.15 hours.

4. The Field Ambulance will parade in front of the Medical Inspection Room at 07.30 hours, to move off at 07.45 hours, to pass the Starting Point at the time above given.

5 Disposal of H T will be as before.
1st Line Transport will be ready to move off at 08.30 hours and will march via Cross Roads 600 yards S E of X in GRAUX, passing through BIOUL at 10.30 hours
2nd Line Transport will move under orders of OC No 4 Coy Div Train
All Spare horses will be harnessed and carry as many trace extensions as possible and will accompany 2nd Line Transport

6. Capt Clarke will be responsible for the collection & Evacuation of sick, arrangements will be as per orders No 19 of 27/11/18

7. Orders for Billeting Party
Major WRIGHT RAMC will act as O/c Billeting Party. Further instructions will be issued later.

8. Surplus stores will be collected by the Brigade H Q Lorry after the Unit has moved off

9. Capt J POTTER M.C. RAMC will inspect the Billets before the Unit moves off

A & L Shields.

Major
, R.A.M.C.
COMDG: 142ND FIELD AMBULANCE.

App XVI

Orders (No 21) by Major A F L SHIELDS RAMC
Commanding No 142 Field Ambulance

29.11.18

Ref NAMUR & MARCHE 1/100000

1. No 142 Field Ambulance will move tomorrow 30th Nov to SKEUVRE. – to pass the Starting Point SPONTIN Station at 09.22 hours

2. Reveille 05.15 hours Breakfast 05.45 hours
A haversack ration will be carried.

3. The Field Ambulance will parade in front of the Orderly Room at 07.30 hours, to move off at 07.45 hours

4. Disposal of H.T. will be as before
1st Line Transport will be ready to move off at 07.45 hours.

5 Loading of wagons will commence at 06.15 hours, to be completed by 07.15 hours.

6. Sick arrangements in charge of Capt CLARKE RAMC will be as usual.

7. Billeting Party – Capt POTTER MC RAMC will * act as Billeting Officer & will arrange to take over Billets occupied by No 7 Field Ambulance in SKEUVRE by 08.00 hours

8 Motor Lorry for surplus stores will be as usual.

9. Major Wright RAMC will inspect all billets before the Unit moves off.

* The NCO i/c Billeting Party will proceed at 07.45 hours to report to Capt POTTER at SKEUVRE on arrival.

A F L Shields

Major, R.A.M.C.
COMDG: 142ND FIELD AMBULANCE.

14

Dec 1918

CONFIDENTIAL

41

121/3481

No. 142 FIELD AMBULANCE.

WAR DIARY FOR MONTH of DECEMBER 1918.

1-1-19.

A.D. Chambers
Lieut-Col.
RAMC
O.C. 142nd F. Amb.

Army Form C. 2118.
Sheet I

Instructions regarding War Diaries and Intelligence Summaries are contained in F. S. Regs., Part II. and the Staff Manual respectively. Title pages will be prepared in manuscript.

WAR DIARY
or
INTELLIGENCE SUMMARY.
(Erase heading not required.)

December 1918 — O.C. No. 142 Field Ambulance

Place	Date	Hour	Summary of Events and Information	Remarks and references to Appendices
SKEUVRE	1/12		Dry cold day	
			A.D.M.S. & D.A.D.M.S. visited these Headquarters	At H.Q.
	2/12		Wet day.	At H.Q.
	3/12		Wet day	App. No. 1
			Orders received for move to RY Chateau tomorrow	At H.Q.
			arrangements made accordingly	
RY Chateau	4/12		Wet day.	App. No. 2
			G.O.C. 9th Inf. Brigade again complimented unit on	
			its smartness on the march	At H.Q.
			Arrived at RY Chateau at 11.20 hours.	
			Orders received for move tomorrow orders issued	
			accordingly.	
	5/12		~~Dry~~ day	App. No. 3
MOINVILLE			Field Ambulance moved to MOINVILLE very long march	At H.Q.
			18 miles, men marched very well, only two fell out	
			Orders received for move ~~tomorrow~~ to FISENNE	
FISENNE	6/12		Dry cold day.	App. No. 4
			Short march reached FISENNE at 1100 hours no men fell out	At H.Q.
			Orders received for move tomorrow to LA FOSSE orders issued accordingly	

(A7092). Wt. W12839/M1293. 750,000. 1/17. D. D. & L., Ltd. Forms/C.2118/14.

Instructions regarding War Diaries and Intelligence Summaries are contained in F. S. Regs., Part II. and the Staff Manual respectively. Title pages will be prepared in manuscript.

WAR DIARY
or
INTELLIGENCE SUMMARY.
(Erase heading not required.)

Army Form C. 2118.

December 1918. OC No 142 Field Ambulance

Place	Date	Hour	Summary of Events and Information	Remarks and references to Appendices
LA FOSSE	7/12		Wet day Unit moved to LA FOSSE arriving at 11.30 hours no men fell out. Orders received for move to ODEIGNE tomorrow orders issued accordingly.	AtL8 App No 5
ODEIGNE	8/12		Dry day. Short march to ODEIGNE no men fell out Orders received for move to VERLEUMONT	App No 6 AtL8
VERLEUMONT	9/12		Very showery day. Unit marched to VERLEUMONT. no men fell out.	AtL8
	10/12		Unit remained at VERLEUMONT. Inspected the Transport at 14.00 found it satisfactory Orders received for move tomorrow to DYFELDT.	App No 7 AtL8
DEYFELDT	11/12		Very wet day. Unit marched to DEYFELDT rained very heavily all the time Now billeted just west of the LUXEMBURG Frontier	App No 8 AtL8
CRUFFLINCHEN	12/12		Wet day. Unit marched to CRUFFLINCHEN crossing the frontier at 9.50 hours. The G.O.C. Division took the salute at the Frontier	App No 9

(A7092) Wt. W12839/M1293 75,000. 1/17. D. D. & L., Ltd. Forms/C.2118/14.

Instructions regarding War Diaries and Intelligence Summaries are contained in F. S. Regs., Part II. and the Staff Manual respectively. Title pages will be prepared in manuscript.

WAR DIARY
or
INTELLIGENCE SUMMARY.

December 1918 *(Erase heading not required.)* [illegible] Field Ambulance

Army Form C. 2118.

Place	Date	Hour	Summary of Events and Information	Remarks and references to Appendices
CRUFFLINGHEN	12/12		And expressed his approval of the turn out of the unit. He told the Brigadier General that it was the smartest & cleanest unit that had passed him today including the Transport.	App 6/10 AHS
			Germans in this village very obliging & willing to help in any way they can.	
			Orders received for move to SCHONBERG tomorrow	
SCHONBERG	13/12		Very wet day.	App 6/11
			Unit marched to SCHONBERG and arrived at 13.00 hours	AHS
			Rained all the way no men fell out.	
			Orders received for march ~~tomorrow~~ to BERK.	
BERK.	14/12		Wet day.	App 6/12
			Unit marched to BERK no men fell out.	
			Orders received for move to BLANKENHEIM ~~tomorrow~~	AHS
BLANKENHEIM.	15/12		Dry day.	App 6/13
			Unit marched to BLANKENHEIM arriving at 14.00 hours	
			Orders received for move tomorrow to EICHERSCHEID ~~tomorrow~~	AHS
			Instructions issued accordingly	

(A7092). Wt. W12839/M1293 750,000. 1/17. D. D. & L., Ltd. Forms/C.2118/14.

WAR DIARY
or
INTELLIGENCE SUMMARY.

Army Form C. 2118.

Instructions regarding War Diaries and Intelligence Summaries are contained in F. S. Regs., Part II. and the Staff Manual respectively. Title pages will be prepared in manuscript.

December 1918. (Erase heading not required.) OC 20th Field Ambulance

Place	Date	Hour	Summary of Events and Information	Remarks and references to Appendices
EICHERCHED	16/12		Cold day - some showers. Unit marched to EICHERCHED arriving at 14.30 hours orders received and issued for move tomorrow to STOTZHEIN	App. No. 14 At HQ
STOTZHEIN	17/12		Dry day Unit marched to STOTZHEIN arriving at 13.00 hours. Roads much better and villages passed through much cleaner and better built. People in village all turned out to see the unit arrive which is rather unusual, have been usually greeted by empty streets & no civilians to be seen. Orders received for move ~~tomorrow~~ to EUSKIRCHEN ~~tomorrow~~. Arrangements made accordingly	App. No. 15 At HQ
EUSKAIRCHEN	18/12		Unit moved to EUSKIRCHEN arriving at 11.20 hours Short march. No men fell out. Orders received for move tomorrow to ZULPICH ~~tomorrow~~ arrangements made accordingly.	App. No. 16 At HQ

(A7092). Wt. W12839/M1293 750,000. 1/17. D. D. & L., Ltd. Forms/C.2118/14.

Instructions regarding War Diaries and Intelligence Summaries are contained in F. S. Regs., Part II. and the Staff Manual respectively. Title pages will be prepared in manuscript.

WAR DIARY
or
INTELLIGENCE SUMMARY.

Army Form C. 2118.

December 1918 *(Erase heading not required.)* O.C. No 142 Field Ambulance

Place	Date	Hour	Summary of Events and Information	Remarks and references to Appendices
ZULPICH	19/12		Very cold day, some showers.	
			Unit marched to ZULPICH arriving at 12.15 hours	AtL8
			no men fell out.	App 17
			Instructions received for move tomorrow to Final area	
			BINSFELD. Orders issued accordingly.	
			Major WRIGHT R.A.M.C. visited final billeting area ~~today~~ today	
			accompanied by ~~Staff~~ Captain 9th Inf Brigade.	
BINSFELD	20/12		Dry day.	
			Unit moved to BINSFELD arriving at 12.45 hours	AtL8
			No men fell out.	
			This is the Final area, the unit remains here until	
			after Christmas. All the men are in very comfortable	
			billets.	
"	21.12.18.		O.C 142nd F.A. returned from leave to U.K. last evening. A Brigade Rest Station of 36 beds is being formed to-day in this village. Sick for evacuation are sent to 17 CCS DURREN. Weather mild-rainy	

A. D. Chambers
Lieut. Col.

(A7092). Wt. W12839/M1293 75,000. 1/17. D. D. & L., Ltd. Forms/C.2118/14.

Instructions regarding War Diaries and Intelligence Summaries are contained in F. S. Regs., Part II. and the Staff Manual respectively. Title pages will be prepared in manuscript.

WAR DIARY
or
~~INTELLIGENCE~~ SUMMARY. O.C.
142nd Field Ambulance.

(Erase heading not required.)

Army Form C. 2118.

Place	Date	Hour	Summary of Events and Information Ref. Map. GERMANY 1/100.000. 1.L.	Remarks and references to Appendices
BINSFELD	22.12.18.		Inspected the unit this morning. All ranks very smartly turned out. Capt CLARKE RAMC proceeded on temporary duty with 1/Northumberland Fusiliers whilst their M.O. is on leave. Scheme of Training - Recreational and Educational is being prepared. Rainy and cold.	(init.)
"	23.12.18.		Organisation for demobilization being carried out. Routine Office work to-day. Weather changeable.	(init.)
"	24.12.18.		Committees have been appointed to organise and supervise games - indoor and outdoor (Recreational Training). Christmas arrangements are being completed to-day. Div. Commander. Brigadier General and ADMS called in evening to wish the ambulance Christmas Greetings.	(init.)
"	25.12.18		Christmas Day. Mens Dinner was served at 12.00 hrs concert at 17.00 hrs. Weather Seasonable - Slight snow and frost.	(init.)
"	26.12.18		With Staff Captain I reconnoitred village of KELZ as a suitable place for the ambulance which is under orders to move to-morrow. The village appears in every way suitable. Cold and frosty. Major A.P.L. SHIELDS left to-night with DDMS VI Corps on a secret mission to BERLIN.	(init.)

(A7092). Wt. W12839/M1293. 75,000. 1/17. D. D. & L., Ltd. Forms/C.2118/14.

Instructions regarding War Diaries and Intelligence Summaries are contained in F. S. Regs., Part II. and the Staff Manual respectively. Title pages will be prepared in manuscript.

WAR DIARY
or
INTELLIGENCE SUMMARY.
(Erase heading not required.)

Army Form C. 2118.

O.C. 142nd Field Ambulance

Place	Date	Hour	Summary of Events and Information Ref. Map. GERMANY 1 L. 1/100,000	Remarks and references to Appendices
KELZ	27.12.18		Ambulance moved to KELZ to-day. This is a good-sized village, accomodation sufficient and comfortable. There is a large hall with several small rooms which will be used as a Rest Station. Rooms are also obtainable for Dining Hall and Lectures. Weather dull and rainy	(E.D.)
"	28.12.18		Demobilization of Pivotal men, Demobilizers and Release Slip men began to-day (and Coalminers). Six left F.A. to-day.	(E.D.)
"	29.12.18		As Senior Officer of district I assume duties of District Commander in accordance with instructions from G.O.C. 9th Inf. Brigade. Orders for civilian population given to Burgomeister who carries out my instructions promptly and efficiently. Rained all day. Mild	(E.D.)
"	30.12.18		Rest Station accomodation for 40 patients (other ranks). Work being done on Rest Station each day. Programmes of Recreational Training are being carried out. 4 men were demobilized to-day. ADMS inspected the unit this afternoon. Confidential Reports on officers sent to ADMS to-day. Mild. Rainy at times	(E.D.)
"	31.12.18		Inter-Section Football Match was played this afternoon. Recreational Training (Indoors) is being carried out. All ranks show great keenness in these games. 2 men were demobilized to-day. Weather cooler	

E.D. Chambers
Lieut-Col RAMC
O.C. 142nd F.A.

(A7092). Wt W12839/M1293 750,000. 1/17. D. D. & L., Ltd. Forms/C.2118/14.

App. No I

Orders (No 22) by Major A F L SHIELDS. RAMC.
Commanding No 142 Field Ambulance.

3.12.18

Ref. MARCHE 1/100 000

1 No. 142 Field Ambulance will move tomorrow, 4th Dec. to RY Château, to pass the starting point, cross roads 300 yds. south of L in LETIGE at 9.30 hours

2 Reveillé 06 00 hours. Breakfast 06 30 hours. Sick parade 07 30 hours.

3 The Field Ambulance will parade in front of Orderly Room at 08.15 hours, to move off at 08 35 hours.

4 Disposal of H Transport will be as before. First line transport will be ready to move off at 08 35 hours.
Second line transport will move off at 09.00 hours

5 Loading of wagons will commence at 07.00 hours, to be completed by 08.00 hours.

6 Sick arrangements will be in charge of Capt. Clarke as usual.

7. Billeting Party. - Major Wright will act as billeting officer and will report to rear party of 76th Inf Bde. at SCY railway at 9.30 hours to take over billets occupied by No 9 F Amb at RY Château

8 Motor lorry for surplus stores will be as usual

9 Capt. Potter RAMC. will inspect all billets before the unit moves off.

A F L Shields
Major
R.A.M.C.
142nd FIELD AMBULANCE.

APP. No 2

No 2 Orders (No. 23) by Major A.H.L. Shields RAMC
Commanding No. 142 Field Ambulance
Ref MARCHE 1/100,000

1. No. 142 Field Ambulance will move tomorrow, 5th inst. to the FRONVILLE, GOENEILLE, BAILLONVILLE area to pass the starting point Road Junction 900 yards N.E. of M in DE L'ABIME at 10.14 hours.

2. Reveille - 5.30 hours.
Breakfasts - 6.00 "
A haversack ration will be carried

3. The Field Ambulance will parade at 7.45 hrs. on road in front of Sergeants' Mess, head of column at the Cross Roads - to move off at 8.00 hours.

4. Loading of wagons will be commenced at 6.30 hours and will be completed by 7.30 hours.

5. Disposal of H.T. will be as usual. All transport will be ready to move off by 8.00 hours.

6. Capt. Clarke RAMC will arrange for the collection and evacuation of all sick. Sick parade will be at 7.00 hours.

7. Capt. Potter M.C. RAMC will act as O/C Billeting Party which will be as usual. Further instructions will be issued later.

8. Lorry for surplus stores as before.

9. Capt. Clarke RAMC will inspect all billets before the unit moves off.

A H L Shields

4/12/18.

Major RAMC.
Comdg. 142 Field Ambulance

Orders (No 24) by Major A. F. L. Shields RAMC
APP. No 3 Commanding No 142 Field Ambulance
Ref MARCHE 1/100000

5/12/18

1. No 142 Field Ambulance will march tomorrow 6th inst to FISENNE - to pass the Starting Point - Railway Crossing 200 yards S W of S in STATION at 10.28 hours
2. Reveille 07.00 hours Breakfast 07.30 hours
3. The Field Ambulance will parade at 09.30 hours to move off at 10.00 hours.
4. Loading of wagons will commence at 08.00 hours to be completed by 09.00 hours
5. Disposal of H.T. will be as usual. All transport will be ready to move off at 09.30 hours
6. Capt Clarke RAMC will arrange for the collection & evacuation of sick
Sick Parade will be at 08.30 hours
7. Major Wright RAMC will act as Officer i/c Billeting Party which will be as usual
The N.C.O. i/c Billeting Party will report to Major Wright at FISENNE at 09.30 hours.
8. Lorry for surplus stores as before
9. Capt Clarke RAMC will inspect all billets before the Unit moves off

A F L Shields
Major, R.A.M.C.
Comdg: 142nd FIELD AMBULANCE

Operation Order

APP No 5

Orders No 25 by Major A.F.L. SHIELDS RAMC.
Commanding No 142 Field Ambulance

6/12/18

Ref MARCHE 1/100000

1. No142 Field Ambulance will march tomorrow the 7th inst to LA FOSSE to pass the Starting Point - Cross Roads 200 yards S of N in ESTINEE -

2. Reveille 05·30 hours - Breakfast 06·00 hours.

3. The Field Ambulance will parade opposite Q.M. Stores at 07·45 hours to move off at 08·00 hours

4. Loading of wagons will commence at 06·30 to be completed by 07·30 hours under the Supervision of Capt POTTER M.C., RAMC.

5. Disposal of H.T. will be as usual
1st Line Transport will be ready to move at 08·00 hours, 2nd Line Transport will be parked outside Q.M. Stores ready to move at 08·30 hours.

6. Capt Clarke RAMC will arrange for the Collection and Evacuation of Sick.
Sick Parade will be at 07·00 hours

7. Major Wright RAMC will act as Officer i/c Billeting Party which will be as usual. The NCO i/c Billeting Party will report to Major Wright at LA FOSSE at 09·30 hours

8. Lorry for surplus stores will be as usual

9. Capt Clarke RAMC will inspect all billets before the Unit moves off.

10. Capt Clarke RAMC will arrange to hand over Billets to the 8th Bde.

A.F.L. Shields
Major
.... , R.A.M.C.
COMDG: 142ND FIELD AMBULANCE

APP No 6.

Orders (No 26) by Major A.F.L. SHIELDS RAMC
Commanding No 142 Field Ambulance.

7.12.18.

Ref MARCHE 1/100 000.

1. No 142 Field Ambulance will march tomorrow the 8th inst to ODEIGNE to be clear of present billets by 10.00 hours

2. Reveille 07.00 hours, Breakfast 07.30 hours

3. The Field Ambulance will parade opposite M.I. Room at 09.25 to move off at 09.40 hours

4. Loading of wagons will commence at 08.00 hours to be completed by 09.00 hours under the supervision of Major WRIGHT RAMC

5. Disposal of H.T. as usual
All Transport will be ready to move with the Unit at 09.40 hours, with the exception of the Cooks' Limber which will leave at 08.30 hours, accompanied by the cooks

6. Capt Clarke RAMC will arrange for the collection and evacuation of sick.
Sick Parade will be at 08.30 hours.

7. Capt Potter MC, RAMC will arrange to take over Billets from Rear Party of No 7 Field Amb'ce at 09.00 hours. Billeting Party will be as usual

8. Capt Clarke RAMC will inspect all billets before the Unit moves off, and will arrange to hand over present billets to the 8th Infantry Brigade.

A.F.L. Shields.

Major

............................, R.A.M.C.
COMDG: 142ND FIELD AMBULANCE

Orders (No 27) by MAJOR AFL SHIELDS RAMC
Commanding No 142 Field Ambulance

APP. No 7

Ref MARCHE 1/100000

8.12.18

1. No 142 Field Ambulance tomorrow the 9th inst to BECH to pass the Starting Point – Cross Roads 500 yds N.W. of J. in JOUBIEVAL

2. Reveille 05.00 Breakfast 05.30 hours. A haversack ration will be carried.

3. The Field Ambulance will parade at 07.15 hours at the corner of the road opposite the Sergeants' Mess to move off at 07.30 hours

4. Loading of wagons will commence at 06.00 hours to be completed at 07.00 hours.

5. Disposal of H.T. as usual
1st Line Transport will move in same order as Personnel.
2nd Line Transport will follow personnel as far as REGNE where NCO i/c will report to OC No 4 Coy 3rd Div Train
All Transport will be ready to move at 07.30 hours

6. Capt Clarke RAMC will arrange for collection and evacuation of Sick
Sick Parade will be at 06.30 hours

7. Major Wright RAMC will act as Officer i/c Billeting
Billeting Party will be as usual and will move off at 07.30. NCO i/c will report to Rear Party of 76 Inf Bde at BECH

8. Capt Clarke RAMC will inspect all Billets before the Unit moves off. ~~and will~~

AFL Shields.
Major

............................, R.A.M.C.
COMDG: 142ND FIELD AMBULANCE

Orders No 28 by Major A F L Shields RAMC
Commanding No 142 Field Ambulance

APP. No. 8

Ref MARCHE 9 1.M.

10.12.18

1. No 142 Field Ambulance will march tomorrow the 11th inst to DEYFELDT to pass the Starting Point - Road Junction 1000 yds E of X in PROVEDROUX at 11.14 hours.

2. Reveille 06.00 Breakfast 06.30 hours
A Haversack Ration will be carried

3. Loading of wagons to commence at 07.00, to be completed by 08.00 hours in charge Capt POTTER MC, RAMC

4. The Field Ambulance will parade at 08.15 on road in front of school, to move off at 08.30 hours.

5. Capt Clarke RAMC will arrange for the collection and evacuation of Sick
Sick Parade will be at 07.30 hours

6. Disposal of H.T. as usual
1st Line Transport will be brigaded & march in same order as personnel
2nd Line Transport will halt at the main road with head of column clear of the main road
All transport will be ready to move at 08.30

7. Major Wright RAMC will act as Officer i/c Billeting Party. Billeting Party will be as usual & NCO i/c will report to Major Wright at DEYFELDT on arrival. Billeting Party will move off at 08.00 hours.

8. Capt Clarke RAMC will inspect all billets before the Unit moves off.

A F L Shields
Major
, R.A.M.C.
COMDG: 142ND FIELD AMBULANCE

APP. No. 9

Orders No. 29. by Major A.T.L. Shields RAMC
Commanding 142 Field Ambulance

Ref. MAP. 1.M. 11/12/18.

1. No. 142 Field Ambulance will march tomorrow, 12th inst. to GRUFFLINGEN, to pass starting point - road junction, 200 yards S. of U in KATZEBUR at 09.37 hours.

2. Reveille at 06.00 hours. Breakfast 06.30 hours.

3. Loading of wagons to commence at 07.00 hours and to be completed by 08.00 hours, in charge of Capt. J. POTTER. M.C., RAMC

4. Field Ambulance will parade at 08.15 hrs at S.E. side of the Crossroads - to move off at 08.30 hours.

5. Capt. CLARKE. RAMC will arrange for the collection and evacuation of sick.
Sick Parade will be at 07.30 hours.

6. Disposal of H.T. as usual.
1st Line Transport will be brigaded and move in same order as personnel, moving off at 08.30 hours.
2nd Line Transport will be ready to move from Q.M. Stores at 08.50 hours.

7. Major WRIGHT. RAMC will act as O i/c Billetting Party. Billetting Party will be as usual and move off at 08.00 hours, and report to Major WRIGHT at GRUFFLINGHEN on arrival.

8. Capt. CLARKE. RAMC will inspect all Billets before the unit moves off, and will arrange to hand over to 8th Infantry Brigade.

A T L Shields

Major RAMC.
[redacted] Commanding 142 Fd. Ambce.

Orders No 30 by Major A F L SHIELDS RAMC

APP. No 10 Commanding No 142 Field Ambulance.

Ref 1. M. 12.12.18

1. No 142 Field Ambulance will move tomorrow the 13th inst. to SCHONBERG, to pass the starting point – Railway Crossing 400 yds S of S in ST VITH at 10.18 hours.

2. Reveille 05.30 Breakfast 06.00 hours
A haversack ration will be carried

3. Loading of wagons to commence at 06.30 to be completed by 07.30 hours

4. The Field Ambulance will parade at 07.50 hours on road outside School House to move off at 08.05 hours

5 Capt Clarke RAMC will arrange for collection and evacuation of sick
Sick Parade will be at 07.00 hours.

6. Disposal of H.T. as usual.
1st Line Transport will be brigaded and march in same order as personnel moving off at 08.05 hrs
2nd Line Transport will be parked at Q.M. Stores ready to move at 09.00 hours.

7. Major Wright RAMC will act as Officer i/c Billeting Party. Billeting Party will be as usual & NCO i/c will arrange to move off at 07.30 hours, reporting to Major Wright on arrival at SCHONBERG.

8. Capt Clarke RAMC will inspect all billets before the Unit moves off and will arrange to hand over Billets to 8th Inf Bde.

A F L Shields

Major
............................, R.A.M.C.
COMDG: 142ND FIELD AMBULANCE

Orders (No 31) by Major A F L. SHIELDS RAMC

APP. No. 11 Commanding No 142 Field Ambulance.

Ref. 1.M. 13.12.18.

1. No 142 Field Ambulance will move tomorrow the 14th inst to BERK – to pass the Starting Point Road Junction 200 yds N of R. in MANDERFELD at 10.12 hours

2. Reveille 05.15 hours Breakfast 05.45
A haversack ration to be carried

3. Loading of wagons to commence at 06.15 to be completed by 07.15 hours.

4. The Field Ambulance will parade at 07.30 hours in road near Orderly Room, to move off at 07.45 hours.

5. Capt Clarke RAMC will arrange for the collection and evacuation of Sick
Sick Parade will be at 06.45 hours

6. Disposal of H.T. as usual.
1st Line Transport will march in same order as personnel at 07.45 hours
2nd Line Transport will be parked at Q.M. Stores ready to move at 08.30 hours.

7. Major Wright RAMC will act as Officer i/c Billeting Party. Billeting Party will be as usual & N.C.O. i/c will arrange to move off at 07.15 hours, reporting to Major Wright on arrival at BERK.

8. Capt Clarke RAMC will inspect all billets before the Unit moves off and will arrange to hand over billets to 8th Inf Bde

A F L Shields
Major

........................, R.A.M.C.
COMDG: 142ND FIELD AMBULANCE

Orders No 32 by Major A.F.L. SHIELDS. RAMC

APP. No. 12 Commanding No 142 Field Ambulance

Ref 1.M. 14.12.18

1. No 142 Field Ambulance will move tomorrow the 15th inst to BLANKENHEIM - to pass the Starting Point Road Junction 1000 yards N.W. of S in STADTKYLL at 11.01 hours.

2. Reveille 06.00 Breakfast 06.30 hours
A haversack Ration will be carried

3. Loading of wagons to commence at 07.00 to be completed by 08.00 hours

4. The Field Ambulance will parade at ~~08.20~~ 08.25 hours opposite M.I. Room to move off at 08.~~30~~ 40 hours

5. Capt Clarke RAMC will arrange for collection and evacuation of Sick
Sick Parade will be at 07.30 hours.

6. Disposal of HT as usual
1st Line Transport will be brigaded & march in same order as personnel - to move off at 08.~~30~~ 40 hours
2nd Line Transport will follow 1st Line as far as KRONNENBURG where they will report to OC No 4 Coy 3rd Div Train

7. ~~Major [illegible]~~ Capt POTTER MC, RAMC will act as officer i/c Billeting Party. The Billeting Party will be as usual & NCO i/c will arrange to move off at 08.15 hours reporting to Capt POTTER on arrival at BLANKENHEIM.

8. Capt Clarke RAMC will inspect all billets before the Unit moves off and will arrange to hand over Billets to 8th Inf Bde.

A F L Shields.
Major. , R.A.M.C.
COMDG: 142ND FIELD AMBULANCE.

Orders No 33 by Major A F L SHIELDS RAMC
APP. No 13 Commanding No 142 Field Ambulance
Ref 1. M. 15.12.18.

1. No 142 Field Ambulance will move tomorrow the 16th inst. to EICHERSCHEID – to pass the Starting Point – Bendin road 1000 yds N. of B in BLANKENHEIM at 10.56 hours

2. Reveille 07.00 Breakfast 07.30
A Haversack Ration will be carried

3 Loading of wagons to commence at 08.15 hours to be completed 09.15 hours

4. The Field Ambulance will parade at 10.00 hours opposite M I Room to move off at 10.15 hours.

5. Capt Clarke RAMC will arrange for collection and evacuation of sick
Sick Parade will be at 08.45 hours

6 Disposal of HT as usual
1st Line Transport will be brigaded and will move in same order as personnel
2nd Line Transport will be parked at QM Stores ready to move at 11.00 hours

7 Capt POTTER M.C., RAMC will act as Officer i/c Billeting Party. The Billeting Party will be as usual & NCO i/c will arrange to move off at 09.30 hours reporting to Capt POTTER on arrival at EICHERSCHEID.

8. Capt Clarke RAMC will inspect all billets before the Unit moves off and will arrange to hand over billets to 8th Inf Bde

A F L Shields.

Major

COMDG: 142ND FIELD AMBULANCE.

Orders No 34 by Major A.F.L. SHIELDS. RAMC
APP. No. 14 Commanding No 142 Field Ambulance.

Ref 1. L. 16. 12. 18

1. No 142 Field Ambulance will move tomorrow the 17th inst to STOTZHEIM – to pass the Starting Point Road Junction in centre of EICHERSCHEID at 10.06 hours.

2. Reveille 07.00 hours Breakfast 07.30 hours. A Haversack Ration will be carried

3. Loading of wagons to commence at 08.00 hours, to be completed by 09.00 hours.

4. The Field Ambulance will parade at 09.40 ~~and~~ at road outside Orderly Room, to move off at 10.06 hours

5. Capt Clarke RAMC will arrange for collection and evacuation of Sick
Sick Parade will be at 08.30 hours.

6. Disposal of H T as usual
1st Line Transport will be brigaded and march in same order as personnel
2nd Line Transport will be parked at Q.M. Stores at 10.30 ready to move at that hour

7. Capt POTTER M.C, RAMC will act as Officer i/c Billeting Party. The Billeting Party will be as usual & N.C.O. i/c will arrange to move off at 08.00 hours, reporting to Capt. POTTER on arrival at STOTZHEIM.

8. Capt Clarke RAMC will inspect all billets before the Unit moves off and will arrange to hand over Billets to 8 Fd Amb ce

A F L Shields.

Major.
, R.A.M.C.
COMDG: 142ND FIELD AMBULANCE

Orders No 35 by Major A F L SHIELDS RAMC

APP. No 13 Commanding No 142 Field Ambulance

17.12.18

Ref 1. L.

1. No 142 Field Ambulance will move tomorrow the 18th inst to EUSKIRCHEN - to pass the Starting Point - Cross Roads 1000 yds N of the Second R in RHEDER at 10.36 hours.

2. Reveille 07.00 hours Breakfast 07.30 hours

3. Loading of wagons to commence at 08.15, to be completed by 09.15 hours

4. The Field Ambulance will parade outside the Orderly Room at 09.50 to move off at 10.10 hours

5. Capt Clarke RAMC will arrange for the Evacuation & collection of Sick
Sick Parade will be at 08.30 hours

6. Disposal of H.T as usual
1st Line Transport move in the same orders as personnel
2nd Line Transport will move behind all 1st Line Transport to the Starting Point where they will halt with the head of the column clear of the cross-roads. - To be collected by OC No 4 Coy 3rd Divl Train.

7. Capt POTTER MC RAMC will act as officer i/c Billeting Party.
The Billeting Party will be as usual.

8. Capt Clarke RAMC will inspect all billets before the Unit moves off.

A F L Shields
Major

, R.A.M.C.
COMDG: 142ND FIELD AMBULANCE

Orders No 36 by Major A.F.L. SHIELDS RAMC

APP. No 16 Commanding No 142 Field Ambulance

Ref 1.L. 18.12.18

1. No 142 Field Ambulance will move tomorrow the 19th inst to ZULPICH – to pass the Starting Point – Cross Roads in EUHENHEIM at 10.23 hours

2. Reveille 07.00 Breakfast 07.30 hours
A Haversack Ration will be carried

3. Loading of wagons will commence at 08.00 hours to be completed by 09.00 hours

4. The Field Ambulance will parade near Men's Billets at 09.15 hours to move off at 09.30 hours

5. Capt Clarke RAMC will arrange for the collection and evacuation of sick
Sick Parade will be at 08.30 hours

6. Disposal of HT as usual
1st Line Transport will march in same order as Personnel.
2nd Line Transport will be parked at Q.M. Stores ready to move at 09.45 hours.

7. Capt POTTER MC RAMC will act as Officer i/c Billeting Party. The Billeting Party will be as usual + NCO will arrange to move off at 08.30 hours reporting to Capt POTTER on arrival at ZULPICH.

8. Capt Clarke RAMC will inspect all billets before the Unit moves off

A F L Shields.
Major.
, R.A.M.C.
COMDG: 142ND FIELD AMBULANCE

Orders No. 37 by Major A. F. L. SHIELDS R.A.M.C.
APP No. 17 Commanding No. 142 Field Ambulance.

Ref. Map. 1.L. 19.12.18.

1. No. 142 Field Ambulance will move tomorrow, 20th inst to the final area BINSFELD to pass the starting point - Level Crossing 800 yards N. of L in ZULPICH, at 09.01 hours.

2. Reveille 05.45 hours; Breakfast 06.15 hours. Haversack Ration will be carried

3. Loading of wagons will commence at 06.45 hrs to be completed by 07.45 hours.

4. The Field Ambulance will parade near the men's Billets at 08.00 hours, to move off at 08.15 hours.

5. Capt. E.R. CLARKE, R.A.M.C., will arrange for the collection and evacuation of sick. Sick Parade will be at 07.15 hours.

6. 1st Line Transport will accompany unit. 2nd Line Transport - instructions issued later.

7. Major C.S.E. WRIGHT, R.A.M.C. will act as O/c Billeting Party. The billeting party will be as usual, leaving at 7.30 - to report to Major WRIGHT on arrival at BINSFELD.

8. Capt. E.R. CLARKE, R.A.M.C., will inspect all Billets before the unit moves off.

AFLShields.

Major, R.A.M.C.
COMDG: 142ND FIELD AMBULANCE.

Jan 1919

Confidential

16/3

ORIGINAL

WD

14/3524

42

War Diary of

O.C. 142nd Field Ambulance

for the month of

January 1919

C.D. Chambers.
Lieut-Col.
RAMC.
O.C. 142nd F. Amb.ce

1-2-19.

Instructions regarding War Diaries and Intelligence Summaries are contained in F. S. Regs., Part II. and the Staff Manual respectively. Title pages will be prepared in manuscript.

WAR DIARY
or
~~INTELLIGENCE SUMMARY.~~
(Erase heading not required.)

Army Form C. 2118.

O.C. 142nd Field Ambulance [illegible] MEDICAL

Place	Date	Hour	Summary of Events and Information	Remarks and references to Appendices
KELZ (GERMANY) 1 L. 1/100,000	1.1.19.		Brigade Rest Station in process of construction - accommodation at present is for 20 beds. Sent in to A.D.M.S. a list of my requirements for improving this site. Weather freezing and frosty. 142nd F.A. played 3rd F.A. and beat them by 2 goals to 1.	E.B. Chamberlain Lt-Col. RAMC
"	2.1.19.		Return of quantities of Hay and Straw and other reports of various non-medical matters called for by 9th Inf. Bde. in my capacity as District Commander of this area & have replied as far as possible in each case. Demobilisation of the unit continues.	[illegible]
"	3.1.19.		I made local requisition on Burgomaster for Stove Wood and various small requirements for the Rest Station which were necessary. These requirements have been produced forthwith and with no difficulty. R.E. requisition not having been notified as ready for issue at the time and the matter was urgent. Weather fine and cold.	[illegible]
"	4.1.19.		Programme of Recreational Training being carried out. Capt Clarke - temporary M.O. i/c 1/N.F.S. is now in medical charge of 4/R.F.S. in addition to his other duties.	[illegible]

(A7092). Wt. W12839/M1293 75,000. 1/17. D. D. & L., Ltd. Forms/C.2118/14.

Instructions regarding War Diaries and Intelligence Summaries are contained in F. S. Regs., Part II. and the Staff Manual respectively. Title pages will be prepared in manuscript.

WAR DIARY
or
~~INTELLIGENCE SUMMARY.~~

(*Erase heading not required.*)

O.C
142nd F. Ambulce

Army Form C. 2118.

Folio 2

MEDICAL

Place	Date	Hour	Summary of Events and Information	Remarks and references to Appendices
KELZ	5.1.19		Routine work. Improvements to Rest Station being carried out. Thirty bed-cots have been obtained locally; also, bricks, stove and labour for making an annexe into a ward for special cases. Fine and cold.	[illegible]
"	6.1.19		142nd FA played 7th FA at football to-day and beat the latter by 2 goals to nil. ADMS was present. Special cases and Officers (sick) have to be evacuated to Group of CCS's at COLOGNE by Divisional Ambulance cars.	[illegible]
"	7.1.19		The Rest Station is now equipped for 30 beds and can be expanded to take up to 40 cases. In my capacity of District Commander of this area (appointed by G.O.C 9th Infantry Brigade) I see the Burgomeister daily about any civil transactions and local difficulties. Passes to travel out of the area are sent by me, after interviewing the applicants with identification cards, to Staff Capt. 9th Inf. Brigade at NORVENICH (with fee of 1 mark attached). They are subsequently returned to me for issue. Weather fine and cold.	[illegible]

(A7092). Wt. W12839/M1293. 75,000. 1/17. D. D. & L., Ltd. Forms/C.2118/14.

Instructions regarding War Diaries and Intelligence Summaries are contained in F. S. Regs., Part II. and the Staff Manual respectively. Title pages will be prepared in manuscript.

WAR DIARY
or
~~INTELLIGENCE~~ SUMMARY.
(Erase heading not required.)

O.C. 142nd F. Ambulance

Army Form C. 2118.

Folio 3.
MEDICAL

Place	Date	Hour	Summary of Events and Information	Remarks and references to Appendices
KELZ	8.11.19.		Transport being overhauled to-day and vehicles are being cleaned and painted. A bath-house in connection with the hospital is being constructed.	
"	9.11.19.		Report of amount of Hay and Straw available in KELZ rendered to 9th Inf. Brigde.	
"	10.11.19.		Bed-cots have been obtained for the hospital - No. of beds 36. Incinerator, Shower-baths and hot water apparatus is being installed. Capt & Q.M. BOWEN RAMC. rejoined the unit.	
"	11.11.19.		Inspected medical equipment to-day	
"	12.11.19.		Received notification from ADMS that DMS. Second Army will inspect 142nd FA to-morrow afternoon.	
"	13.11.19.		DMS. Second Army with DDMS VIth Corps, and ADMS 3rd Divn inspected the ambulance to-day. The DMS expressed his satisfaction at the smartness of the personnel, transport and horses; at the cleanliness and completeness of the hospital; and at the cleanliness of the kitchens - He visited all the kitchens namely Hospital, Personnel, Sergeants and Officers messes, in turn - also the Recreation Room and Q.M. Stores.	

(A7092). Wt. W12839/M1293. 750,000. 1/17. D. D. & L., Ltd. Forms/C.2118/14.

Instructions regarding War Diaries and Intelligence Summaries are contained in F. S. Regs., Part II. and the Staff Manual respectively. Title pages will be prepared in manuscript.

WAR DIARY
or
~~INTELLIGENCE SUMMARY.~~
(Erase heading not required.)

Army Form C. 2118.

O. C.
142nd Fd Ambce
Folio 4
MEDICAL.

Place	Date	Hour	Summary of Events and Information	Remarks and references to Appendices
KELZ	14.1.19.		As S.M.O. "B" group I visited 4th R. Fusiliers at BLATSHEIM and 13th Kings Liverpools at KERPEN and saw the medical officers in charge of each regiment. I inspected billets, cook houses and latrines. Owing to lack of material, work in Sanitation has not progressed in some of the smaller units – improvised arrangements have been made and are in use.	[illegible]
"	15.1.19.		Ambulance personnel were medically inspected to-day by Major WRIGHT and Capt POTTER. Instructions regarding lectures in Venereal Prophylaxis were sent out to M.O's to-day – also notes re Sanitation were sent to 9th Inf. Brigade for circulation to unit Commanders.	[illegible]
"	16.1.19.		Routine office work. Nothing of importance to note.	[illegible]
"	17.1.19.		Lectures on Venereal Prophylaxis are being given as under:– 13th Kings – on 17th, 4th R.Fs on 18th, 1st N.Fs on 19th.	[illegible]
"	18.1.19.		Obtained apparatus from Adv. Depot Med. Stores for fitting up irrigation and prophylactic treatment in medical inspection rooms in "B" group.	[illegible]

(A7092). Wt. W12839/M1293. 750,000. 1/17. D. D. & L., Ltd. Forms/C.2118/14.

Instructions regarding War Diaries and Intelligence Summaries are contained in F. S. Regs., Part II. and the Staff Manual respectively. Title pages will be prepared in manuscript.

WAR DIARY
or
~~INTELLIGENCE SUMMARY.~~
(Erase heading not required.)

O.C. 142nd F. Ambulance. MEDICAL.

Army Form C. 2118.

Folio 5

Place	Date	Hour	Summary of Events and Information	Remarks and references to Appendices
KELZ	19.1.19.		Medical arrangements - 142nd F.A. - drawn up to-day. Separate accommodation for Rose Measles is difficult to obtain - further search in the district is being made. Weather colder.	Appendix I. (CW)
"	20.1.19.		Capt. CLARKE. RAMC. is detailed as M.O. to 13th Kings in addition to his present duties, whilst Capt. LEIGH is on leave. Made out revised scale of equipment for a F. Amb. and sent it in to DADMS in compliance with instructions. Weather fine, dry and cold	(CW)
"	21.1.19.		A new Cook-house has been completed. It has been made entirely by personnel and with materials from R.E. yard. The former cookhouse not being a very suitable site.	(CW)
"	22.1.19		Have detailed one or more men to understudy all important branches in the ambulance in view of demobilization. Both Sergt. Clerks were demobilized to-day. The unit is about 110 under strength. A lecture on demobilization and reconstruction was given at 14.30 hrs. to-day by Capt. BICKLEY - 4th/R. Fusiliers. The unit paraded for this lecture. weather very cold & frosty	(CW)

(A7092). Wt. W12839/M1293. 750,000. 1/17. D. D. & L., Ltd. Forms/C.2118/14.

Instructions regarding War Diaries and Intelligence Summaries are contained in F. S. Regs., Part II. and the Staff Manual respectively. Title pages will be prepared in manuscript.

WAR DIARY
or
~~INTELLIGENCE SUMMARY.~~ O.C.
(*Erase heading not required.*)
142nd Field Ambulce.

Army Form C. 2118.
Folio 6
MEDICAL

Place	Date	Hour	Summary of Events and Information	Remarks and references to Appendices
KELZ	23.1.19		Represented to A.D.M.S. the serious shortage of personnel in this unit caused by demobilization and large numbers on leave – no reinforcements are coming up. The unit can barely carry on with the numbers available to-day. Both Sergt. clerks were demobilized.	(initials)
"	24.1.19		Instructions re demobilising through D.G.M.S. for RAMC and through D.S.&T. for R.A.S.C. received. The A.D.M.S. notified me that steps were being taken to lay down the irreducible minimum strength of a F. Amb. Weather very cold during the last 2 days.	(initials)
"	25.1.19		Routine Office work. This has increased lately beyond all anticipation – necessitated by (1) Reports on Training and Education (2) Reports of military nature required by 9th Inf. Brigde for district of KELZ. (3) Work in connection with Civilian Passes and daily interviews with Burgomaster. (4) Administration of Brigade Rest Station. (5) Administration of "B" Group and Artillery Units attached to 3rd Division. Out-door inspections of the latter have likewise to be carried out weekly. With the decreasing personnel available in the unit – it is found very difficult to efficiently carry on some of the above work. A ruling as to future strength of the unit is greatly needed. Weather continues very cold.	(initials)

(A7092) Wt. W12839/M1293 750,000. 1/17. D. D. & L., Ltd. Forms/C.2118/14.

Instructions regarding War Diaries and Intelligence Summaries are contained in F. S. Regs., Part II. and the Staff Manual respectively. Title pages will be prepared in manuscript.

WAR DIARY
or
~~INTELLIGENCE SUMMARY.~~
(*Erase heading not required.*)

Army Form C. 2118.

O.C.
142nd Field Amb^ce

Folio 7
MEDICAL.

Place	Date	Hour	Summary of Events and Information	Remarks and references to Appendices
KELZ	26.1.19.		The ambulances of 3rd Div. played the KRRC in the first round of the Divisional Cup-Tie this afternoon at the Barracks. Duren It was a keenly contested match and resulted in a draw - no goals scored on either side. Snow during afternoon	(initials)
"	27.1.19.		Major WRIGHT. RAMC. proceeded on 14 days leave to U.K. to-day. Capt. MANN. RAMC. returned from leave to U.K. to-day. Capt. CLARKE. RAMC. handed over medical charge of 4/R.F.s. to Capt. McGEEHIN. MC. RAMC. on his return from leave to-day. An inspection of 23rd and 40th Bgdes R.F.A. was carried out yesterday by Major WRIGHT. These units as well as all others in "B" Group which have Medical Inspectn Rooms have been fitted up with Blue Lamp Rooms. Weather cold - more snow	(initials) (initials)
"	28.1.19.		As the downfall of snow prevented Football to-day - an organised snowball fight took place and was a great success - 50 men taking part - with officers in command of opposing sides. In the evening a Boxing Tournament took place - which was very popular - many men volunteering as competitors. It is hoped to arrange a similar display every week. Slight thaw in evening	(initials)

(A7092). Wt. W12839/M1293. 750,000. 1/17. D. D. & L., Ltd. Forms/C.2118/14.

Instructions regarding War Diaries and Intelligence Summaries are contained in F. S. Regs., Part II. and the Staff Manual respectively. Title pages will be prepared in manuscript.

WAR DIARY
or
~~INTELLIGENCE SUMMARY.~~ O. C. 142nd F. Amb.ce

(Erase heading not required.)

Army Form C. 2118.

Folio 8
MEDICAL.

Place	Date	Hour	Summary of Events and Information	Remarks and references to Appendices
KELZ.	29.1.19.		The football match between KRRC and 8th Div. F Ambce combined Team took place ~~at~~ on the 142nd F.A. ground at KELZ, this afternoon. It was again, a very close game, but in the second half, resulted in a win for the F.Ace by 2 goals to nil. A musical concert was held in the evening – 15 items (all from the unit) were included in the programme, and was well attended by the unit.	(ebc)
"	30.1.19.		A lecture on Demobilization was given at 18.00 hrs by C.O. – The lecture lasted 1 hour and 40 minutes. The history of Demobilization and Resettlement, the procedure for applications – special and ordinary – were discussed – and questions put by the men after the lecture were answered and settled.	(ebc)
"	31.1.19.		Monthly returns rendered to-day. New War Establishment for a F. Amb. has been published and returns of strength of unit are now rendered in accordance with it. The health of the unit has been excellent during the past month. Since the introduction of spray-baths and laundry facilities – a high standard of cleanliness has been maintained. E.B. Chambers Lieut-Col. RAMC O.C. 142nd F. Ambce	

(A7092). Wt. W12839/M1293. 750,000. 1/17. D. D. & L., Ltd. Forms/C.2118/14.

142 FIELD AMBULANCE. MEDICAL ARRANGEMENTS. Appendix 1

1. No.142 Field Ambulance will collect sick from "B" Group, and, in addition from the following Units :-

23rd Bde. R.F.A. .... STOCKHEIM.
40th Bde. R.F.A. ....KREUZAU.
3rd.D.A.C. R.F.A. ....LENDERSDORF.
3rd. M.G.C. ....DUREN (barracks)
20th. K.R.R. .... " "

Capt. J. Potter, R.A.M.C. will be M.O. i/c Hospital.

Only those cases of ordinary sickness (non-contagious), likely to recover within ten days, will be retained. Other cases (except those for whom special arrangements are notified in these arrangements) will be evacuated forthwith to No. 17 C.C.S. DUREN.

All Officers for evacuation will be sent to No. 36 C.C.S. COLOGNE.

All evacuations will be carried out by Motor Transport of No. 142 F.A , the N.C.O. i/c Ambulance Cars being notified on prescribed evacuation, a slip of the number and nature of cases for evacuation, and the time the transport is required.

2. DENTAL CASES.

Medical Officers i/c Units in "B" Group will arrange to send to No. 142 F.A., on Fridays, patients requiring Dental Treatment.
Each man must be in possession of the unexpired portion of the day's rations, plus rations for the next day.
Each man must be in possession of his A.B. 64.

Patients are not admitted to F.A., but particulars are to be taken and entered in a special book.

Patients are sent to C.C.S. for treatment, accompanied by Nominal Rolls in DUPLICATE. The Dental Surgeon will write disposal of patients on one roll, and return it to 142 F.A. by Motor Cyclist, who will call from 142 F.A. the following day.

Patients shewn as detained at C.C.S. are then shewn as "admitted to F.A. and evacuated to C.C.S.

Patients returned to their own Units are not officially admitted to F.A. books, but their Units are notified of the steps that have been taken.

3. VENEREAL CASES.

Gonorrhoea cases. Adequate means for treatment of such cases, pending investigation required for identification purposes by the A.P.M., will be provided. As soon as this has been completed, the case will be evacuated to C.C.S.

Venereal ~~cases~~ Sores. All cases suffering from venereal sores will be dispatched with as little delay as possible, necessitated by investigation for identification purposes, to No. 43 C.C.S. COLOGNE.
(see attached pro-forma)

4. SCABIES CASES.

Scabies cases will be evacuated to 6th Corps Scabies Station, No. 37 F.A. COLOGNE.

The N.C.O. i/c Hospital will render a written notification daily to the Orderly Room by 17.00 hours of the number of scabies Cases awaiting evacuation.

5. ROSE MEASLES.

Cases of "Rose Measles" occurring in the Division will be treated at No. 142 F.A. Cases sent by Nos. 7 & 8 F.A. will be recorded as "transferred from No. ..........F.A."

6. A.F.W 3428.

In all cases of Accidental or S.I. Injuries A.F.W3428 will be rendered, accompanied by a signed statement by the patient stating how the injury occurred. In no case will the patient be evacuated until the Medical Officer has satisfied himself that these documents have been completed.

10/1/19.

(Sd. G.O. Chambers,
Lieut-Col., R.A.M.C.
Commanding 142 Field Ambulance.

CONFIDENTIAL

21

Feb. 1919

140/3524

Original

VII 43

WAR DIARY OF

O.C. 142ND FIELD AMBULANCE,

FOR THE MONTH OF

FEBRUARY 1919

C. D. Chambers
Lieut-Col.
RAMC
O.C. 142nd F. Amb

1-3-19.

Army Form C. 2118.

WAR DIARY
or
INTELLIGENCE SUMMARY.
(Erase heading not required.)

Instructions regarding War Diaries and Intelligence Summaries are contained in F. S. Regs., Part II. and the Staff Manual respectively. Title pages will be prepared in manuscript.

February.

O.C. 142nd F. Ambulance

Folio 1

MEDICAL

Place	Date	Hour	Summary of Events and Information	Remarks and references to Appendices
KELZ	1.2.19.		Lieut. Col. G.O. Chambers RAMC proceeded on ~~leave~~ short leave to Paris. Capt H.L. MANN RAMC assumed temporary command	AHS
	2.2.19.		Frost still holds, cold dry day.	AHS
	3.2.19.		Capt. E.R. Clarke RAMC. gave a lecture on Demobility etc to all men of the unit. Maj. A.F.L. SHIELDS RAMC returned from temporary duty with DDMS. VI Corps at Berlin and assumed temporary command. DADMS 3rd Division visited this unit today and informed me that the G.O.C. 3rd Div would inspect this unit on 12th February 1919.	AHS
	4.2.19.		Cold dry day. ~~Large~~ hut for formation of a Hospital arrived today	AHS

D. D. & L., London, E.C. (A8004) Wt. W1771/M231 750,000 5/17 Sch. 52 Forms/C2118/14

Army Form C. 2118.

Instructions regarding War Diaries and Intelligence Summaries are contained in F. S. Regs., Part II. and the Staff Manual respectively. Title pages will be prepared in manuscript.

WAR DIARY
or
INTELLIGENCE SUMMARY.
(*Erase heading not required.*)

February 1919 — O.C. No 142 Field Ambulance — Sheet II

Place	Date	Hour	Summary of Events and Information	Remarks and references to Appendices
KELZ.	5/2/19.		Cold dry day, some snow.	AtLS
	6/2/19.		Frost still holds, cold. Brigadier Gen. Potter G.O.C. 9th Inf Brigade inspected this unit at 12 hours today and was entirely satisfied with all the arrangements of the Ambulance. Ten surplus horses (surplus to new Establishment) left today for remount depot.	AtLS
	7/2/19		Weather very cold. Visited No 4 Coy 3rd Div Train arranged for M.O. to lecture on Venereal disease and for prophylactic equipment to be fitted up.	AtLS
	8/2/19		Cold day frost holds.	AtLS

D. D. & L., London, E.C.
(A5004) Wt. W1771/M2 31 750,000 5/17 Sch. 52 Forms/C2118/14

Army Form C. 2118.

Instructions regarding War Diaries and Intelligence Summaries are contained in F. S. Regs., Part II. and the Staff Manual respectively. Title pages will be prepared in manuscript.

WAR DIARY
or
INTELLIGENCE SUMMARY.
(*Erase heading not required.*)

February 1919. O.C. No 144 Field Ambulance. Sheet III

Place	Date	Hour	Summary of Events and Information	Remarks and references to Appendices
KELZ.	9/2/19.		Beautiful day. L/Cpl CHIFFINCH and 4 men proceeded to DUREN to take over from No 6 Field Ambulance, to act as a holding party.	AtkS
	10/2/19.		Weather frost still holds. Sgt SMITH RAMC. delivered a lecture on "Poultry Farming". Aeroplane descended beside village today owing to engine trouble arranged for a guard to look after it until it could be moved.	AtkS
	11/2/19		Bright sunny day. Capt. E.R. CLARKE RAMC. detailed and left today, to take over Rest Station DUREN from No 6 Field Ambulance	AtkS
	12/2/19		Weather warm day thaw has set in. Visited DUREN and arranged with Capt E.R. CLARKE RAMC. to accommodate 20 sick if required in the site ~~formerly~~ which he occupying at present.	AtkS

D. D. & L., London, E.C. (A8094) Wt. W1771/M2031 750,000 5/17 Sch. 52 Forms/C2118/14

Instructions regarding War Diaries and Intelligence Summaries are contained in F. S. Regs., Part II. and the Staff Manual respectively. Title pages will be prepared in manuscript.

WAR DIARY
or
INTELLIGENCE SUMMARY.
February 1919 (*Erase heading not required.*) O.C. No 142 Field Ambulance

Army Form C. 2118.

Sheet XV

Place	Date	Hour	Summary of Events and Information	Remarks and references to Appendices
KELZ.	12/2		Visited A.D.M.S. 3rd Division Lieut Col. G. O. CHAMBERS M.C. RAMC returned from Paris leave and resumes command.	A+LS
	13/2.		Warm day, thaw continues Maj. Gen. DEVERELL CB G.O.C. 3rd Division inspected this unit today, accompanied by the G.O.C 9th Inf Brigade Brig Gen POTTER. and the D.A.Q.M.G. 3rd Div. The Major General expressed his high approval with the organization of the Unit, the feeding arrangements & comfort of the patients and of the personnel, the condition of the horses & smartness of the transport—	A+LS
	14/2.		Warm day Visited 9th Inf Brigade and discussed certain routine arrangements with the G.O.C. 9th Inf Bgde	A+LS

(A8604) Wt. W1771/M2 31 750,000 5/17 Sch. 52 Forms/C2118/14 D. D. & L., London, E.C.

Instructions regarding War Diaries and Intelligence Summaries are contained in F. S. Regs., Part II. and the Staff Manual respectively. Title pages will be prepared in manuscript.

WAR DIARY
or
INTELLIGENCE SUMMARY.
(Erase heading not required.)

Army Form C. 2118.

February 1919 — O.C. No 142 Field Ambulance — Sheet V

Place	Date	Hour	Summary of Events and Information	Remarks and references to Appendices
KELZ	15/2.		Dull day some showers Visited ADMS 3rd Div DUREN and discussed with him the question of the retention of men necessary for the carrying on of the Routine work of the unit. He informed me that the subject was under consideration and a definite policy to be followed would be issued by ADMS 6th Corps in the course of a few days.	A.T.S.
	16/2.		Weather very showery As No 8 Field Ambulance Rest Station closed down temporarily today, arranged to take in the sick from No 8 Field Ambulance. Case of Foot & Mouth Disease which was reported in the village was notified to ADMS. All precautions were taken.	A.T.S.
	17/2.		Wet day. Visited 23rd Brigade RFA inspected the sanitary arrangements found that cook houses were not clean, instructed that they should be removed and that meat-safes should be provided.	

D. D. & L., London, E.C. (A8004) Wt. W1771/M2 31 750,000 5/17 Sch. 52 Forms/C2118/14

Army Form C. 2118.

Instructions regarding War Diaries and Intelligence Summaries are contained in F. S. Regs., Part II. and the Staff Manual respectively. Title pages will be prepared in manuscript.

WAR DIARY
or
INTELLIGENCE SUMMARY.
(*Erase heading not required.*)

February 1919. DC. No 142 Field Ambulance Sheet VI

Place	Date	Hour	Summary of Events and Information	Remarks and references to Appendices
KELZ.	18/2		Wet day. Lecture by Sgt A.L. SMITH RAMC on 'Poultry Farming'. Orders received from G.O.C. 9th Inf Brigade to the effect that 13th Kings Liverpool Regt would move tomorrow en route for COLOGNE and that all other units of the Brigade Group would move during week-end. Medical arrangements issued accordingly for the march.	
	19/2		Weather - dry day. Lecture on Venereal Prophylaxis was given by Maj. A.F.L. SHIELDS to all men of the unit	AFLS
	20/2		Weather - some showers. ~~Ma~~ Capt. E.C. BOWEN. lectured on Advantages of Army Life.	AFLS
	21/2.		Weather dry cold.	

D. D. & L., London, E.C. (A8604) Wt. W1771/M231 750,000 5/17 Sch. 52 Forms/C2118/14

Army Form C. 2118.

Instructions regarding War Diaries and Intelligence Summaries are contained in F. S. Regs., Part II. and the Staff Manual respectively. Title pages will be prepared in manuscript.

WAR DIARY
or
INTELLIGENCE SUMMARY.
(Erase heading not required.)

February 1919. O.C. No 142 Field Ambulance. Sheet VII

Place	Date	Hour	Summary of Events and Information	Remarks and references to Appendices
KELZ.	21/2		Arranged for Maj. A.F.L. SHIELDS Ramc and Capt & Q.m E.C. BOWEN. to go to EHRENFELD today to make arrangements re taking over stores etc from No 4 Field Ambulance Guards Division from whom we take over on Tuesday 25th Feb.	
		P.m.	O.C. No 4 Field Ambulance visited this unit & I showed him over the Hospital, Billets etc. I arranged with him, to send a Holding Party to EHRENFELD on Monday 24th Feb	AFLS
	22/2		Weather – Heavy showers in the morning, brighter in afternoon. Arranged for packing of wagons, preparatory to move on Monday, to be started at 9 am Sunday 23rd February. R.A.M.C. Divisional Football Team played 1st Gordons in Semi-Final of Divisional Competition but were beaten by 3–2 by the Gordons who had a much stronger team.	AFLS
	23/2.		Weather – dry cold. Made arrangements with 3rd Div "Q" to have two motor lorries put at my disposal tomorrow for the move	AFLS

2353 Wt. W2544/1454 700,000 5/15 D. D. & L. A.D.S.S./Forms/C. 2118.

Instructions regarding War Diaries and Intelligence Summaries are contained in F. S. Regs., Part II. and the Staff Manual respectively. Title pages will be prepared in manuscript.

WAR DIARY
or
INTELLIGENCE SUMMARY.
(Erase heading not required.)

Army Form C. 2118.

Sheet VIII

February 1919. OC No 142 Field Ambulance

Place	Date	Hour	Summary of Events and Information	Remarks and references to Appendices
KELZ.	23/2		Issued necessary instructions for move to KERPEN tomorrow.	AHD
KERPEN.	24/2.		The Field ambulance in charge of Maj. A F L Shields marched to KERPEN today arriving at 13.30 hours. Unit billeted in the School. Sent Quartermaster (Capt. E.C. BOWEN) to EHRENFELD to take over Billets from No 4 Field Ambulance. Instructions received for move to EHRENFELD ~~tomorrow~~ Orders issued accordingly.	AHD.
EHRENFELD	25/2		Weather – heavy rain all morning, stopped about noon. Unit marched to EHRENFELD passing starting point at 9.15 hours, good march, no men fell out. Billets satisfactory. Arranged for collection of sick from 1/9th D. L. Infantry (Pioneer Battn) according to instructions received from A.D.M.S. 3rd Div.	AHD

D. D. & L., London, E.C. (A8004) Wt. W1771/M2 31 750,000 5/17 Sch. 52 Forms/C2118/14

Instructions regarding War Diaries and Intelligence Summaries are contained in F. S. Regs., Part II. and the Staff Manual respectively. Title pages will be prepared in manuscript.

WAR DIARY
or
INTELLIGENCE SUMMARY.
(*Erase heading not required.*)

Army Form C. 2118.

Sheet IX

February 1919. O.C. No 142 Field Ambulance

Place	Date	Hour	Summary of Events and Information	Remarks and references to Appendices
EHRENFELD	26/2		weather – warm sunny day. Invitation received from 4th Battn Guards M. G. Regt – inviting as many men as possible to a Kinema Show of Official German War Films. Detailed a party to attend this Show which was at 11.00 hours. the men enjoyed the entertainment	a.t.l.
	27/2.		weather – showery, cold. Arranged for civilian swimming baths at EHRENFELD to be used two mornings per week by the men of this unit	a.t.l.
	28/2		weather – wet day Brig. Gen. POTTER G.O.C. 9th Inf Brigade inspected these Headquarters, Hospital, Billets etc. The Ambulance Rest Station comprises part of the Civilian Hospital in the VOGELSANGER STRASSE EHRENFELD. It is quite up to date in modern requirements. Accomodation for 2 officers – 37 other Ranks.	

C. D. Chambers
Lieut Col RAMC
O.C. 142nd F. Amb.

D. D. & L., London, E.C. (A8004) Wt. W1771/M31 750,000 5/17 Sch. 52 Forms/C2118/14

CONFIDENTIAL

Mar. 1919

12

ORIGINAL

Vol 44

140/3551.

WAR DIARY OF

O.C. 142 FIELD AMBULANCE

FOR THE MONTH OF

MARCH 1919

DATE 31-3-19.

A D Chambers

LIEUT-COL. R.A.M.C.

O.C. 142 FIELD AMBULANCE.

Army Form C. 2118.

WAR DIARY
or
~~INTELLIGENCE SUMMARY.~~

Sheet I

Instructions regarding War Diaries and Intelligence Summaries are contained in F. S. Regs., Part II. and the Staff Manual respectively. Title pages will be prepared in manuscript.

March 1st 1919 (Erase heading not required.) O.C. No 142 Field Ambulance

Place	Date	Hour	Summary of Events and Information	Remarks and references to Appendices
EHRENFELD	1/3.		weather - fine warm day. Gave a Lecture on "Venereal Prophylaxis" to 1/5 West Yorks Regt. who have arrived to relieve the 13th Battn Kings Liverpool Regt. A pay Parade was held today all men in the unit attending. at.L.S. Capt C.E. CLARKE Rame rejoined from temporary duty with APM DUREN.	[illegible]
	2/3.		weather - warm sunny day. ~~All~~ In accordance with instructions received ~~the~~ time was altered at 23.00 hours last night and Clocks were put on one hour. D.A.D.M.S. 3rd Division visited this unit today at.L.S.	[illegible]
	3/3.		weather - warm sunny day very wet in afternoon	at.L.S. [illegible]
	4/3.		weather - wet day. Capt. C.E. CLARKE Rame inspected all "Blue Lamp Rooms" in 9th Inf Brigade, found most of these complete, arranged for others to be completed as per instructions. at.L.S.	

Instructions regarding War Diaries and Intelligence Summaries are contained in F. S. Regs., Part II. and the Staff Manual respectively. Title pages will be prepared in manuscript.

WAR DIARY
or
~~INTELLIGENCE SUMMARY.~~
(Erase heading not required.)

Army Form C. 2118.

Sheet II

March 1919 — O.C. No 142 Field Ambulance

Place	Date	Hour	Summary of Events and Information	Remarks and references to Appendices
EHRENFELD	5/3		weather – dry day.	
			arranged for Capt E.C. CLARKE RAMC to visit HQ 9th Inf. Brigade to ascertain numbers of other ranks who require vaccination	
			Arranged for Maj A.T. SHIELDS RAMC to visit 1/4 York & Lancs Regt who arrived in this Brigade 4/3/19 to arrange for collection of sick, lecture on Venereal Prophylaxis and to inspect the Blue Lamp Room.	
			Capt. H.L. MANN RAMC has been unwell for two days arranged for him to be removed into a Comfortable room in Hospital where he would have proper attention	(initialled)
	6/3.		weather – very wet day	
			Capt. E.C. CLARKE RAMC visited No 4 Coy 3rd Div Train to arrange for the proper equipment of a Blue Lamp Room.	(initialled)

D. D. & L., London, E.C. (A8004) Wt. W1771/M2 31 750,000 5/17 Sch. 52 Forms/C2118/14

Instructions regarding War Diaries and Intelligence Summaries are contained in F. S. Regs., Part II. and the Staff Manual respectively. Title pages will be prepared in manuscript.

WAR DIARY
or
~~INTELLIGENCE~~ SUMMARY.
(Erase heading not required.)

Army Form C. 2118.

March 1919. OC No 142 Field Ambulance Sheet III

Place	Date	Hour	Summary of Events and Information	Remarks and references to Appendices
EHRENFELD	7/3.		weather – good ADMS. & D.A.D.M.S. 3rd Division visited this unit today and inspected Hospital, billets etc they were quite satisfied with the condition of the unit.	A.H.S.
	8/3.		Weather still remains good Reconnoitred the area of the STADTGART in accordance with orders received from ADMS to ~~fun~~ choose a site for a Collecting Post in the event of civil disturbances in COLOGNE. Called at 9th I Bgde HQ and discussed with the G.O.C. 9th I.B. the arrangements	A.H.S.
	9/3		weather – good 12 Other Rank reinforcements arrived for duty with this unit	
	10/3.		Weather – good weather continues. Arranged for the taking over of another ward for purpose of Convalescent patients in this Hospital.	A.H.S.
	11/3.		Weather – good.	

D. D. & L., London, E.C. (A8004) Wt. W2771/M2 31 750,000 5/17 Sch. 52 Forms/C2118/14

Instructions regarding War Diaries and Intelligence Summaries are contained in F. S. Regs., Part II. and the Staff Manual respectively. Title pages will be prepared in manuscript.

WAR DIARY
or
INTELLIGENCE SUMMARY.
(Erase heading not required.)

Army Form C. 2118.

Sheet IV

March 1919. O.C. No [illegible] Field Ambulance

Place	Date	Hour	Summary of Events and Information	Remarks and references to Appendices
EHRENFELD	12/3.		13 other Ranks arrived today for duty with this unit and were posted to various Sections.	
			The Divisional RAMC Football team represented the Division in the Semi final of 2nd Army Cup and beat VI Corps Troops 2 – 0	
			Capt J. POTTER MC RAMC returned from temporary duty with 2nd Royal Scots.	
	13/3.		Weather – remains good.	
	14/3		Weather – good.	
			D.D.M.S. VI Corps accompanied by D.A.D.M.S. VI Corps inspected the Hospital today. He found everything in order & was quite satisfied with the general arrangements. ARLS	
	15/3		Weather – good weather continues	

D. D. & L., London, E.C. (A8004) Wt. W1771/M2031 750,000 5/17 Sch. 52 Forms/C2118/14

Instructions regarding War Diaries and Intelligence Summaries are contained in F. S. Regs., Part II. and the Staff Manual respectively. Title pages will be prepared in manuscript.

WAR DIARY
or
~~INTELLIGENCE SUMMARY.~~
(Erase heading not required.)

Army Form C. 2118.

March 1919 O.C. 142 Field Ambulance Sheet V

Place	Date	Hour	Summary of Events and Information	Remarks and references to Appendices
EHRENFELD	16/3		Played final of Corps football Competition v. 35 Bde R.G.A. Result 0-0 after extra time 1-1. Very hard game 4 men of the unit in the team	M
	17/3		Replay of Cup Tie Result 2-0. Cup presented by Corps Commander	M
			3. O.R. Reinforcements reported for duty with unit	M
	18/3		Weather rather cold	
	19/3		Major A.F.L. Shields detached for temporary duty as DADMS Northern Division M	
	20/3.		Semi final of 2nd Army Cup v R.A.S.C. 2nd Army H.Q. Result won 5-1.	
			1 O.R. Reinforcement reported for duty M	
	21/3		A.D.M.S. Northern Division inspected Hospital + also inspected the Medical arrangements of 1/5 West Yorks 1/6 West Yorks + Northern Machine Gun Battalions. He was quite satisfied with all except the 1/6 West Yorks whose Blue Lamp Room was unsatisfactory M	

D. D. & L., London, E.C.
(A8004) Wt. W1771/M2-31 750,000 5/17 Sch. 52 Forms/C2118/14

Instructions regarding War Diaries and Intelligence Summaries are contained in F. S. Regs., Part II. and the Staff Manual respectively. Title pages will be prepared in manuscript.

WAR DIARY
or
~~INTELLIGENCE SUMMARY.~~
(*Erase heading not required.*)

Army Form C. 2118.

Sheet VI

March 1919 — OC 142 Field Ambulance

Place	Date	Hour	Summary of Events and Information	Remarks and references to Appendices
EHRENFELD	22/3		A.D.M.S. accompanied by SMO group inspected Medical arrangements of 1/9 Durham Light Infantry and 1/4 Yorks & Lancs Regt. and found them satisfactory except the Blue Lamp Room of 9 DLI.	
	23/3		Weather becoming colder. Wire from Division that all leave & demobilization stopped on account of strike.	
	25/3		Divisional Commander accompanied by ADMS. inspected the Hospital & Mens billets and expressed satisfaction with all arrangements.	
	24/3		Semi final of Army Football Cup + 1st Cameron Highlanders v R.A.M.C. Northern Division won by the former 4-0. A special train was provided to convey spectators to BONN & large crowds availed themselves of it. 1 OR Reinforcement reported for duty	
	26/3.		Capt H L Mann appointed in temporary Medical charge of 9th DLI & Northern Div. R.E. in place of 2 officers demobilized	

D. D. & L., London, E.C.
(A8004) Wt. W1771/M2-31 750,000 5/17 Sch. 52 Forms/C2118/14

Instructions regarding War Diaries and Intelligence Summaries are contained in F. S. Regs., Part II. and the Staff Manual respectively. Title pages will be prepared in manuscript.

WAR DIARY
or
~~INTELLIGENCE~~ SUMMARY.
(Erase heading not required.)

Army Form C. 2118.

Sheet VII

March 1919 — OC 142 Field Amb

Place	Date	Hour	Summary of Events and Information	Remarks and references to Appendices
EHRENFELD	27/3		Sanitary inspection of unit today by Capt POTTER.	
	28/3		Weather very cold & snowing	
	29/3		Nil	
	30/3		Snow still falling	
	31/3		ADMS inspected animals & animal accounts & found everything satisfactory	
			Capt Clarke RAMC admitted to Hospital sick	

E D Chambers
Lieut Col.
O.C. 142nd F. Amb.

D. D. & L., London, E.C.
(A8004) Wt. W1771/M2031 750,000 5/17 Sch. 52 Forms/C2118/14

CONFIDENTIAL

apr. 1919

ORIGINAL

WAR DIARY OF

O.C. 142 FIELD AMBULANCE

FOR THE MONTH OF

APRIL. 1919

H. L. [illegible]

CAPT. R.A.M.C.

COMMANDING 142 FIELD AMBULANCE.

Army Form C. 2118.

Instructions regarding War Diaries and Intelligence Summaries are contained in F. S. Regs., Part II. and the Staff Manual respectively. Title pages will be prepared in manuscript.

WAR DIARY
or
~~INTELLIGENCE~~ ~~SUMMARY.~~
(Erase heading not required.)

O.C. 142 Field Ambulance

Sheet I

Place	Date	Hour	Summary of Events and Information	Remarks and references to Appendices
EHRENFELD	1/4/19		1 O.R. reported for duty with this unit. Capt Clarke admitted to Hosp.	
"	2/4/19		Weather very bright & sunny. ~~Capt Clarke admitted to Hosp.~~	
	3/4/19		Weather remains bright Capt Clarke discharged from Hosp.	
	4/4/19		Lt. Col. G.O. Chambers R.C. S.M.O. Group, inspected sanitation of all units in the group. Everything satisfactory including all Blue Lamp Rooms, except a new building taken over by 1/5th West Yorks for the reception of a new draft of 400. The sanitary arrangements were unsatisfactory and a report was made to A.D.M.S. Northern Division	
	5/4/19		Capt Potter detailed to visit M.G. Battn temporarily vice Capt Dowling R.C. on leave.	
	6/4/19		Weather warm & sunny	
	7/4/19		3rd Machine Gun Battalion left Brigade group today & are attached to 76th Inf. Bde.	
"	8/4/19		1/6 W. Yorks moved to BARTEL STRASSE GYMNASIUM EHRENFELD today. Weather warm and sunny	

G.O. Chambers
Lt. Col.

D. D. & L., London, E.C.
(A8004) Wt. W1771/M2031 750,000 5/17 Sch. 52 Forms/C2118/14

Instructions regarding War Diaries and Intelligence Summaries are contained in F. S. Regs., Part II. and the Staff Manual respectively. Title pages will be prepared in manuscript.

WAR DIARY
or
~~INTELLIGENCE SUMMARY.~~

(*Erase heading not required.*) O.C. 142nd F. Amb^ce

Army Form C. 2118.

Sheet II.

Place	Date	Hour	Summary of Events and Information	Remarks and references to Appendices
EHRENFEID	9.4.19.		Capt. Potter M.C. proceeded on leave today. Weather very fine	(init.)
			Routine Hospital work. Nothing of importance to record.	(init.)
"	10.4.19.		Fire Orders revised and published. Standing Orders for 142nd F.A.	
"	11.4.19.		in the event of Civil Disturbances read out on parade (9 am 12th inst)	(init.)
"	12.4.19.		Brig.-Gen. CAREY C.B., C.M.G. visited OC this morning to discuss the question of disciplinary measures re Ven. Disease. It was decided that two disciplinary measures of precautions should be submitted to the G.O.C. Northern Division as follows:- 1. It should be made a punishable offence if the man infected cannot identify the house and give its address as required by APM Report and "A" Branch Report. 2. A system of card-slips with man's name, No, Reg. Date should be introduced in every unit and a locked "letter-box" provided into which the men will drop their cards filled in immediately after using the Blue Lamp Room. Hour of using the latter will be stated on these cards. The cards will be collected every morning by MO and kept by him for record. Weather dull & cooler	(init.)

D. D. & L., London, E.C.
(A8004) Wt. W1771/M2'31 750,000 5/17 Sch. 52 Forms/C2118/14

Instructions regarding War Diaries and Intelligence Summaries are contained in F. S. Regs., Part II. and the Staff Manual respectively. Title pages will be prepared in manuscript.

WAR DIARY
or
~~INTELLIGENCE SUMMARY.~~ O.C.

(Erase heading not required.) 142nd Field Ambulance.

Army Form C. 2118.

Sheet III

Place	Date	Hour	Summary of Events and Information	Remarks and references to Appendices
EHRENFELD	13.4.19		Attended a Court of Enquiry at ADMS Office this morning regarding ~~the~~ deficiency of 1000 marks on a requisition for cash drawn from F Cashier Second Army on 10-3-19. Weather rainy and mild.	(initials)
"	14.4.19.		Visited No 7 F Amb. at RHIEL this morning. DADMS called in afternoon to discuss medical arrangements in Defence Scheme. Weather rainy and windy	(initials)
"	15.4.19		Nothing of note to-day. Pay-day. Weather very changeable	(initials)
"	16.4.19		ADMS - Col. F.J. McCLENNAN. DSO - called to bid farewell to the unit on his departure to-day. Heavy rain.	(initials)
"	17.4.19.		D.M.S. Second Army accompanied by ADMS. Northern Division inspected the Rest Station. The DMS expressed his satisfaction on the general arrangements and appearance of the hospital. Divisional inspection of Cookhouses takes place to-day.	(initials)
"	18.4.19.		142nd FA obtained 2nd place (Second Prize) in unit Cookhouse Competition. Visited ADMS this morning. Weather fine and mild.	(initials)

D. D. & L., London, E.C.
(A8004) Wt. W1771/M2 31 750,000 5/17 Sch. 52 Forms/C2118/14

Army Form C. 2118.

Instructions regarding War Diaries and Intelligence Summaries are contained in F. S. Regs., Part II. and the Staff Manual respectively. Title pages will be prepared in manuscript.

WAR DIARY
or
~~INTELLIGENCE~~ ~~SUMMARY~~.

(*Erase heading not required.*)

O.C. 142nd Field Ambulance — Sheet IV

Place	Date	Hour	Summary of Events and Information	Remarks and references to Appendices
EHRENFELD.	19.4.19.		Nothing of note to-day. Weather fine.	(initials)
"	20.4.19		Attended a conference of OC's F.A's at ADMS Northern Div. this morning. There is a possibility of the division moving further into GERMANY towards ESSEN. — Medical arrangements were discussed regarding this move. During the afternoon Maj. General BABTIE V.C. and Maj. General THOMPSON KCMG inspected the hospital. The former expressed his complete satisfaction with the medical arrangements therein. Weather fine & fresh.	(initials)
"	21.4.19		Routine work to-day. Weather very fine.	(initials)
"	22.4.19.		Attended Conference of DMS. Army of the Rhine at 64 CCS this morning (10.30 a.m.). Maj. Genl. BABTIE was present and gave a farewell address. All DDsMS. ADsMS and OsC. Medical Units in the Army were present. Maj. Genl. THOMPSON discussed various subjects on medical organisation. See appendix I	(initials)
"	23.4.19.		Inspected F.A's and 59th Sanitary Section of VI Corps, i.e. Demobilisation Registers today in accordance with instructions received from DDMS VI Corps	(initials)

D. D. & L., London, E.C. (A8004) Wt. W1771/M2-31 750,000 5/17 Sch. 52 Forms/C2118/14

Instructions regarding War Diaries and Intelligence Summaries are contained in F. S. Regs., Part II. and the Staff Manual respectively. Title pages will be prepared in manuscript.

WAR DIARY
or
~~INTELLIGENCE SUMMARY.~~
(*Erase heading not required.*)

O.C. 142nd Field Ambulance

Army Form C. 2118.

Sheet V

Hour, Date, Place	Summary of Events and Information	Remarks and references to Appendices
EHRENFELD. 24.4.19	Capt. J. POTTER. MC RAMC has been granted 3 days extra leave. He returns on the 27th inst. Completed inspections of unit Demobilization Rosters to-day and rendered the report direct to DDMS VIth Corps.	
" 25.4.19	Lieut Col G. O. Chambers M.C. R.A.M.C. granted leave to United Kingdom.	RAC
" 26.4.19	Routine work only today.	RAC
" 27.4.19	Sunday divine services.	RAC
" 28.4.19	Pay parade. Weather dull & cold.	
" 29.4.19	A.D.M.S. Northern Division visited ambulance, spoke to the men on demobilization and inspected horse lines & men's quarters.	
" 30.4.19	Nothing of note to record. Weather very cold.	

R.A. [illegible] Capt RAMC

CONFIDENTIAL

May 1919

ORIGINAL

WAR DIARY OF

O.C. 142 FIELD AMBULANCE

FOR THE MONTH OF

MAY. 1919.

C.W. Chambers.
Lieut-Col., R.A.M.C.
O.C. 142 Field Ambulance

Instructions regarding War Diaries and Intelligence Summaries are contained in F. S. Regs., Part II. and the Staff Manual respectively. Title pages will be prepared in manuscript.

WAR DIARY
or
~~INTELLIGENCE SUMMARY.~~
(*Erase heading not required.*)

O.C. 142nd Field Ambulance

Army Form C. 2118.

Sheet I

Hour, Date, Place	Summary of Events and Information	Remarks and references to Appendices
Ehrenfeld. 1. 5. 19.	Attended A.D.M.S. Office to discuss detail of forthcoming ceremonial parade. Capt J. Potter M.C. R.A.M.C. doing duty as M.O. i/c Northern Div. R.E. Capt Name doing duty as M.O. i/c 1/6th West Yorks.	[illegible]
2.5.19.	Routine ambulance duties. Wet day.	[illegible]
3.5.19.	The three Field Ambulances practised ceremonial parade at HQrs No 7 Field Ambulance A.D.M.S. Northern Div. taking the parade.	[illegible]
4.5.19.	Sunday. Divine Services	[illegible]
5.5.19.	Paraded with No 7 & No 8 Field ambulances and took part in Divisional practice of forthcoming ceremonial parade.	[illegible]

(73989) W4141—463. 400,000. 9/14. H.&J.Ltd. Forms/C. 2118/10.

Instructions regarding War Diaries and Intelligence Summaries are contained in F. S. Regs., Part II. and the Staff Manual respectively. Title pages will be prepared in manuscript.

WAR DIARY
or
~~INTELLIGENCE SUMMARY~~.
(Erase heading not required.)

O.C. 142nd Field Ambulance

Army Form C. 2118.

Sheet II

Hour, Date, Place	Summary of Events and Information	Remarks and references to Appendices
Ehrenfeld. 6.5.19.	Nothing of importance today.	[illegible]
" 7.5.19.	Paraded men for ceremonial parade at 36. C.C.S. All very smart.	[illegible]
" 8.5.19.	Forty men of the ambulance paraded with No 7 & 8 Field Ambulance under A.D.M.S. Northern Division & took part in ceremonial parade & march past. Reviewing officer His Royal Highness the Duke Connaught. Twenty men of the ambulance paraded at 36. C.C.S. under Capt Dowling R.A.M.C (acting D.A.D.M.S Northern Division) & took part in ceremonial parade, reviewing officer His Royal Highness the Duke of Connaught.	[illegible]

Instructions regarding War Diaries and Intelligence Summaries are contained in F. S. Regs., Part II. and the Staff Manual respectively. Title pages will be prepared in manuscript.

WAR DIARY
or
~~INTELLIGENCE SUMMARY.~~
(*Erase heading not required.*)

O.C. 142nd Field Ambulance

Army Form C. 2118.

Sheet III

Hour, Date, Place	Summary of Events and Information	Remarks and references to Appendices
Erlenbach 9. 5. 19.	Routine duties today. Weather fine & hot.	[illegible]
" 10. 5. 19.	Attended Conference of D.M.S. Rhine Army. 1st Subject of discussion R.A.M.C. War Memorial. Resolutions of Meeting published & copies filed. Afterwards various instructions were given by D.M.S. Lt-Col. Chambers M.C. R.A.M.C. granted 5 days extension of leave. 20 O.Rs on Rhine Steamer Trip.	[illegible]
" 11. 5. 19.	Sunday, Divine services.	[illegible]
" 12. 5. 19.	Pay parade.	[illegible]
" 13. 5. 19.	Capt Mitchell R.A.M.C. M.O. i/c 1/4th Yorks and Lancs acted as Orderly Officer in the afternoon & evening.	[illegible]
" 14. 5. 19.	Nothing to record today.	[illegible]

Army Form C. 2118.

WAR DIARY
or
~~INTELLIGENCE SUMMARY~~.
(*Erase heading not required.*)

O.C. 142nd Field Ambulance

Sheet IV

Instructions regarding War Diaries and Intelligence Summaries are contained in F.S. Regs., Part II. and the Staff Manual respectively. Title pages will be prepared in manuscript.

Hour, Date, Place	Summary of Events and Information	Remarks and references to Appendices
Ehrenfeld 15.5.19.	Weather fine & very hot.	W.A.
" 16.5.19.	Lieut. Col. G.O. Chambers M.C. RAMC returned from leave in U.K.	W.A.
" 17.5.19.	Orders received from ADMS Northern Division that 142nd F. Ambulance will be disbanded as a reduction of 3 to 2 FA's per division in Rhine Army has been made.	G.O. Chambers Lt-Col
" 18.5.19.	In view of No 8 F.Amb. (Regular unit) being composed chiefly of demobilizable Officers and men, most of the personnel of 142nd F.Amb. will be transferred to that unit. 50 men from 1/4 Yorks and Lancs. arrived yesterday for temporary duty with 142nd FA. This is being done for all medical units to enable the releasable RAMC to be demobilized	

Instructions regarding War Diaries and Intelligence Summaries are contained in F. S. Regs., Part II. and the Staff Manual respectively. Title pages will be prepared in manuscript.

WAR DIARY
or
INTELLIGENCE ~~SUMMARY~~.
(*Erase heading not required.*)

Army Form C. 2118.

O.C. 142nd Field Ambulance
Sheet V

Hour, Date, Place	Summary of Events and Information	Remarks and references to Appendices
EHRENFELD. 19.5.19.	The unit is to be disbanded in the course of the next week. No 8 FA will take over the hospital and present site of 142nd FA. Weather continues fine.	[illegible]
" 20-5-19.	Instructions received from ADMS that No 8 F.Amb. is to be disbanded instead of 142nd FA.	[illegible]
" 21-5-19.	Visited units of London Div. re inspection of Demob.n Rosters. Attended conference of O's C. Field Amb.ces at office of DDMS VI Corps in afternoon – when scheme of advance, in the event of Refusal of Peace Terms, was given out.	[illegible]
" 22.5.19	Inspection of units' Demob. Rosters continued. Capt. SLATER RAMC. posted to this amb. for duty.	[illegible]
" 23.5.19	Exchanged 2 Amb. wagons with those of No 8 F.A. as latter's are in better condition. Held a parade at 14-00 hrs of unit and re-organised the Bearer Division which now consists of 15 Bearer Squads (including att.d Infantry)	[illegible]

(73989) W4141—463. 400,000. 9/14. H.&J.Ltd. Forms/C. 2118/10.

Instructions regarding War Diaries and Intelligence Summaries are contained in F.S. Regs., Part II. and the Staff Manual respectively. Title pages will be prepared in manuscript.

WAR DIARY
or
~~INTELLIGENCE SUMMARY~~.
(*Erase heading not required.*)

Army Form C. 2118.

O.C. 142nd Field Ambulance

Sheet VI.

Hour, Date, Place	Summary of Events and Information	Remarks and references to Appendices
EHRENFELD. 24.5.19.	Completed Inspection of Demob^n Rosters of CCS's to-day. Weather continues very fine and warm. Capt. SLATER RAMC posted to 52nd North^d Fusiliers for duty.	[illegible]
" 25.5.19	Routine office work to-day. Scheme of Advance into GERMANY received & acknowledged.	[illegible]
" 26.5.19.	Inspected Demob. Rosters of No 13 B. Depot Med Stores No 2 Adv. Depot Med. Stores. No 20 MAC and No 25 Sanitary Section.	[illegible]
" 27.5.19.	Rendered consolidated report on Demob^n Rosters to-day. Weather Sultry and dull.	[illegible]
" 28.5.19	Visited 1st Northern Brigade H.Q. and met the G.O.C. Brig. Gen. KENNEDY C.M.G. Medical arrangements in the event of civil Disturbances and in the case of an advance were discussed - OC. 142nd FA. being S.M.O. of 1st North^n Inf. Brigade as well as 2nd North^n Inf. Brigade - as	

Instructions regarding War Diaries and Intelligence Summaries are contained in F. S. Regs., Part II. and the Staff Manual respectively. Title pages will be prepared in manuscript.

WAR DIARY
or
~~INTELLIGENCE SUMMARY~~.
(Erase heading not required.)

Army Form C. 2118.

O.C. 142nd Field Ambulance
Sheet VII

Hour, Date, Place	Summary of Events and Information	Remarks and references to Appendices
EHRENFELD 28-5-19.	No 8 Field Ambulance is now broken up. In the event of a move - one Section of the Ambulance personnel will proceed by lorry with the Advancing Troops (in lorries and busses) of 1st Northern Brigade. The remainder of the Ambulance will proceed with the 2nd Northern Brigade by route march.	(initials)
" 29-5-19.	Conferred with OC 7th F. Amb. re the painting of Horse Ambulance wagons. A uniform scheme was arranged and a report sent to the ADMS. Weather continues very fine.	(initials)
" 30-5-19.	No further information received re movement of troops. A draft of 8 infantry trained in H.T. duties have arrived from Northern Divisional Train to replace RASC (HT) personnel demobilised. A few of them have had experience of horses in civic life - but the majority	

Instructions regarding War Diaries and Intelligence Summaries are contained in F. S. Regs., Part II. and the Staff Manual respectively. Title pages will be prepared in manuscript.

WAR DIARY
or
~~INTELLIGENCE SUMMARY~~.
(Erase heading not required.)

Army Form C. 2118.

O.C. 142nd Field Ambulance

Sheet VIII

Hour, Date, Place	Summary of Events and Information	Remarks and references to Appendices
EHRENFELD. 30-5-19	have only had a week's training before being sent to this unit. Held a conference with Officers of 142nd FA. re Scheme of Advance.	[initials]
" 31-5-19	Demobilisation has been continuing satisfactorily. only 34 RAMC 7. RASC (MT) 4. (HT) and 3 P.B. remain in the unit. The draft of 50 Infantry from 1/4 York. and Lancs. have taken to their new duties satisfactorily and many of them give promise of making useful RAMC orderlies in the near future. The health of the 2nd Northern Brigade during the month under review, has been good. There has been very little sickness. Scabies and Venereal Disease do not appear to be more prevalent. Admissions for the former (Scabies) are lower than they have been for some time. Weather - remarkably fine month very little rain.	[signature] Lieut-Col RAMC O.C. 142nd F Amb.

(73989) W4141—463. 400,000. 9/14. H.&J.Ltd. Forms/C. 2118/10.

CONFERENCE AT 64 C.C.S.,

by D.M.S., ARMY OF THE RHINE.

Date 22/4/19. Time 10,30 hrs.

Present:-

MAJOR GENERAL S.H. THOMPSON. K.C.M.G. Etc.
MAJOR GENERAL S.W. BABTIE. V.C. Etc.
All D.Ds.M.S., A.Ds.M.S., O.C's. Medical Units.

The following subjects were discussed by D.M.S. :-

No.1. Decentralising of Hospitals. All C.C.S's. and Stationary Hospitals will shortly be administered by D.D's.M.S. Corps.

No.2. Demobilisation. The minimum strength to maintain in Medical Units will shortly be reduced from 75% to 60%.
Men with longest service are to be given priority in being demobilised. There are 60 Officers and 1000 Other Ranks R.A.M.C. coming to Rhine Army as reinforcements.
Volunteers from Units other than R.A.M.C. in the Rhine Army, may soon be [redacted] accepted for Medical Units and will be transferred to the R.A.M.C. if they prove suitable.

No.3. Indents on Medical Stores. O.C's. Medical Units will personally make out indents for Medical Stores which are to be submitted to A.Ds.M.S. for countersignature once a week.
Drugs on charge will be substituted where ever possible for those requisitioned.

No.4. Collection of Sick. Horse Ambulance Wagons will be used as much as possible in the collection of sick.

No.5. Venereal Disease. Other Ranks will go to No.25 Genl Hospital, which will shortly open in Cologne.
Officers will go to No.36. C.C.S.
This class of case will in no way be treated differently (regarding care, respect, etc.) to any other class of patient.
They will not be penalised whilst in Hospital or in any way made to feel their unfortunate position.

No.6. "SCABIES" Cases will be treated in every way like any other patients.

No.7. Medical Inspections. M.O's. should inspect a Company at a time and not attempt to inspect a whole Battalion at once.

MAJOR GENERAL BABTIE made a speech in which he expressed satisfaction at the Medical Arrangements in the Army of the Rhine.

WAR DIARY
Appendix No 1

C.D. Chambers.

LIEUT-COL., R.A.M.C.,
COMMANDING 142 FIELD AMBULANCE.

NOTE.
This appendix should have been included with War Diary for month of April.
CDC

June 1919

142 Field Ambulance

28031 W3125/M2250 1000m 6/17 M.R.Co.,Ltd. (1367) Forms W3091. Army Form W. 3091.

Cover for Documents.

19. Returns (a) Armies - 1st Army

Natures of Enclosures.

Statistics of Wounded.

various operations in May 1915
operations in June 1915
" Neuve Chapelle May 1915
British & Indians. proportionate losses between during operations May 1915

Statistics

Notes, or Letters written.

Instructions regarding War Diaries and Intelligence Summaries are contained in F. S. Regs., Part II. and the Staff Manual respectively. Title pages will be prepared in manuscript.

WAR DIARY
or
~~INTELLIGENCE SUMMARY.~~
(*Erase heading not required.*)

Army Form C. 2118.

O.C. 142nd F. Ambulance. Sheet 1

Hour, Date, Place	Summary of Events and Information	Remarks and references to Appendices
EHRENFELD. COLOGNE. June 1st 1919	Routine ambulance work. Weather fine Conference at DMS Office this morning and warm.	G.D. Chambers Lieut-Col
" June 2nd	Inspected Horse Lines and Transport. All G.S. wagons are being re-painted.	(init)
" June 3rd	Programme of RAMC Training drawn up for all retainable RAMC. and att. Infantry to attend. Weather changeable - rainy at times	(init)
" June 4th	Lectured personnel on general subjects today. O.C. No 7 F.A. called and discussed medical arrangements in the event of an advance. Monthly auditing and stock-taking of Canteen Accounts carried out by C.O. and Capt Potter MC RAMC this morning.	(init)
" June 5th	Inspected a plot of land at BICKENDORF for grazing Horses and mules. D.A.P.M. Northern Division carried out an identification parade of unit this afternoon. Pte HUTCHINSON 4 York & Lancs was recognised in connection with an offence contrary to A.R.O. 2627. (and picked out)	(init)

(73989) W4141—463. 400,000. 9/14. H.&J.Ltd. Forms/C. 2118/10.

Instructions regarding War Diaries and Intelligence Summaries are contained in F. S. Regs., Part II. and the Staff Manual respectively. Title pages will be prepared in manuscript.

WAR DIARY
or
~~INTELLIGENCE SUMMARY~~.
(Erase heading not required.)

Army Form C. 2118.

O.C. 142nd Field Ambulance
Sheet II.

Hour, Date, Place	Summary of Events and Information	Remarks and references to Appendices
EHRENFELD. 6.6.19	Inspected Cookhouse and men's billets at the School House. Weather - Changeable	[illegible]
" 7.6.19	Summary of Evidence taken in the case of Pte Hutchinson. Capt Mann gave evidence at a Court-Martial 1/5 W. Yorks. Weather very warm	[illegible]
" 8.6.19	Draft of 7 releasable men RAMC arrived from No 8 F.A. Whit-Sunday. Weather very hot & close	[illegible]
" 9.6.19	Transport being overhauled during the next few days - General holiday proclaimed by the C in C. Weather warm but fresh.	[illegible]
" 10-6-19	Office Routine Work. Nothing special to report.	[illegible]
" 11.6.19	Nothing Special to report. Hot and close. Inspected Guard rooms in Cologne.	[illegible]
" 12.6.19	Visited Brig. Gen. Carey CB. 2nd Inf. Brigade.	[illegible]
" 13.6.19	Attended lecture by Command Paymaster at Rhiel in the morning and conference at office of DDMS in the afternoon.	[illegible]
" 14-6-19	Routine work to-day 8 men demobilised to-day	[illegible]

Instructions regarding War Diaries and Intelligence Summaries are contained in F. S. Regs., Part II. and the Staff Manual respectively. Title pages will be prepared in manuscript.

WAR DIARY
or
~~INTELLIGENCE SUMMARY.~~
(Erase heading not required.)

Army Form C. 2118.

Sheet III
O.C. 142nd Field Ambulance

Hour, Date, Place	Summary of Events and Information	Remarks and references to Appendices
EHRENFELD 15-6-19	Weekly returns rendered to-day - Eight men demobilized. Weather very hot & close	[initials]
" 16-6-19	Period of Armistice expires on Friday 20th - Peace Terms have not yet been signed by Germany. Preparations for moving Northern Division over the RHINE are ready. All officers re-called from leave. Health inspection of unit held at 11-00 hrs to-day	[initials]
" 17-6-19	Units preparing to move forward under instructions detailed in Brigade Orders for the advance. No orders received up to 15-00 hrs to-day. Have ordered H transport to load up Mobilization Equipment and have confined all ranks to barracks.	
16-00 hrs.	Orders received from ADMS. to evacuate all sick to-day. Orders received from 1st and 2nd Northern Inf. Brigades that J-2 day will be to-morrow 18th inst. Operation Order No I. re move of ambulance issued. Weather very hot and close	[initials]

(73989) W4141—463. 400,000. 9/14. H.&J.Ltd. Forms/C. 2118/10.

Instructions regarding War Diaries and Intelligence Summaries are contained in F. S. Regs., Part II. and the Staff Manual respectively. Title pages will be prepared in manuscript.

WAR DIARY

or

~~INTELLIGENCE SUMMARY.~~

(*Erase heading not required.*)

Army Form C. 2118.

Sheet IV

O.C. 142nd F. Ambulance.

Hour, Date, Place	Summary of Events and Information	Remarks and references to Appendices
EHRENFELD 18.6.19	In view of my acting as S.M.O. 1st N. Inf. Brigade in addition to 2nd N. Inf. Brigade I have detailed Capt Mann to act as O.C. "A" Section (including H.Q.) to march with 2nd North. Inf. Brigade. Capt Dowling MC has been sent to 142nd F.A. and will accompany him. I shall proceed with 1st N. Inf. Brigade by Motor Transport with Capt. Potter MC as O.C. Bearers "B" Section. "A" Section with Horse Transport moved at 07.30 hrs this morning with 2nd North. Inf. Brig by route march to ~~[illegible]~~ DÜNWALD. "B" Section remains to day at EHRENFELD but moves off in the morning by motor Lorry.	
" 19.6.19.	"B" Section with light Medical and Surgical equipment in 4 motor Lorries moved off at 07.30 hrs. 3 large ambulance cars and 1 Ford (remainder of M.T. sent on yesterday to "A" Section) together with 5 MAC. cars and 1 car attached from Cavalry Division - followed the Lorries.	

(73989) W4141—463. 400,000. 9/14. H.&J.Ltd. Forms/C. 2118/10.

Instructions regarding War Diaries and Intelligence Summaries are contained in F. S. Regs., Part II. and the Staff Manual respectively. Title pages will be prepared in manuscript.

WAR DIARY
or
~~INTELLIGENCE SUMMARY.~~ 142nd F. Ambulance

(Erase heading not required.)

Army Form C. 2118.

Sheet V

Hour, Date, Place	Summary of Events and Information	Remarks and references to Appendices
EHREN FELD to DURSCHIED (J-1 day). 19.6.19	The whole convoy in charge of myself joined "Motor Flying Column" of 1st Northern Inf. Brigade at NEUE BRIDGE - COLOGNE - and proceeded to DURSCHIED - KURTEN road, arriving there about noon. MAC cars evacuate sick from ambulance to CCS's - COLOGNE. Visited "A" Section in the afternoon at HILGEN where they marched to-day. All are in billets and quite well accomodated. "B" Section are bivouacking by the road side in an orchard. Weather fine and warm.	[illegible]
DURSCHIED. to KURTEN 20.6.19	1st North Brig. HQ. are at KURTEN. To-day whole Brig. Group moved up to near KURTEN. "B" Section (142 FA) located about 3/4 mile South of KURTEN beside road in a very pleasantly situated place - a small river at the further end of the field in which unit is bivouacked gives ample washing facilities. ~~Visited "A" Section in afternoon at HILGEN~~ [illegible] MO. Hussar Squadron in evening at DELLING	[illegible]

(73989) W4141—463. 400,000. 9/14. H.&J.Ltd. Forms/C. 2118/10.

Instructions regarding War Diaries and Intelligence Summaries are contained in F. S. Regs., Part II. and the Staff Manual respectively. Title pages will be prepared in manuscript.

WAR DIARY
or
~~INTELLIGENCE SUMMARY.~~
(*Erase heading not required.*)

Army Form C. 2118.

Sheet VI

O.C. 142nd Field Ambulance

Hour, Date, Place	Summary of Events and Information	Remarks and references to Appendices
KURTEN. 20-6-19.	Duration of armistice extended to Monday 23rd so troops will not move forward at present. D.D.M.S. VIth Corps Colonel ENSOR C.B CMG DSO visited unit in afternoon.	
" 21-6-19.	Visited VI Corps "A" re Court of Enquiry, also visited "A" Section at HILGEN in the afternoon. Medical arrangements for 142nd FA have just been received from GOC 2nd North Inf. Brigade which I am forwarding to ADMS together with my report in the matter as this is purely a ~~[illegible]~~ question of medical administration. Weather cooler some rain	
" 22-6-19.	Capt Mann and Capt Potter went to COLOGNE to attend a Court of Enquiry at 36 CCS this morning. Issued standing orders for camp to day. MAC evacuate sick to COLOGNE these cars are attached to the unit for this purpose – Two men of 52nd N.F.s were wounded early yesterday morning suffering from G.S. Wounds (accidental) due to Lewis Gun instruction)	

Instructions regarding War Diaries and Intelligence Summaries are contained in F. S. Regs., Part II. and the Staff Manual respectively. Title pages will be prepared in manuscript.

WAR DIARY
or
~~INTELLIGENCE SUMMARY~~.
(Erase heading not required.)

O.C. 142nd Field Ambulance.

Army Form C. 2118.

Sheet VII

Hour, Date, Place	Summary of Events and Information	Remarks and references to Appendices
KURTEN. 23-6-19	Route March for "B" Section this morning. Inspected Sanitary arrangements of 1st Inf Brigade Units. ADMS called in the afternoon. Germans given till 7 P.M to sign Peace Terms. Arrangements are being made for a early and rapid advance should they fail to do so. Arranged for with Brigade Major (1st N 9. Brig) to issue orders that riverwater must not be used for drinking purposes, unless chlorinated.	Weather cooler. much rain
" 24-6-19.	Visited "A" Section 142nd FA at HILGEN this afternoon and inspected Sanitary arrangements of 1/6th W. Yorks. with their new M.O. – Capt. HILL RAMC. Stretcher and Squad Drill carried out by "B" Section in the morning. The men are now all in tents with 2 blankets per man. The personnel of "A" Section are in billets. News received early this morning that the Germans have decided to sign the Peace Terms.	very wet and cold. all day

Army Form C. 2118.

Instructions regarding War Diaries and Intelligence Summaries are contained in F. S. Regs., Part II. and the Staff Manual respectively. Title pages will be prepared in manuscript.

WAR DIARY
or
~~INTELLIGENCE SUMMARY.~~
(Erase heading not required.)

OC.
142nd Field Ambulance
Sheet VIII

Hour, Date, Place	Summary of Events and Information	Remarks and references to Appendices
KURTEN. 25-6-19	Nothing of importance to note. Troops are still bivouacing around KURTEN. Weather unsettled.	[illegible]
" 26-6-19	Situation remains the same. Peace Terms still unsigned. Very wet and cold	[illegible]
" 27-6-19	Orders received re. withdrawal of Troops to former billets in COLOGNE - if Peace is signed. Situation in the evening not clear. Preparations are being made for the advance to continue tomorrow morning as German delegates have not yet signified their assent to sign.	[illegible]
" 28-6-19	German delegates have decided to sign and are at VERSAILLES to-day. Officially reported at 18.00 hrs that Peace has been signed this afternoon. Orders regarding move back to COLOGNE received. Move begins tomorrow. Main body of Troops move back on 30th inst. Weather very wet and cold.	[illegible]

(73989) W4141—463. 400,000. 9/14. H.&J.Ltd. Forms/C. 2118/10.

Army Form C. 2118.

WAR DIARY
or
~~INTELLIGENCE SUMMARY.~~
(Erase heading not required.)

O.C.
142nd F. Ambulce.

Sheet XXI

Instructions regarding War Diaries and Intelligence Summaries are contained in F. S. Regs., Part II. and the Staff Manual respectively. Title pages will be prepared in manuscript.

Hour, Date, Place		Summary of Events and Information	Remarks and references to Appendices
KURTEN	29.6.19.	Visited HQ and "A" Section 142nd FA at HILGEN this morning. Have sent an advance party by lorry to-day from "B" Section – KURTEN – to EHRENFELD to prepare former billets and hospital for taking over by Ambulance tomorrow. Arrangements made for the march of 1st and 2nd Northern Brigades to COLOGNE. Weather finer but cold	
" EHRENFELD	30-6-19.	"A" and "B" Sections 142nd Field Ambulce moved back to COLOGNE to-day and joined up at 98 VOGELSANGER STRASSE, EHRENFELD, where the hospital is being opened for reception of sick again – OC, 142nd FA is acting as SMO 1st and 2nd Northern Brigades as heretofore. Forwarded Subscription of 142nd FA for RAMC War Memorial to ADMS Northern Division – Amount subscribed was £14.14.8d. Weather still cold and unsettled	

CONFIDENTIAL

July 1919

+ Aug 1919

Original

War Diary of

O.C. 142nd Field Ambulance

for the month of

JULY 1919.

142nd FIELD AMBULANCE
No. 1.8.19.
Date
R.A.M.C.

C. D. Chambers
Lieut. Col., R.A.M.C.
COMDG: 142nd FIELD AMBULANCE.

Army Form C. 2118.

Instructions regarding War Diaries and Intelligence Summaries are contained in F. S. Regs., Part II. and the Staff Manual respectively. Title pages will be prepared in manuscript.

WAR DIARY

or

~~INTELLIGENCE SUMMARY.~~

(Erase heading not required.)

O.C. 142nd Field Ambulance

Folio 1

Place	Date	Hour	Summary of Events and Information	Remarks and references to Appendices
EHRENFELD (COLOGNE)	1.7.19		142nd F. Amb. Rest Station opened for reception of sick of 1st and 2nd Northern Infantry Brigades at 98 VOGELSANGER STRASSE. The Rest Station is in a Civilian Hospital - 5 wards have been taken over. accomodation (beds) 42. C D Chambers Lieut Col.	
"	2.7.19		Captain G.F. ALLISON MC. RAMC. posted to duty with this ambulance to-day.	CDC
"	3.7.19.		General holiday for the Army of the Rhine proclaimed to-day.	CDC
"	4.7.19		Spare Wheels, rims and Stepney wheel have been stolen from the Ambulance Cars of this unit during the night 3/4th inst. D.A.P.M. Northern Div. was notified at once.	CDC
"	5.7.19		Capt. G.F. ALLISON proceeded for duty as M.O. i/c. 20th Durham Light Infantry to-day.	CDC
"	6.7.19.		Routine Ambulce work. Nothing important to record.	CDC
"	7.7.19.		Large increase in number of Scabies cases observed - especially from 51st North'd Fusiliers. Investigation being made. Weather during the last week has been very unsettled - and below normal temperature for this time of year.	CDC

Instructions regarding War Diaries and Intelligence Summaries are contained in F. S. Regs., Part II. and the Staff Manual respectively. Title pages will be prepared in manuscript.

WAR DIARY
or
~~INTELLIGENCE SUMMARY.~~
(Erase heading not required.)

O.C. 142nd Field Ambulance

Army Form C. 2118.

Folio 2.

Place	Date	Hour	Summary of Events and Information	Remarks and references to Appendices
EHRENFELD	8.7.19		Winter Clothing and Surplus blankets handed in to I.C.S. Fort VI to-day – also Surplus Ordnance Equipment to D.A.D.O.S Northern Division.	(initials)
"	9.7.19.		Inspected Demobilization Rosters of medical units in accordance with instructions received from DDMS VIth Corps. The inspection will be continued to-morrow.	(initials)
"	10.7.19.		Evacuated a case of ? Diphtheria – from VI Corps Cyclist Battn to 37 CCS to-day. Precautions taken. Inspected Demobn Rosters during the day.	(initials)
"	11.7.19.		Completed inspection of Demobn Rosters of Rhine Army units (medical) to-day. Weather remains unsettled.	(initials)
"	12.7.19.		Forwarded report re Inspection of Demobn Rosters to DDMS VIth Corps to-day. High rate of Scabies admissions continues.	(initials)
"	13.7.19.		Wire received from 37 CCS this afternoon that case evacd on 10th inst has been diagnosed Diphtheria. Informed by wire ADMS, Sanitary Section and VIth Corps Cyclist Battalion.	(initials)

D. D. & L., London, E.C. (A8004) Wt. W1771/M2 31 750,000 5/17 Sch. 52 Forms/C2118/14

Instructions regarding War Diaries and Intelligence Summaries are contained in F. S. Regs., Part II. and the Staff Manual respectively. Title pages will be prepared in manuscript.

WAR DIARY
or
~~INTELLIGENCE SUMMARY.~~
(Erase heading not required.)

O.C. 142nd Field Ambulance.

Army Form C. 2118.

Folio 3.

Place	Date	Hour	Summary of Events and Information	Remarks and references to Appendices
EHRENFELD	14.7.19.		Routine Ambulance duties to-day. Weather fine and warm.	(init)
"	15.7.19.		Information received that Northn Division and VI Corps Eliminating Trials for Cav. Div. Horse Show are to be held on July 17th at the EXERCIOR PLATZ. Very little time to prepare vehicles and horses for them. One H-Ambul. Wagon and 1 G.S. Wagon will, however, be entered.	(init)
"	16.7.19.		Working all day on the above vehicles and horses. There is great difficulty in getting horses shod and vehicles repaired owing to having no Shoeing Smith, Farrier, or artificers in the unit. No 4 Co RASC which has been detailed to look after this unit has not been able to do this owing to pressure of work etc. The present arrangements are very unsatisfactory.	(init)
"	17.7.19.		One horse shod at 0600hrs - the morning of the Show: another pair were shod last night by No 3 Company. Both entries were turned down at the Eliminating Trials to-day.	(init)

Instructions regarding War Diaries and Intelligence Summaries are contained in F. S. Regs., Part II. and the Staff Manual respectively. Title pages will be prepared in manuscript.

WAR DIARY
or
~~INTELLIGENCE SUMMARY.~~ O.C. 142nd Field Ambulance

(*Erase heading not required.*)

Army Form C. 2118.

Folio 4.

Place	Date	Hour	Summary of Events and Information	Remarks and references to Appendices
EHRENFELD.	18.7.19.		Daily lectures are being given to the Infantry attached to this unit. These men are showing generally very great keenness in RAMC work and are making good progress. Weather unsettled – cooler.	(CEO)
"	19.7.19.		Have arranged with OC 402 Water Tank Coy. for 6 men to attend a series of lectures and demonstrations in water duties. General holiday owing to Peace Celebrations – proclaimed to-day.	(CEO)
"	20.7.19		Rendered report on high sick wastage of 51st N.F's to ADMS also on 4 attached Infantrymen (9th D.L.I's) to be returned to their unit on account of indifferent and bad characters as being unfit for transfer to the RAMC.	(CEO)
"	21.7.19.		Inspected Demobilisation Rosters of some units for month of July to-day. Weather fresh and fine.	(CEO)
"	22.7.19.		Continued Inspection of Demobn Rosters to-day. Capt. Bowen RAMC – Q.M. of this unit – examined by a Medical Board at 36 CCS to-day – on instructions from ADMS. Weather very wet all day.	(CEO)
"	23.7.19		Nothing of importance to note.	(CEO)
"	24.7.19		The attached Infantrymen are making good progress in RAMC training the majority have been recommended for transfer.	(CEO)

D. D. & L., London, E.C. (A8004) Wt. W1771/M2231 750,000 5/17 Sch. 52 Forms/C2118/14

Instructions regarding War Diaries and Intelligence Summaries are contained in F. S. Regs., Part II. and the Staff Manual respectively. Title pages will be prepared in manuscript.

WAR DIARY
or
~~INTELLIGENCE SUMMARY.~~
(Erase heading not required.)

O.C. 142nd Field Ambulance

Army Form C. 2118.

Folio 5

Place	Date	Hour	Summary of Events and Information	Remarks and references to Appendices
EHRENFELD	25-7-19.		Attended a lecture by Command Paymaster on new Pay and Mess Book method of accounts which come into operation on August 1st. Weather Cold and changeable	(Ecd)
"	26-7-19.		Nothing of importance to note.	(Ecd)
"	27-7-19.		Nothing special to note. Weather continues changeable	(Ecd)
"	28-7-19		Work of painting Amb. wagon G.S. wagon and L.G.S. wagon for Rhine Army Horse Show is proceeding. Very good work is being done	(Ecd)
"	29.7.19		Routine duties only to record.	(Ecd)
"	30.7.19.		Held Court of Enquiry under instructions from DDMS VI Corps re an ambul. car becoming damaged by fire at No 7. FA	(Ecd)
"	31.7.19.		Unable to attend DMS Conference today owing to Court having to reassemble for further evidence. Notified ADMS accordingly. The Sick Rate for 1st & 2nd Northern Inf. Brigades has improved during the past month. There is a marked decline in diseases of all kinds except for Venereal Disease which remains about stationary. Scabies incidence is improving. The battalions that were chiefly affected with this complaint are now very much better through energetic steps having been taken.	E.C. Chambers Lieut Col RAMC

(A7092). Wt W12839/M1293 75,000 1/17. D. D. & L., Ltd. Forms/C.2118/14.

Instructions regarding War Diaries and Intelligence Summaries are contained in F. S. Regs., Part II. and the Staff Manual respectively. Title pages will be prepared in manuscript.

WAR DIARY
or
~~INTELLIGENCE SUMMARY.~~ O.C.
(Erase heading not required.) 142nd Field Ambulance

Army Form C. 2118.

Folio 1.

Place	Date	Hour	Summary of Events and Information	Remarks and references to Appendices
EHRENFELD.	1.8.19.		Routine hospital work. Nothing of importance to note. Weather fine. Trekking Tattoo practice in STADTWALD to-night.	G.O. Chambers Lt.Col
			Capt. H.L MANN RAMC granted 14 days leave to U.K.	
"	2.8.19.		Cavalry Horse Show begins to-day. (Race meeting to-day)	
"	3.8.19.		Nothing to note routine work.	
"	4.8.19.		Eliminating trial for Horse Amb. Wagons held this morning. ADMS & DADVS as judges No 7. Ambulance decided to enter. General holiday to-day.	
			Cavalry Horse Show to day.	
"	5.8.19.		Routine Office work.	
"	6.8.19.		Practice Review Parade of Combined Field Ambulance held at No 7 F.A. this afternoon at RHIEL.	
			Authority granted for Capt. H.L MANN to wear Badges of Rank of Major pending notification in Gazette.	
"	7.8.19.		Practice Review VIth Corps held at EXERCIER PLATZ MERHEIM to-day	
"	8.8.19.		Routine Office work to-day.	

(A7092). Wt W12839/M1293. 750,000. 1/17. D. D. & L., Ltd. Forms/C.2118/14.

Instructions regarding War Diaries and Intelligence Summaries are contained in F. S. Regs., Part II. and the Staff Manual respectively. Title pages will be prepared in manuscript.

WAR DIARY
or
~~INTELLIGENCE SUMMARY.~~
(Erase heading not required.)

Army Form C. 2118.

Folio 2

O.C.
142nd Field Ambulance.

Place	Date	Hour	Summary of Events and Information	Remarks and references to Appendices
EHRENFELD.	9.8.19		Routine work only. ADMS. Colonel FAICHNIE AMS. proceeded on leave. I am appointed A/ADMS during his absence and have assumed these duties to-day.	
"	10.8.19		Nothing of importance to note.	
"	11.8.19		Practice Review held to-day at STADT SPIELPLATZ. DURENER STRASSE. Unit inspected by G.O.C. Northern Division.	
"	12.8.19.		Capt. RICHARDSON reported for duty with this unit.	
"	13.8.19		Capt. GOODWIN is acting M.O. i/c 1/6 W. Yorks and R.E. units Northern Div. during the absence of Capt. HILL.	
"	14.8.19.		Practice Parade held to-day in anticipation of Review on 18th inst. by Army Council of Rhine Army.	
"	15.8.19		Called on DDMS VI Corps. Colonel McCARTHY. AMS.	
"	16.8.19.		Routine Ambulance work only. Weather has been very hot and fine all the week.	
"	17.8.19.		Held a Parade of Combined F. Amb. at RHIEL to-day.	

(A7092). Wt W12839/M1293 75,000. 1/17. D. D. & L., Ltd. Forms/C.2118/14.

Instructions regarding War Diaries and Intelligence Summaries are contained in F. S. Regs., Part II. and the Staff Manual respectively. Title pages will be prepared in manuscript.

WAR DIARY
or
~~INTELLIGENCE SUMMARY.~~
(Erase heading not required.)

O.C. 142nd Field Ambulance.

Army Form C. 2118.

Folio 3

Place	Date	Hour	Summary of Events and Information	Remarks and references to Appendices
EHRENFELD.	18.8.19.		Review of Rhine Army held at EXERCIER PLATZ - MERHEIM this morning at 11.00 hrs - RT HON. WINSTON CHURCHILL M.P. held the Review. The combined Field Amb. of Northern Division represented the RAMC. I was in command. Capt. CROCROFT and Capt POTTER. M.C., were in charge of half companies. Lieut & QM. WILKINSON was officer i/c transport. 50 men from No 7 & 142 F Ambs respectively together with NCOs. made a total of 110 on parade. The Ambulance marched past in good line and presented a smart appearance on parade. The weather was fine and warm. Over six thousand troops took part in this review. Major MANN returned from leave to-day.	(initialled)
"	19.8.19.		Rhine Army Horse Show (Second Day) held at MERHEIM (KALK). A motor ambulance car of this unit won 3rd Prize. Lt Col. McSHEEHY (OC No 7 F Amb) returned from leave to-day. Weather very hot.	(initialled)
"	20.8.19		Routine Office work only. Weather very hot.	(initialled)

Instructions regarding War Diaries and Intelligence Summaries are contained in F. S. Regs., Part II. and the Staff Manual respectively. Title pages will be prepared in manuscript.

WAR DIARY
or
~~INTELLIGENCE SUMMARY.~~
(Erase heading not required.)

OC 142nd Field Ambulance.

Army Form C. 2118.

Folio 4.

Place	Date	Hour	Summary of Events and Information	Remarks and references to Appendices
EHRENFELD	21.8.19		D.D.M.S. VIth Corps inspected 142nd Field Ambulance yesterday 11 o'clock including the hospital and men's billet at School House.	EOD
"	22.8.19.		Commenced monthly inspection of Unit Demobn Registers to-day. Capt. Potter MC RAMC proceeded on leave 21.8.19.	EOD
"	23.8.19		Pay Day for unit to-day. Inspection of Demob. Rosters continued. Weather changeable, cooler.	EOD
"	24.8.19.		Most of attached infantrymen have now been transferred to RAMC – a few remaining names of ~~suitable~~ men have been forwarded for approval – those considered unsuitable have been returned to their units.	EOD
"	25.8.19		Inspection of Unit Demob. Rosters continued – otherwise nothing to note. Weather very wet all day	EOD
"	~~26.8.19~~ EOD		Held Board on two officers today as A/ADMS. referred one for examination by Specialist at 36 CCS.	EOD
"	26.8.19		Nothing of importance to record. Weather fine.	EOD

Instructions regarding War Diaries and Intelligence Summaries are contained in F. S. Regs., Part II. and the Staff Manual respectively. Title pages will be prepared in manuscript.

WAR DIARY

or

~~INTELLIGENCE SUMMARY.~~

(Erase heading not required.)

Army Form C. 2118.

O.C.
142nd Field Ambulance.

Folio 5

Place	Date	Hour	Summary of Events and Information	Remarks and references to Appendices
EHRENFELD	27.8.19.		Report on Demobilization Rosters - sent to DDMS VIth Corps to-day. Routine Hospital work. C.O's Parade of unit held this morning.	
"	28.8.19.		Visited G.O.C. 1st and 2nd Northern Inf. Brigades this morning and reported on the health of the two Brigades. The Sick Admission Rate is much lower than it has been for several months past. Venereal Disease remains about the same.	
"	29.8.19		Inspected Hospital and School House to-day - Weather Cooler. Unit Pay Parade this afternoon. Major MANN was in charge of Pay Duties. Weather cool - rain at times	
"	30.8.19.		Nothing of importance to note to-day.	
"	31.8.19.		Most of the Infantrymen attached to the unit have now been transferred to the RAMC - many of them are quite capable and efficient and should make good progress in the Corps. The unit is now under more stable conditions than it has been for some months past - general efficiency is quite good.	[illegible] Lieut-Col. RAMC

(A7092). Wt W12839/M1293- 750,000. 1/17. D. D. & L., Ltd. Forms/C.2118/14.

Sept: 1919

142nd Field Ambulance.

Instructions regarding War Diaries and Intelligence Summaries are contained in F. S. Regs., Part II. and the Staff Manual respectively. Title pages will be prepared in manuscript.

WAR DIARY
or
~~INTELLIGENCE SUMMARY.~~ O.C. 142nd Field Ambulance

(Erase heading not required.)

Army Form C. 2118.

Folio 1.

Place	Date	Hour	Summary of Events and Information	Remarks and references to Appendices
EHRENFELD (GERMANY)	1-9-19		Time table forecasting moves of Rhine Army units to U.K. received. The North. Division will be the last division to leave GERMANY - due to go about October 24th. Inspected hospital to-day. G.O.Chambers Lieut Col	
"	2.9.19		Called on OC North. Div. M.T. Co. to point out serious shortage of M.T. drivers. A driver is promised for the unit in 3 or 4 days time. Inspected Sanitary Arrangements of above unit. Weather fine & hot.	[initials]
"	3.9.19		Inspected School House (billet of 142nd F. Amb) also Transport parked there. A new incinerator (brick) is being built in the yard.	[initials]
"	4.9.19		Inspected Horse Lines of unit this morning. Several animals require attention by Shoeing-Smith as soon as possible. Capt. T. Potter M.C. RAMC granted 4 days extension of leave in U.K. CO's Parade was held yesterday morning at 0900hrs — Very fine day.	[initials]
"	5.9.19		Unit paid out to-day by Major H.L. Mann RAMC. A Soldier of North. Div MT Co. brought into hospital dead G.S.W. head S.I. body sent to Mortuary of No 36 CCS under instructions of DDMS VI Corps. Weather very fine.	[initials]

(A9175) Wt W2358/P360 600,000 12/17 D. D. & L. Sch. 52a. Forms/C2118/15.

Instructions regarding War Diaries and Intelligence Summaries are contained in F. S. Regs., Part II. and the Staff Manual respectively. Title pages will be prepared in manuscript.

WAR DIARY
or
~~INTELLIGENCE SUMMARY.~~
(Erase heading not required.)

O.C. 142nd Field Ambulance.

Army Form C. 2118.

Folio 2

Place	Date	Hour	Summary of Events and Information	Remarks and references to Appendices
EHRENFELD	6.9.19		Inspected Sanitary Arrangements of 51st & 52nd Northumberland Fusiliers 1st North. Inf. Brigade. There is some overcrowding in one or two of the company billets (in disused Cinema Halls). Ventilation is not sufficient in one of them. I have reported this to 1st Inf. Bnge.	[illegible]
"	7.9.19		Routine Ambulance duties. Weather continues fine & warm	[illegible]
"	8.9.19		Physical drill for men at 8.30 hrs. A Tug o' war team is being trained to enter into No 7 F. Amb. Sports next Wednesday, 10th	[illegible]
"	9.9.19		Capt. Potter MC, returned from leave to-day.	[illegible]
"	10.9.19		C.O's Parade held at 09.00 hrs. 142nd F.A. won the tug o war competition against No 7 F. Amb. during the afternoon.	[illegible]
"	11.9.19		Routine Ambulance duties. Weather continues very hot.	[illegible]
"	12.9.19		Pay Parade this afternoon. Major Mann was in charge as a/ADMS. I held a Medical Board on an Officer this morning re disability from old G.S. wounds. Squad and Company drill took place this morning. Major Mann took the parade. Horse exercise is daily supervised by me.	[illegible]

(A9175) Wt. W2358/P360 600,000 12/17 D. D. & L. Sch. 52a. Forms/C2118/14.

Army Form C. 2118.

Instructions regarding War Diaries and Intelligence Summaries are contained in F. S. Regs., Part II. and the Staff Manual respectively. Title pages will be prepared in manuscript.

WAR DIARY
or
~~INTELLIGENCE~~ SUMMARY. O.C. 142nd Field Ambulance

Folio 3

(Erase heading not required.)

Place	Date	Hour	Summary of Events and Information	Remarks and references to Appendices
EHRENFELD	13-9-19		Visited G.O.C. Northern Division this morning, as a/ADMS and discussed medical situation & health of the troops. Held meeting in Ambulance to arrange for Athletic Sports next month. Unit photographed this morning, into event of my going on leave tomorrow (crossing on 15th) Major H.L. MANN, RAMC will act as O.C. during my absence.	[illegible]
"	14.9.19		Lieut. Col. Chambers M.C. RAMC handed over to me temporary command of unit as he expects to go to U.K. on leave this afternoon.	[illegible]
"	15.9.19		Lieut. Col. Chambers M.C. RAMC O.C. of unit proceeded on leave yesterday. Capt. Potter M.C. RAMC giving evidence at G.C.M & away all day, visited sick of 17th Lancers myself. Held meeting of Sports committee to arrange events for unit sports.	[illegible]
"	16.9.19		Weather fine & hot, arranged football match between unit and 2nd Northern Inf. Bde.	[illegible]
"	17.9.19		Capt. Richardson relieved from seeing sick of R.A.O.C. at Artillery Depot	[illegible]

Instructions regarding War Diaries and Intelligence Summaries are contained in F. S. Regs., Part II. and the Staff Manual respectively. Title pages will be prepared in manuscript.

WAR DIARY
or
~~INTELLIGENCE SUMMARY.~~
(*Erase heading not required.*)

O.C. 142 Field Ambulance

Army Form C. 2118.

Folio 4.

Place	Date	Hour	Summary of Events and Information	Remarks and references to Appendices
EHRENFELD	17.9.19.		(cont) duty to be carried out by No 7. F.A., to start tomorrow.	
			Played football match with 2nd Inf. Bde H.Qrs., lost 3-0.	
"	18.9.19.		Rhine Army Boxing finals took place, I was present as medical officer to the proceedings.	
"	19.9.19.		Pay parade today. Routine ambulance work only.	
"	20.9.19.		Visit A.D.M.S to discuss medical arrangements for evacuation of sick from 53rd Northumberland Fusiliers who are proceeding to Brühl. Arrangement made for 30 M.A.C. to evacuate. Last meeting of Rhine Army Jockey Club races.	
"	21.9.19.		Sunday. Divine services. Weather very cold.	
"	22.9.19.		Had meeting of Sports committee.	
"	23.9.19.		Lt-Col. G.O. Chambers M.C. RAMC returned from U.K. to hand over unit to me before reporting for duty in Egypt.	
			The unit played a football match with H.Divl.T. Coy & won 4-2.	
"	24.9.19.		Lieut Col. G.O. Chambers M.C. RAMC returned to U.K. & handed over command of unit to me.	
"	25.9.19.		O.C. 140th Field Ambulance inspected unit registers.	

(A9175) Wt W2358/P360 600,000 12/17 D. D. & L. Sch. 52a. Forms/C2118/13.

Instructions regarding War Diaries and Intelligence Summaries are contained in F. S. Regs., Part II. and the Staff Manual respectively. Title pages will be prepared in manuscript.

WAR DIARY
or
~~INTELLIGENCE SUMMARY.~~
(Erase heading not required.)

O.C. 142 Field Ambulance

Army Form C. 2118.

Folio 5.

Place	Date	Hour	Summary of Events and Information	Remarks and references to Appendices
Ehrenfeld	26.9.19		Pay parade today	H.G.A.
"	27.9.19.		Saturday. Unit played football match against 2nd Bde H'Qrs Lost 6–1	H.G.A.
"	28.9.19.		Sunday, divine services today, very wet day.	H.G.A.
"	29.9.19.		2 Bde Signal Office closed down, unit office no longer in telephone communication	H.G.A.
"	30.9.19		Unit football function match at Blucher Park. Weather fine but cold	H.G.A.

(A9475) Wt W2358/P360 600,000 12/17 D. D. & L. Sch. 52a. Forms/C2118/15.

(6392) Wt. W6192/P875 1,500,000 4/18 McA & W Ltd (E 2815) Forms W3091/4. Army Form W.3091.

Cover for Documents.

Confidential

Nature of Enclosures.

War Diary

142nd Field Ambulance

October 1st, 1919 — October 31st 1919

Notes, or Letters written.

October 1919.

CONFIDENTIAL

[illegible]

142nd Field Ambulance.

Original Copy of War Diary

For the Month of October. 1919

142nd FIELD AMBULANCE
No. ....
31/10/19
— R. A. M. C. —

[illegible signature]

Major. ...., R.A.M.C.

[illegible]: 142nd FIELD AMBULANCE

Instructions regarding War Diaries and Intelligence Summaries are contained in F. S. Regs., Part II. and the Staff Manual respectively. Title pages will be prepared in manuscript.

WAR DIARY
or
INTELLIGENCE ~~SUMMARY~~. O.C. 142nd Field Ambulance

(*Erase heading not required.*)

Army Form C. 2118.

Folio 1.

Place	Date	Hour	Summary of Events and Information	Remarks and references to Appendices
EHRENFELD	1.10.19.		Held a meeting of Football Committee to select team for match in 2nd Bde competition.	H.L.R.
"	2.10.19		Lieut Col McCammon visited ambulance in connection with the training of infantry transferred to R.A.M.C.	H.L.R.
			I attended lecture by D.M.S Rhine Army.	
			Football match with B Coy 1/4 York & Lancs Lost 6-0.	H.L.R.
"	3.10.19.		Col. O'Grady A.D.M.S Northern Division inspected unit. Pay parade today.	
"	4.10.19.		Routine ambulance only nothing of interest to record	H.L.R.
"	5.10.19.		Sunday today Divine Services.	H.L.R.
"	6.10.19.		Under instructions from Northern Division D.L.I. attached to unit are to return to their unit for demobilization, this includes 10 men working in the unit & necessitates many alterations in unit duties, great difficulty is found to find enough men to carry out ambulance duties & at the same time allow a proportion of men to get instruction in the wards	H.L.R.

(A9175) Wt W2358/P360 600,000 12/17 D. D. & L. Sch. 52a. Forms/C2118/15.

Instructions regarding War Diaries and Intelligence Summaries are contained in F. S. Regs., Part II. and the Staff Manual respectively. Title pages will be prepared in manuscript.

WAR DIARY
or
~~INTELLIGENCE SUMMARY.~~ O.C. 143rd Field Ambulance

(*Erase heading not required.*)

Army Form C. 2118.

Folio 2.

Place	Date	Hour	Summary of Events and Information	Remarks and references to Appendices
EHRENFELD.	6.10.19 (cont.)		and attend lectures	H.E.A.
"	7.10.19.		Ten men of D.L.I attached to unit for transfer to R.A.M.C. were sent back to their unit for the purpose of Demobilization.	H.E.A.
"	8.10.19.		Football match between Unit and 2nd Bde T.M.B. Won 1–0.	H.E.A.
"	9.10.19.		Nothing to record, routine ambulance duties only.	H.E.A.
"	10.10.19.		Pay parade today. Unit inspected for scabies & lice	H.E.A.
"	11.10.19.		Four men proceeded to concentration camp for demobilization	H.E.A.
"			Played football match against 2nd N. Inf. Bde. Won 3–1.	
"	12.10.19.		Sunday today. Divine Service Four proceeded to No 1 Concentration camp for demobilization.	H.E.A.
"	13.10.19		Weather very cold. Routine ambulance duties today, nothing of special interest to record.	H.E.A.
"	14.10.19.		Nothing of special interest to record today	H.E.A.
"	15.10.19.		Eight men proceeded to concentration camp for the purpose of Demobilization. Unit played football match with No 3 Coy	H.E.A.

(A9475) Wt W2358/P360 600,000 12/17 D. D. & L. Sch. 52a. Forms/C2118/15.

Instructions regarding War Diaries and Intelligence Summaries are contained in F. S. Regs., Part II. and the Staff Manual respectively. Title pages will be prepared in manuscript.

Army Form C. 2118.

WAR DIARY
or
INTELLIGENCE SUMMARY.
(Erase heading not required.)

O.C. 142 Field Ambulance.

Folio No 3

Place	Date	Hour	Summary of Events and Information	Remarks and references to Appendices
EHRENFELD	15.10.19		Horfham Div Train. Lost 5–1.	RDL
"	16.10.19.		Routine Ambulance Duties. Nothing of interest to record.	RDL
"	17.10.19.		Pay day today.	RDL
"	18.10.19.		D.D.M.S. VI Corps visited unit & inspected the hospital.	RDL
"	19.10.19.		Sunday. Divine Services.	RDL
"	20.10.19.		I was detailed as president of Court of Enquiry held at 10 am No 7. F.A. Riehl Barracks.	RDL
"	21.10.19.		Routine ambulance duties only today.	RDL
"	22.10.19.		Played football match against No 7 Field Ambulance at Riehl Barracks. Lost 2–0. Reinforcements sent for R.A.S.C. H.T.	RDL
"	23.10.19.		12 Heavy Draught horses & 2 Riders sent as reinforcements.	RDL
"	24.10.19.		More horses sent to complete establishment.	RDL
"	25.10.19.		I proceeded to Riehl barracks to reassembled court of enquiry held on 20.10.19.	
"	26.10.19		Capt. W. J. Dowling R.C.R.A.M.C. joined the unit for duty. Sunday	RDL

Instructions regarding War Diaries and Intelligence Summaries are contained in F. S. Regs., Part II. and the Staff Manual respectively. Title pages will be prepared in manuscript.

WAR DIARY
or
~~INTELLIGENCE~~ SUMMARY.
(*Erase heading not required.*)

O.C. 142nd Field Ambulance

Army Form C. 2118.

Folio No 4

Place	Date	Hour	Summary of Events and Information	Remarks and references to Appendices
EHRENFELD	26.10.19		Cont. today, Divine Services.	[illegible]
"	27.10.19.		Very wet day, routine ambulance duties. D.D. of R to inspect horses which are now up to establishment.	[illegible]
"	28.10.19		Received orders to take over No 2 CCS. Went down to No 2 CCS. with G.R.	
"	29.10.19.		Party of 1 Officer & 24 men sent to 2. C.S.S to take over duties.	[illegible]
Cologne.	30.10.19.		Took over buildings & patients of No. 2. C.S.S; 50 reinforcements sent to unit, 25 actually reported for duty, the others being on leave or on detached duty.	[illegible]
"	31.10.19.		Pay parade. Six more reinforcements sent to unit, all reported for duty.	[illegible]

(A9475) Wt W2358/P360 600,000 12/17 D. D. & L. Sch. 52a. Forms/C2118/15.

www.ingramcontent.com/pod-product-compliance
Lightning Source LLC
Chambersburg PA
CBHW080853010526
44117CB00014B/2244
* 9 7 8 1 4 7 4 5 0 4 3 6 2 *